THE
EVERYTHING®
LOW-
CHOLESTEROL
COOKBOOK

LAURA LIVESEY

of TheConfidenceKitchen.com

200 HEART-HEALTHY RECIPES FOR REDUCING CHOLESTEROL AND LOSING WEIGHT

ADAMS MEDIA

NEW YORK   LONDON   TORONTO   SYDNEY   NEW DELHI

To the forward-thinking cardiologists, doctors, and scientists who inspired me to feel confident in my ability to heal my body without prescription drugs. And to my blog readers, whose excitement about their new lease on life motivates me daily.

Acknowledgments

I cannot say thank you enough to the innovative doctors who went against the grain of our prescription drug– and surgery-based healthcare system to suggest that it was possible (and indeed preferable!) for patients to utilize food and lifestyle as powerful medicine. Thank you to my recipe testers, including the team at LiveseySolar. And to Frieda (my mom!) for inspiring a love of healthy food.

Adams Media
An Imprint of Simon & Schuster, Inc.
100 Technology Center Drive
Stoughton, Massachusetts 02072

Copyright © 2023 by Simon & Schuster, Inc.

All rights reserved, including the right to reproduce this book or portions thereof in any form whatsoever. For information address Adams Media Subsidiary Rights Department, 1230 Avenue of the Americas, New York, NY 10020.

An Everything® Series Book.

Everything® and everything.com® are registered trademarks of Simon & Schuster, Inc.

First Adams Media trade paperback edition March 2023

ADAMS MEDIA and colophon are trademarks of Simon & Schuster.

For information about special discounts for bulk purchases, please contact Simon & Schuster Special Sales at 1-866-506-1949 or business@simonandschuster.com.

The Simon & Schuster Speakers Bureau can bring authors to your live event. For more information or to book an event contact the Simon & Schuster Speakers Bureau at 1-866-248-3049 or visit our website at www.simonspeakers.com.

Interior layout by Kellie Emery
Interior photographs by James Stefiuk
Nutritional analysis by Alex Briceno

Manufactured in the United States of America

1 2022

Library of Congress Cataloging-in-Publication Data has been applied for.

ISBN 978-1-5072-2017-7
ISBN 978-1-5072-2018-4 (ebook)

Many of the designations used by manufacturers and sellers to distinguish their products are claimed as trademarks. Where those designations appear in this book and Simon & Schuster, Inc., was aware of a trademark claim, the designations have been printed with initial capital letters.

This book is intended as general information only, and should not be used to diagnose or treat any health condition. In light of the complex, individual, and specific nature of health problems, this book is not intended to replace professional medical advice. The ideas, procedures, and suggestions in this book are intended to supplement, not replace, the advice of a trained medical professional. Consult your physician before adopting any of the suggestions in this book, as well as about any condition that may require diagnosis or medical attention. The author and publisher disclaim any liability arising directly or indirectly from the use of this book.

Always follow safety and commonsense cooking protocols while using kitchen utensils, operating ovens and stoves, and handling uncooked food. If children are assisting in the preparation of any recipe, they should always be supervised by an adult.

Contains material adapted from the following title published by Adams Media, an Imprint of Simon & Schuster, Inc.: *The Everything® Low-Cholesterol Cookbook* by Linda Larsen, copyright © 2008, ISBN 978-1-59869-401-7.

Dear Reader,

Sometimes, without our knowing, food can cause unintended consequences. Will it cause wrinkles, pimples, or plaque buildup in your arteries? Until I started learning about what causes heart disease, my body felt like a black box: I knew its functions but not exactly how it worked.

When I was diagnosed with familial hypercholesterolemia several years ago, I started to understand my body. I found **astonishing research** on lifestyle solutions that allowed me to reduce my key disease markers by 56 percent. On my blog, TheConfidenceKitchen.com, I wrote about what I was learning and shared heart-healthy recipes. Soon, my readers also shared stories like: "I just got my results back and I have lowered my LDL cholesterol to the point where they are no longer recommending medication," and "I had my labs run again (four weeks after my heart attack) and the results were amazing!"

The **most important discovery** I found is that researchers in the past five years have further clarified that there is one metric that affects all systems: the amount of sugar in our blood. My goal with *The Everything® Low-Cholesterol Cookbook* is to help you **feel amazing** by building habits that keep your blood sugar stable all day long. And of course, to give you delicious and satisfying recipes that make those habits easy.

I'm rooting for your health transformation!

Laura Livesey

P.S. Get free videos and support for your transformation at TheConfidenceKitchen.com/Thrive.

Welcome to the Everything® Series!

These handy, accessible books give you all you need to tackle a difficult project, gain a new hobby, comprehend a fascinating topic, prepare for an exam, or even brush up on something you learned back in school but have since forgotten.

You can choose to read an Everything® book from cover to cover or just pick out the information you want from our four useful boxes: Questions, Facts, Alerts, and Essentials. We give you everything you need to know on the subject, but throw in a lot of fun stuff along the way too.

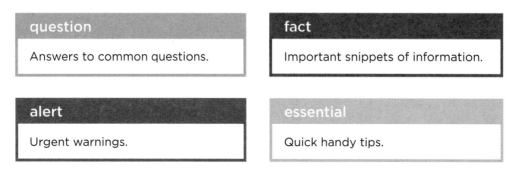

question	fact
Answers to common questions.	Important snippets of information.

alert	essential
Urgent warnings.	Quick handy tips.

We now have more than 600 Everything® books in print, spanning such wide-ranging categories as cooking, health, parenting, personal finance, wedding planning, word puzzles, and so much more. When you're done reading them all, you can finally say you know Everything®!

PUBLISHER Karen Cooper

MANAGING EDITOR Lisa Laing

ASSOCIATE COPY DIRECTOR Casey Ebert

PRODUCTION EDITOR Jo-Anne Duhamel

ACQUISITIONS EDITOR Lisa Laing

SENIOR DEVELOPMENT EDITOR Lisa Laing

EVERYTHING® SERIES COVER DESIGNER Erin Alexander

Contents

CHAPTER 7: WEEKEND WONDERS 133

CHAPTER 8: DIPS, SMALL PLATES, AND SIDES 155

Introduction

If you're reading this, it's likely that you, or someone you know, has been diagnosed with high cholesterol. You probably received a typical cholesterol test report giving you the levels of your total cholesterol, LDL cholesterol (so-called "bad" cholesterol), HDL cholesterol (so-called "good" cholesterol), and triglycerides. You might be wondering whether you should take prescription drugs like statins, go on a diet, or switch up your lifestyle. It's normal to have a lot of questions at this stage!

The short answer is that experts estimate that a whopping 60–90 percent of your heart-health risk factors can be dramatically improved by changing your lifestyle. This is great news because it's not your genetics that holds all the cards! Your habits can determine your destiny.

When it comes to the treatment of heart disease risk factors, a heart-healthy diet and lifestyle, versus cholesterol-lowering drugs called statins, is now considered the best treatment protocol for the vast majority of patients. A March 2022 study on statin use, published in the *British Medical Journal* by a team of researchers from Australia, Denmark, Ireland, and the US, performed a meta-analysis of twenty-one randomized clinical trials undertaken between 1987 and 2021. They found that the relationship between LDL cholesterol reduction by the common cholesterol-lowering statin drugs and the risk of death, heart attack, and stroke is "weak or inconsistent." A few people, such as middle-aged men with existing coronary artery disease, do still benefit from cholesterol-lowering medications, but prescription drugs come with side effects that you'll want to avoid, if possible. While high cholesterol (including high LDL) is no longer considered the most important risk factor for heart disease (it's actually the ratio between your triglycerides and your HDL levels), you can put your high-cholesterol diagnosis to great use as a powerful wake-up call to review and update your health habits.

What habits should you look at? Over the last decade, there have been huge scientific advancements in the understanding of heart disease, and due to this, government recommendations have changed dramatically. Plants are still wonderful and should fill the majority of your plate. But the low-fat and high-carbohydrate method of eating for heart health is now defunct. Healthy fats are crucial to get on your plate, and often. Protein is also moving into center stage. It's an important tool to help you live longer. And with the increase in fats and proteins comes a recommended decrease in carbohydrates (sugar, refined carbohydrates, and even some previously recommended whole grains). Carbohydrates can spike your blood sugar, which over time is a key factor in creating the insulin resistance that ultimately drives heart disease.

You can do a lot with just one easy change. At every meal, eat at least a few spoonfuls of vegetables (fiber) first, then protein, fats, starches, and sugars (in that order). A 2015 study conducted by Cornell University found that the order in which you eat different types of foods has a dramatic impact on your body. By eating fiber first at every meal, you reduce the overall glucose spike of that meal by 73 percent, as well as your insulin spike by 48 percent, which is comparable to the effect of diabetes medication! This one habit change works whether you have diabetes or not, and has helped thousands of people lose weight. Try eating the Best Basic Salad (Chapter 9) at the start of your lunches and dinners to put this into practice. And eat dessert (sugars) at the end of a meal, as opposed to on an empty stomach.

Whether you're dealing with high cholesterol, high blood pressure, or extra weight around your middle, you'll find two hundred easy and satisfying recipes to help make your transition to a heart-healthy lifestyle more doable.

Start the day with high-protein foods that contain fiber. Try a Chocolate Mint Protein Smoothie (Chapter 2) or a Broccoli and Feta Egg Bake (Chapter 3). Make a batch of Tahini Sweet Potatoes with Chicken and Broccoli (Chapter 5) early in the week so you've got several days' worth of epic lunches ready to go in your refrigerator. You'll also find lots of ideas for expanding your weeknight dinner options, from Lemony Tabouleh with Salmon (Chapter 6) to Warm Kale and Halloumi Salad (Chapter 9). On the weekend, there are some special things to try, like Za'atar Roast Chicken (Chapter 7) and Parmesan Truffle Mash (Chapter 8) or Quinoa and Cranberry–Stuffed Mini Pumpkins (Chapter 7). And of course, there are healthy choices for dessert, including Sweet Potato Brownies (Chapter 11) and Matcha Panna Cotta with Chocolate Sauce (Chapter 11).

Along the way, *The Everything® Low-Cholesterol Cookbook* will teach you about powerful foods and nutrients that can dramatically reduce your risk for heart disease. And with the tasty and satisfying recipes in this collection, you don't have to worry about feeling deprived as you change your eating habits. You can turn your high-cholesterol diagnosis into good news by using it as a reason to finally make those healthy changes you've been meaning to make. Take the first step today, and after thirty days of heart-healthy eating, you'll be amazed at how good you feel!

CHAPTER 1

Food Is Medicine

Each year millions of people are affected by diseases such as cancer, heart disease, type 2 diabetes, and Alzheimer's disease (often called type 3 diabetes), all of which are linked to a common condition called insulin resistance. An excess of dietary carbohydrates and simple sugars can cause insulin resistance. In this chapter, you'll learn how to build a heart-healthy plate with plenty of fiber-rich vegetables, protein, and healthy fats, along with a small amount of other carbohydrates. You'll uncover a handful of simple habits like consuming vinegar, cinnamon, and salt daily, as well as changing the order and timing of your meals. You'll also find tips on day-to-day changes like getting enough sleep, exercising in two intentional ways, reducing stress, and staying connected with people you love. Overall, every small change you make contributes to reducing cholesterol levels, lowering and reversing insulin resistance, decreasing excess weight, increasing energy, and looking many years younger. Let's get started!

Cholesterol and Fat Are Not the Enemies

For years, people believed that dietary fat and cholesterol were the key drivers of heart disease and that sugar was harmless. However, research conducted in the last few decades has upended that hypothesis.

Isn't LDL Cholesterol Bad?

In 2015, the US Dietary Guidelines Advisory Committee removed its long-standing warnings to limit dietary cholesterol, stating that "cholesterol is not a nutrient of concern for overconsumption." In more than a few major studies, LDL cholesterol levels were found to be uncorrelated with whether people had heart attacks or not. A 2001 study by the Arizona Heart Institute and Foundation showed that there was no correlation between the levels of total LDL cholesterol and the degree of calcified plaque in blood vessels.

While it was traditionally thought that high LDL cholesterol as a whole was "bad" and a predictor of heart disease complications, 2019 research from Ohio University suggests that the real predictor of complications may be a particular smaller sized subclass of LDL cholesterol called LDL pattern B (LDLb).

Stop Avoiding Fat

Many studies compare low-fat to normal-fat diets. Considering what you've likely seen in the media, it might be surprising to hear that a low-fat diet is not the winner when it comes to improving heart health.

> **essential**
>
> The best predictor of heart disease is to measure the ratio between your triglycerides and your HDL levels. A study published in the American Heart Association journal *Circulation* found that those people with the highest triglyceride to HDL cholesterol ratios had a sixteen times greater risk of heart disease than those with the lowest ratios. Ideally, you want to bring your triglycerides down to a 2:1 ratio. So if your triglycerides are 100 mg/dL, your HDL cholesterol should be 50 mg/dL. Bring triglycerides down with a higher-fat-lower-carb eating pattern.

A 2018 study published in the *American Journal of Clinical Nutrition* followed nearly three thousand adults aged sixty-five and older for more than twenty years. Those with a higher consumption of whole-fat dairy products had a lower risk of death from all causes, as well as a lower risk of heart disease. The Women's Health Initiative (WHI), was the largest dietary trial of a low-fat diet ever commissioned. Forty-nine thousand women were studied over a decade while they ate less meat and fat while eating more fruits, vegetables, and whole grains. The women failed to lose weight and failed to see a significant reduction in their risk for heart disease.

Similar results across multiple studies show low-fat diet groups exhibiting negative cardiac health indicators including weight gain, higher triglycerides (which increase the dangerous LDLb type of cholesterol), and lower heart-healthy HDL cholesterol.

Cholesterol-Reducing Medications

Many people with elevated levels of cholesterol are prescribed a statin, a drug that blocks the production of an enzyme your liver uses to create cholesterol. However, research shows that unless you are a middle-aged man with existing coronary artery disease, you will be unlikely to significantly improve your heart health with statins. Statins can cause muscle aches, headache, or nausea, and in rare cases, cognitive and memory problems, depression, and most alarmingly, insulin resistance and diabetes. The good news is that when you add successful heart-healthy habits into your life, you can get the equivalent of a daily statin dose (plus hundreds of other positive benefits), without the side effects.

Familial Hypercholesterolemia

Familial hypercholesterolemia (FH) is a genetic variation that impacts about one in every two hundred fifty people. People with FH have twenty times the risk for heart disease and tend to develop serious heart disease in their thirties and forties. If your family members such as parents, aunts, uncles, or siblings have had a heart attack at a very young age, or you show signs of high cholesterol (LDL greater than 190) or signs of small, yellowish fatty deposits in the skin around your eyes (called xanthelasma), then you need to change your habits urgently. You might benefit from a consultation with a functional medicine doctor who can suggest personalized supplements, diet and lifestyle interventions, as well as medications if needed.

Sugar and Insulin Resistance

Insulin, a hormone produced by the pancreas, is responsible for regulating blood sugar levels. When you eat carbohydrates, your body breaks down the food into glucose, which is then absorbed into the bloodstream. In response, the pancreas releases insulin into the bloodstream. This insulin helps to move the glucose from the bloodstream into the cells, where it is used for energy. Excessive intake of carbohydrates (sugars) leads to fat storage and eventually insulin resistance. If you have insulin resistance, your cells become resistant to the action of insulin, and as a result, more and more insulin is required in order to move the glucose from the bloodstream into the cells. This can lead to a buildup of excess body fat, dangerous levels of glucose in the blood, blood vessel inflammation, and heart disease.

Blood Sugar Spikes

Your blood sugar can fluctuate greatly throughout the day, depending on what you eat, how stressed you are, how much alcohol you've had to drink, and how much exercise you've done. When your blood sugar spikes, it means that there is a sudden and temporary increase in blood sugar levels.

One common source of blood sugar spikes is carbohydrates. When you eat foods that are high in carbohydrates, they are broken down into glucose and enter the bloodstream, often causing blood sugar levels to rise rapidly. Blood sugar spikes can also be caused by stress. When you feel stressed, your body releases hormones that cause the body to break down stored glucose into energy. This can lead to a sudden increase in blood sugar levels. Medications like some corticosteroids and beta-blockers can cause blood sugar levels to rise. Finally, remaining sedentary after eating can cause a spike. After a glucose spike occurs, the good news is that you can flatten this glucose curve by taking a walk after eating. Prevention, however, is the best medicine. Reducing your carbohydrate consumption will lower the total number of dangerous glucose spikes. While a few blood sugar spikes are not necessarily harmful in the short term, if you frequently eat high-carbohydrate meals (like pasta, pizza, sandwiches, crackers, or desserts) this can lead to long-term health problems. But don't despair, there are delicious low-carbohydrate recipes for all of these foods in the chapters that follow.

Insulin Resistance Drives Inflammation

Cholesterol, particularly LDL, has an affinity for inflammation. When high blood sugars eventually cause inflammation in your blood vessel walls (endothelium), cholesterol will migrate over and attach to the inflamed endothelium. The small dense LDL particles can slip in underneath the endothelial lining and begin to collect. That's when it begins to become a problem.

This is why cholesterol was originally associated with heart disease. Cholesterol was misidentified as the driver of heart disease because it was always found inside plaque-filled arteries. But what happened first was inflammation, caused by insulin resistance. Without inflammation in your body, circulating cholesterol is not usually going to cause problems. And that's why sugar has overtaken dietary and blood cholesterol levels as the key focus of heart disease prevention.

Habits over Genetics

While some genes can predispose you to obesity, type 2 diabetes, or heart disease, changes including diet, stress, exposure to toxins, and exercise can cause chemical changes in your DNA that literally turn good genes on and bad genes off. In short, your genes load the gun, but your environment and habits pull the trigger.

So which habits should you pick up to dramatically improve your health? The best habits are ones that you actually do. Following are ten dietary habits that you can act on very easily, alongside using the recipes in this book. After following these habits for one month, you should feel better, look better, and have more energy. If you continue for two to three months, you should see big improvements in your cholesterol, triglycerides, insulin, and blood glucose levels.

- **Eat fiber before carbs.** At every meal, try to eat foods in this order: vegetables (fiber) first, then protein, fats, starches, and sugars. This tip alone can reduce the glucose spike from that meal, by 73 percent.
- **Eat vinegar before meals.** Consuming 1–2 tablespoons of apple cider vinegar before each meal can reduce a post-meal blood glucose response by 11 percent and the insulin response by 16 percent.
- **Get enough protein.** Eating a diet higher in protein has been found to reduce several cardiometabolic risk factors significantly, and it can help you lose weight. Try to include at least 30 grams of protein at each meal, especially breakfast.
- **Eat healthy fat.** A higher-fat diet (35 percent of calories from fat) is healthy, safe, and highly effective in fighting obesity, diabetes, and heart disease. Choose natural fats like avocados, nuts, seeds, and olives as well as omega-3-rich fatty acid containing foods like chia, flax and hemp seeds, wild fish, pasture-raised beef, and grass-fed butter.
- **Avoid unhealthy fats.** Avoid high omega-6-rich containing vegetable oils,

including canola, sunflower, safflower, corn, and soybean oils, to reduce inflammation. Also, avoid trans fat and the fats in processed meats. Swap these for the healthy fats listed earlier.

- **Eat cinnamon daily.** Eating ¼–1 teaspoon of cinnamon per day can slow the release of insulin into your bloodstream. Add it to oatmeal, yogurt, smoothies, and roasted vegetables or meats.
- **Eat salt, not sugar.** Recent studies show that salt appears to improve cells' ability to use glucose, and consuming salt enhances the dilation of the blood vessels. The optimal range for sodium intake is about 1⅓–2⅔ teaspoons for healthy adults.
- **Don't drink sugar.** Avoid drinking sweet tasting liquids of any kind. Studies show that even diet sodas are linked to weight gain, diabetes, and heart problems.

---

fact

A 2018 study by Dr. David Ludwig, a professor at the Harvard T.H. Chan School of Public Health, compared three types of diets and found that the participants who followed a lower-carb-higher-fat diet had a two to three times higher resting metabolic rate. A reasonably lower-carb diet can increase the rate at which you burn calories, even when you are doing nothing.

- **Eat earlier in the day.** In healthy men and women, eating a meal at 8 p.m. leads to a 29 percent greater peak glucose response than eating the same meal at 8 a.m. Start and end your eating window earlier in the day.
- **Eat lower-carbohydrate meals.** Start by building a habit of one low-carb meal a day. Once you've nailed one meal, move to two a day and so on until all your meals and snacks are lower in carbohydrates. Build in some "cheat days" so you can look forward to any foods you really miss.

Eat More Plants

The stars of your personal heart-healing journey are plants! A plant-heavy diet can reduce the risk of chronic disease and increase longevity. They are a source of polyphenols, which can reduce your risk of heart disease, diabetes, and cancer. Polyphenols are a category of chemicals that naturally occur in plants. They're powerful antioxidants that prevent or reverse cell damage. This damage is linked to insulin resistance, inflammation, and chronic disease.

Researchers have identified over eight thousand polyphenols in nature, and it's one of the reasons why you've been told to "eat the rainbow" of plants. The more variety of polyphenols you can take in, the more healing pathways you can activate in your body.

Plant fiber helps to regulate your blood sugar levels by slowing down your body's absorption of glucose and preventing a sugar spike. There are two types of plant fiber. Soluble fiber dissolves in water to form a gel-like substance. This type of fiber can help you to lower cholesterol and glucose levels. Insoluble fiber does not dissolve in water and helps to add bulk to the stool, promoting regularity. Both types of fiber are important for maintaining a healthy digestive system. Fiber-rich foods are an important part of a heart-healthy diet, and you will benefit by prioritizing them, and starting each meal with fiber first.

---

fact

Did you know that the chemicals in plants regulate gene expression? Each plant contains different chemicals. Each chemical acts like a unique key to unlock a specific door which triggers how your genes behave, helping to "turn on" the genes that promote good health and "turn off" the genes that promote illness. This is why plants can actually "heal" your body, and the more of them you eat, the more healing you can activate. Dark chocolate, spinach, beets, and bok choy are all particularly good at improving the health of your blood vessel lining (the endothelium).

As you add more plants to your diet, make sure you include a variety of choices. Try new lettuce varieties and different types of eggplant, squashes, or apples instead of the ones you normally eat. When you eat more plant diversity, including more strange or new (to you) vegetables and fruits, you get the benefit of new chemicals that can switch on more healing in your body.

The Best Heart-Healthy Ingredients

Scientists haven't found the "perfect diet" yet but in 2014, Dr. David Katz and colleagues from the Yale School of Medicine reviewed hundreds of scientific studies on the health effects of different diets, including low-fat, low-carb, low-glycemic, Mediterranean, mixed balance, paleo, vegetarian, and vegan. While there wasn't an absolute winner, the healthiest diets consisted of:

- Minimally processed foods and foods direct from nature
- Mostly plants
- Animal products from animals that ate as natural a diet as possible, as would be found in wild settings

Human responses to diet vary enormously, yet for the majority of Americans who are overweight, the most rigorous science strongly supports a diet restricted in carbohydrates and higher in fiber, protein, and fat as the best tool for combating metabolic syndrome. Following are lists of heart-healthy ingredients you should include in your eating plan:

The Best Heart-Healthy Ingredients

VEGETABLES
- Arugula
- Asparagus
- Beet greens
- Bok choy
- Broccoli
- Cabbage
- Carrots
- Collard greens
- Eggplant
- Endive
- Green beans
- Kale
- Mushrooms
- Onions
- Red onions
- Red peppers
- Romaine lettuce
- Spinach
- Squash
- Sweet potatoes
- Swiss chard
- Tomatoes
- Zucchini

HEALTHY FATS
- Avocado oil
- Coconut oil
- Extra-virgin olive oil
- Grass-fed butter or ghee
- Nut butters (almond, cashew, peanut, walnut)
- Sesame oil

ANIMAL-BASED PROTEINS
- Anchovy fillets
- Free-range chicken
- Free-range eggs
- Grass-fed gelatin and collagen powder
- Grass-fed, pasture-raised beef
- Grass-fed whey protein powder
- Mackerel
- Sardines
- White-fleshed fish (cod, flounder, hake, halibut, pollack)
- Wild Alaskan salmon
- Yogurt with bioactive cultures

PLANT-BASED PROTEINS
- Duckweed
- Edamame beans
- Macroalgae and microalgae (like spirulina)
- Nori seaweed
- Tempeh
- Tofu

FRESH FRUITS
- Apples
- Apricots (fresh or dried)
- Avocados
- Bananas
- Blackberries
- Blueberries
- Cantaloupe
- Cherries
- Grapefruit
- Kiwis
- Lemons
- Limes
- Mangoes (sparingly)
- Oranges
- Pineapple (sparingly)
- Raspberries
- Strawberries
- Watermelon
- Beans and legumes
- Black beans
- Chickpeas
- Lentils (green, puy, red)
- Navy beans
- Pinto beans
- Red beans
- Split peas
- White beans

NUTS AND SEEDS
- Almonds
- Brazil nuts
- Chia seeds
- Flaxseeds
- Hazelnuts
- Hemp seeds
- Pumpkin seeds
- Sesame seeds
- Sunflower seeds
- Walnuts

GRAINS
- Barley
- Buckwheat
- Oats
- Quinoa
- Rye

DRINKS
- Coffee
- Dandelion tea
- Green tea
- Hibiscus tea
- Licorice and cinnamon tea
- Red wine (sparingly)
- Rooibos tea
- Water

HERBS, SPICES, AND CONDIMENTS
- Basil
- Cacao powder (raw)
- Cilantro
- Cinnamon
- Citrus zest
- Crushed red pepper flakes
- Dark chocolate
- Dill
- Garlic
- Ginger
- Oregano
- Parsley
- Rosemary
- Tamari
- Thyme
- Turmeric

VINEGARS AND SWEETENERS
- Apple cider vinegar
- Balsamic vinegar (no-sugar-added)
- Dates
- Maple syrup
- Monk fruit sweetener
- Raw honey
- Stevia sweetener (pure extract without fillers)

In general:

- Eat as many fibrous vegetables as you can and make a game of filling your plate with a variety of colors and shapes at each meal. To fast-track your heart-healthy eating, avoid starchier vegetables like potatoes and corn which are associated with weight gain.
- Choose low-glycemic fresh fruits like cherries, apples, blueberries, strawberries, pears, peaches, or grapefruit. Dried fruits are high in sugar and should be used very sparingly.
- Avoid processed and packaged foods, even if they're described as "healthy" on the label.
- Don't be afraid of olive oil and other healthy fats. Animal products can be part of a heart-healthy diet when they are raised in a way that preserves their omega-3 fatty acids and other healthy fats.
- Eat wild-caught fish (not grain fed in farms), free-range cattle and poultry (not grain fed), and whole milk and eggs from free-range animals.
- Replace some of the meat in your diet with plant-based proteins like tofu, tempeh, and edamame beans.
- Eat grains sparingly. Most grains tend to wreak havoc with your blood sugar, which contributes to insulin resistance.
- Reduce your use of sweeteners to avoid sugar spikes.
- Add add flavor and micronutrients with fresh herbs and spices. They're potent antioxidants and disease fighters.

Healthy Lifestyle Choices

Your lifestyle choices have a big impact on your heart health. Eating a healthy diet, maintaining a healthy weight, sleeping well, exercising regularly, destressing, socializing, and avoiding tobacco products are all great ways to keep your heart in top condition.

Sleep

Studies show that short sleep duration or poor quality of sleep is associated with plaque development. If you're not getting seven to eight hours of sleep each night, it can affect your body's ability to use insulin and absorb glucose.

Move

Exercise is one of the most effective ways to ensure healthy arteries. Passive stretching can help the vascular system and improve blood flow. Similar results can be found with Pilates and yoga exercises. Studies show that weight training is better for you than aerobic workouts if you want to preserve muscle mass, which is particularly important for older adults. Lean muscle mass can be lost through aerobic workouts without weight training.

Destress

Stress can be as important a risk factor for heart disease as smoking or high blood pressure. Plaque development can speed up when you are under stress. According to a study published in the *Journal of the American*

Heart Association, regular daily meditation can reduce your risk of heart attack and stroke. Researchers found that people who meditate regularly have a lower risk of diabetes, stroke, and heart disease than those who did not have a regular relaxation routine.

Connect, Socialize, and Love

Increasing your connection to others through committed relationships, diverse groups of friends, hobby groups, sports, and interests is a great way to increase your well-being. Researchers from the University of York found that loneliness and social isolation are linked to a 29 percent increased risk of a heart attack. And the American Heart Association suggests that if you have a healthy partner relationship, you significantly reduce your risk for heart disease.

You Can Do This

Health is not a binary situation. It's a continuum, and you're moving either toward health or toward disease every single day. Pick up a few of the "toward health" habits, and you'll swing the balance of your life over to the healthy side. The rewards for this come quickly.

The recipes in this cookbook are designed to help you lower insulin levels, lower triglycerides, reduce belly fat, decrease inflammation, slow down aging, and look and feel more youthful. With daily healthy habits in place, your skin will glow. Your energy will come back. Your excitement for life will increase.

These are not small things. This is about you reclaiming the life that you are meant to live.

essential

Cooking regularly is easier when you have the right tools. A fine Microplane grater is indispensable for zesting citrus and grating spices every day. A food processor can speed up daily vegetable preparation so that you can shred things like carrots and beets in seconds. And a high-speed blender is essential for smoothies. Immersion blenders are also an efficient way to blend soups.

To make this work, you need a strong "why" to keep motivated when the inevitable setbacks come. This isn't a perfect solution, and you'll still have bad days. You'll eat sugar. You'll eat trans fat. You won't get enough sleep. These don't matter if they are one-offs. It's not what you do once in a while that matters. It's what you do consistently. Just hit the reset button the next day, and start moving your body toward health again.

Your habits can save your life. Savor the process of setting them up. Praise your smallest efforts and don't try to do everything in the first week. Just pick one habit (it doesn't matter which one), and start doing it. Keep doing it for a week or two. Then pick up another one. That's the secret to healing your heart. Seven baby steps this week. Thirty baby steps next month. Three hundred sixty-five baby steps this year. Start today with one.

CHAPTER 2

Super Smoothies and Drinks

Lemon Water Day Starter

SERVES 1

Per Serving

Calories	10
Fat	0g
Sodium	0mg
Carbohydrates	3g
Fiber	1g
Sugar	1g
Protein	0g

WHY LEMON WATER?

Drinking a large glass of lemon water first thing every morning will boost your alertness, increase energy levels, and improve your overall well-being. Lemon juice helps to reduce LDL cholesterol and increase HDL, while reducing inflammation. You could also use 1 tablespoon of apple cider vinegar instead of the lemon, for even more benefits, however most people prefer the taste of lemon juice.

Almost every mainstream health guru advises drinking lemon water to start your day. It's an easy habit to incorporate for a quick win, first thing in your morning. If you have time, it's nice to stir in a little splash of hot water from the kettle to warm it up.

1½ cups cold water

½ medium unwaxed organic lemon

Pour water into a large glass. Squeeze lemon half into glass and drink immediately.

Strawberry Grapefruit Beauty Boost Smoothie

Besides being great for your heart, this beautiful and tasty smoothie will have your skin starting to look more radiant after about a week of daily smoothies. If you're using frozen strawberries, omit the ice.

1 small ruby red grapefruit, peeled

1 cup strawberries, hulled

½ medium avocado, peeled and pitted

¼ cup packed fresh mint leaves

¼ cup chopped fresh parsley

1 cup unsweetened raw coconut water

3 ice cubes

1 Place all ingredients in a high-speed blender. Blend on high for 30 seconds or until smooth.

2 Pour into a large glass and drink immediately.

SERVES 1

Per Serving

Calories	320
Fat	12g
Sodium	85mg
Carbohydrates	55g
Fiber	11g
Sugar	35g
Protein	7g

GRAPEFRUIT LOWERS BLOOD PRESSURE

In a 2012 study conducted by the University of Arizona, participants who consumed fresh Rio Red grapefruit daily for six weeks saw a significant reduction in their blood pressure and cholesterol levels. Note that grapefruit can react with certain blood-thinning and cholesterol medications, affecting their potency. If you're on these medications, check with your doctor before adding grapefruit to your diet.

Essential Green Smoothie

SERVES 1

Per Serving

Calories	170
Fat	6g
Sodium	110mg
Carbohydrates	29g
Fiber	7g
Sugar	19g
Protein	3g

WHY GREEN SMOOTHIES?

Green smoothies are a great way to give your body the nutrients it needs. Fruity smoothies are often high in sugar, which can cause inflammation. The fiber in greens helps you to avoid inflammation. It's a great idea to add a scoop of grass fed whey protein powder to smoothies for sustained energy and satiation. Be sure to rotate your recipes and ingredients and allow yourself a few smoothie-free days every week to enjoy other nutrient-dense foods.

The high fiber content in spinach, apples, and avocados can help to lower cholesterol levels quickly and promote heart health when added to your daily routine.

1 cup packed baby spinach

½ medium apple, cored

¼ medium avocado, peeled and pitted

1 cup unsweetened raw coconut water

3 ice cubes

1 Place all ingredients in a high-speed blender. Blend on high for 30 seconds or until smooth.

2 Pour into a large glass and drink immediately.

Tropical Spirulina Smoothie

SERVES 1

Per Serving

Calories	320
Fat	13g
Sodium	135mg
Carbohydrates	50g
Fiber	5g
Sugar	31g
Protein	7g

SPIRULINA

This blue-green algae is one of the most powerful foods, packing a serious punch in both protein and antioxidants. Spirulina has a similar amino acid profile to eggs. Phycocyanin gives the algae its unique blue-green color and helps protect your cholesterol and body from oxidative damage.

Spirulina is a great addition to green smoothies, but it has a bit of a seaweedy taste, that you can cleverly hide with mangoes and bananas. Start small by adding 1 teaspoon for a big antioxidant boost, and then add more as you get used to the taste. If you're using an unfrozen banana, add a handful of ice to the blender.

1 cup packed baby spinach

1 small banana, peeled, chopped, and frozen

½ cup mango chunks

¼ cup full-fat coconut milk

¾ cup unsweetened raw coconut water

2 tablespoons lime juice

1 teaspoon spirulina powder

1 Place all ingredients in a high-speed blender. Blend on high for 30 seconds or until smooth.

2 Pour into a large glass and drink immediately.

Kiwi Sunflower Smoothie

Kiwi skin contains a lot of great nutrition. You don't need to peel them for this smoothie—just wash them and cut off the hard ends.

1 cup unsweetened almond milk

½ cup drained organic silken tofu

2 kiwis, skin on, ends trimmed

1 large Medjool date, pitted

2 tablespoons shelled raw sunflower seeds

2 tablespoons shelled hemp seeds

2 tablespoons lime juice

1 Place all ingredients in a high-speed blender. Blend on high for 30 seconds or until smooth.

2 Pour into a large glass and drink immediately.

SERVES 1

Per Serving

Calories	510
Fat	24g
Sodium	140mg
Carbohydrates	62g
Fiber	10g
Sugar	42g
Protein	19g

KIWIFRUIT

Kiwifruit, or kiwi, contains almost double the amount of vitamin C than oranges, along with a good amount of fiber and potassium. Kiwis appear to increase HDL cholesterol, reduce other blood triglycerides (fats), and reduce your chance of blood clots, all of which can ultimately reduce your risks over time for atherosclerosis. The fruit also helps manage blood pressure.

Raspberry Coconut Smoothie

SERVES 1

Per Serving

Calories	460
Fat	27g
Sodium	125mg
Carbohydrates	28g
Fiber	11g
Sugar	12g
Protein	35g

RAVISHING RASPBERRIES

Animal studies suggest that when raspberries are consumed alongside a high-fat diet, they help to lower blood sugar levels and improve insulin response. This may be because raspberries contain tannins, plant compounds that inhibit the enzymes that break down starches. Raspberries are also rich in polyphenols, plant compounds that have been shown to reduce the signs of aging and improve balance and strength.

This is a creamy, satisfying start to your day that will give you long-lasting energy and stamina. Try pouring it into a bowl and topping with whole raspberries and toasted coconut flakes.

1 cup raspberries

1 small banana, peeled and chopped

¼ cup full-fat coconut milk

¼ cup whole-milk plain Greek yogurt

1 tablespoon almond butter

1 (¼-cup) scoop grass-fed whey protein powder (20 grams protein)

3 ice cubes

1 Place all ingredients in a high-speed blender. Blend on high for 30 seconds or until smooth.

2 Pour into a large glass and drink immediately.

Cacao Berry Shake

This is a very tempting beverage! Using both frozen berries and frozen banana will give you a thick, ice cream–like smoothie. Add a scoop of grass-fed whey protein powder for a nutritional boost.

1 cup packed baby spinach

1 cup frozen mixed berries

1 small banana, peeled, chopped, and frozen

1 cup unsweetened almond milk

1 tablespoon raw cacao powder

1 tablespoon shelled hemp seeds

1 tablespoon almond butter

1 Place all ingredients in a high-speed blender. Blend on high for 30 seconds or until smooth.
2 Pour into a large glass and drink immediately.

SERVES 1

Per Serving

Calories	400
Fat	19g
Sodium	220mg
Carbohydrates	50g
Fiber	11g
Sugar	25g
Protein	11g

RAW CHOCOLATE (CACAO)

Raw cacao is different from the regular cocoa you grew up with. The raw stuff has forty times the antioxidant power of blueberries! Regular cocoa, also called Dutch processed cocoa, has been heated and processed. A 2010 study in the *Journal of Agricultural and Food Chemistry* notes that the heat during Dutch processing decreases the beneficial cardiovascular ingredients in cacao by between 80 and 98 percent, so look for raw cacao powder in the store.

Sunshine Smoothie

Say hello to a bright orange shot of morning sunshine in a glass! This is a zesty and enjoyable way to get more ginger and turmeric in your diet.

½ medium carrot, peeled and grated

½ medium apple (any type), cored and sliced

2 teaspoons shredded fresh ginger

5 walnut halves

1 large Medjool date, pitted

1 teaspoon ground turmeric

1 cup unsweetened raw coconut water

3 ice cubes

1 Place all ingredients in a high-speed blender. Blend on high for 30 seconds or until smooth.

2 Pour into a large glass and drink immediately.

SERVES 1

Per Serving

Calories	250
Fat	7g
Sodium	85mg
Carbohydrates	48g
Fiber	6g
Sugar	38g
Protein	3g

TURMERIC

Studies suggest that the active ingredient in turmeric, curcumin, may protect against heart disease by reducing inflammation and improving cholesterol levels. Turmeric gives curry its characteristic yellow color and is a member of the ginger family.

Acai Antioxidant Blast

SERVES 1

Per Serving

Calories	360
Fat	13g
Sodium	75mg
Carbohydrates	57g
Fiber	14g
Sugar	34g
Protein	7g

REMARKABLE ROMAINE

It's important to switch up the greens you use in your smoothies for nutrient variety. Romaine lettuce adds a lovely mild sweet flavor that works well with berries. It has a high amount of fiber and vitamins A, C, and K. Vitamin C helps to prevent the oxidation of LDL cholesterol, while fiber binds with cholesterol in the intestines and prevents it from being absorbed into the bloodstream.

Acai is one of the world's top ten antioxidants; it tastes like a lovely mixture of blackberries and dark chocolate. This smoothie is great with 1 tablespoon of raw cacao added. Add 1/4 cup more water if the drink is too thick.

1 cup frozen mixed berries

1 small banana, peeled, chopped, and frozen

2 cups packed torn romaine leaves

1 cup unsweetened raw coconut water

5 raw almonds

5 walnut halves

1 tablespoon acai powder

1 Place all ingredients in a high-speed blender. Blend on high for 30 seconds or until smooth.

2 Pour into a large glass and drink immediately.

Glowing Skin Smoothie

It's really worth taking the extra minute to zest the orange before peeling it. It adds a zingy flavor to the sweet-tart mango. This smoothie can be made without one or more of the seeds if you don't have them on hand.

1 cup packed baby spinach

1 cup unsweetened raw coconut water

¾ teaspoon grated orange zest

½ medium orange, peeled

½ medium lime, peeled

¼ cup chopped mango

¼ small cucumber

¼ medium avocado, peeled and pitted

1 tablespoon shelled raw pumpkin seeds

½ tablespoon chia seeds

½ tablespoon ground flaxseed

5 ice cubes

1 Place all ingredients in a high-speed blender. Blend on high for 30 seconds or until smooth.

2 Pour into a large glass and drink immediately.

SERVES 1

Per Serving

Calories	290
Fat	13g
Sodium	130mg
Carbohydrates	41g
Fiber	11g
Sugar	22g
Protein	9g

VITAMIN A

While you're improving your heart health, you can also dramatically improve your skin with the same diet and lifestyle changes. If you drink a green smoothie like this one every day, you may be surprised to see how quickly your skin responds to the influx of nutrients. This smoothie contains ten times the daily requirement for vitamin A, and because it's a fat-soluble vitamin, you can store up moderate amounts of vitamin A for when you'll need it.

Chocolate Mint Protein Smoothie

SERVES 1

Per Serving

Calories	460
Fat	15g
Sodium	200mg
Carbohydrates	59g
Fiber	7g
Sugar	31g
Protein	28g

WHY PROTEIN POWDER?

It's beneficial to add 25–35 grams of protein powder (usually 1 scoop, but check the package label for details) to every smoothie. Studies show that people who drink a protein smoothie every day have lower levels of cholesterol. Choose a protein powder without artificial additives (like flavor or sweeteners) and with high-quality ingredients such as grass-fed whey protein. If you're avoiding dairy products, try one made with pea protein.

Enjoy this chocolatey shake for a healthy breakfast that tastes like dessert. The protein helps flatten the curve of the sugar released from the banana and date. If you're using an unfrozen banana, add a handful of ice to the blender.

1 cup packed fresh mint leaves

1 small banana, peeled, chopped, and frozen

1 large Medjool date, pitted

1 tablespoon tahini

1 tablespoon raw cacao powder

1 cup unsweetened almond milk

1 (¼-cup) scoop grass-fed whey protein powder (20 grams protein)

1 Place all ingredients in a high-speed blender. Blend on high for 30 seconds or until smooth.

2 Pour into a large glass and drink immediately.

Green Fat-Burner Smoothie

This creamy smoothie is a fat burner thanks to the low sugar and the matcha green tea. If you're new to green smoothies, add a date or banana chunk for more sweetness.

1 cup packed baby spinach

½ small avocado, peeled and pitted

1 cup unsweetened almond milk

2 tablespoons lime juice

¼ cup full-fat coconut milk

2 tablespoons shelled hemp seeds

1 teaspoon matcha green tea powder

1 Place all ingredients in a high-speed blender. Blend on high for 30 seconds or until smooth.

2 Pour into a large glass and drink immediately.

SERVES 1

Per Serving

Calories	460
Fat	39g
Sodium	190mg
Carbohydrates	20g
Fiber	10g
Sugar	3g
Protein	14g

MATCHA GREEN TEA

Studies of matcha show it can promote heart health and even aid in weight loss. Like green tea, matcha comes from the *Camellia sinensis* plant. However, matcha farmers cover their tea plants twenty to thirty days before harvest to avoid direct sunlight. This increases chlorophyll production (for a darker green hue) and boosts amino acid content. ConsumerLab.com reports that matcha contains between two to five times more antioxidant catechins per cup than regular green tea.

Watermelon Smoothie

SERVES 1

Per Serving

Calories	290
Fat	9g
Sodium	120mg
Carbohydrates	35g
Fiber	5g
Sugar	22g
Protein	24g

COLLAGEN POWDER

Collagen production naturally decreases as we age, which can cause wrinkles, joint pain, and unhealthy blood vessels. There are twenty-eight types of collagen, but 90 percent of body collagen are types I and III, which are the major components of skin, hair, nails, muscles, tendons, ligaments, bones, gums, teeth, eyes, and blood vessels. To counteract collagen loss, look for a multi-type collagen supplement that includes at least types I and III.

This refreshing smoothie is packed with fiber, healthy fat, and protein from the collagen powder. The amount of protein in collagen powder brands varies widely. Check your label and add enough collagen powder to get 20 grams of protein. You can use sunflower seeds instead of cashews.

2 tablespoons lime juice

1½ teaspoons grated lime zest

2 cups chopped watermelon

1 cup chopped cucumber

½ cup packed fresh mint leaves

10 whole raw, unsalted cashews

1 (¼-cup) scoop collagen powder (20 grams protein)

5 ice cubes

1 Place all ingredients in a high-speed blender. Blend on high for 30 seconds or until smooth.
2 Pour into a large glass and drink immediately.

Peach Ginger Smoothie

A scoop of collagen or grass-fed whey protein powder added to this delicious breakfast shake will give you an essential morning shot of 20 to 30 grams of protein. If this fruit-packed smoothie is too thick, add a few tablespoons of water and blend again.

1 large peach, pitted and chopped (peeled if not organic)

1 small banana, peeled and chopped

1 cup packed baby spinach

1 tablespoon grated fresh ginger

1 tablespoon almond butter

¼ cup full-fat coconut milk

1½ teaspoons lemon juice

3 ice cubes

1 Place all ingredients in a high-speed blender. Blend on high for 30 seconds or until smooth.

2 Pour into a large glass and drink immediately.

SERVES 1

Per Serving

Calories	390
Fat	22g
Sodium	90mg
Carbohydrates	48g
Fiber	8g
Sugar	28g
Protein	9g

PROTECTIVE GINGER

Ginger is a spice that has been used in cooking for thousands of years. In addition to its culinary uses, ginger is also prized for its unique medicinal properties. Even in tiny quantities, ginger is a rich source of antioxidants, including gingerols and shogaols. These compounds help to scavenge harmful free radicals, protect cells from damage, promote healthy cholesterol levels, and reduce inflammation.

Blueberry Kale Crunch

SERVES 1

Per Serving

Calories	270
Fat	12g
Sodium	150mg
Carbohydrates	41g
Fiber	7g
Sugar	22g
Protein	6g

KALE IS KING

Studies have shown that kale can help to lower cholesterol, improve heart health, and reduce the risk of certain types of cancer. One cup of kale is powerful and provides well over 6,000IU of vitamin A, which is two to three times more than the minimum recommended dietary intake (RDI) for most people! It also provides almost a whole day's RDI for vitamin C! Use kale in smoothies and salads or make crispy savory kale chips in the oven.

This smoothie is great before or after a workout with a scoop of protein added. Blueberries, banana, and nut butter taste amazing together and help you to sneak in the super-healthy kale. If you're using an unfrozen banana, add a handful of ice to the blender.

1 cup chopped kale

1 small banana, peeled, chopped, and frozen

½ cup frozen blueberries

1 teaspoon almond butter

1 cup unsweetened almond milk

1 tablespoon shelled raw sunflower seeds

1 Place kale, banana, blueberries, almond butter, and almond milk in a high-speed blender. Blend on high for 30 seconds or until smooth.

2 Pour into a large glass, sprinkle with sunflower seeds, and drink immediately.

Fast Homemade Nut Milk

SERVES 16

Per Serving

Calories	60
Fat	4.5g
Sodium	0mg
Carbohydrates	1g
Fiber	1g
Sugar	0g
Protein	3g

WHY HOMEMADE NUT MILK?

Most store-bought non-dairy milks (like almond and oat milk) contain added sugar, flavors, thickeners, stabilizers, and emulsifiers (like carrageenan), which can cause a blood sugar overload and trigger inflammation in the gut. Give homemade nut milks a good shake before using as the solids will separate from the water as it sits in the refrigerator.

Hemp or cashew milk add a delicious nutrition boost to smoothies. For extra flavor, add 1 teaspoon each raw honey and vanilla extract, along with a pinch of salt. Nut milk isn't just for smoothies—use it like any other type of milk.

1 cup shelled hemp seeds or raw cashews

4 cups filtered water

1. If using cashews, soak in water overnight, then rinse and drain.
2. Place all ingredients in a high-speed blender. Blend on high for 30 seconds or until smooth.
3. Pour into a 1-quart glass bottle and store in the refrigerator for up to 5 days.

Mint Green Iced Tea

A pitcher of this flavorful iced tea in the refrigerator is a strategic tool to help you enjoy the many benefits of green tea, including weight loss and heart health. Make a big batch and sip it throughout the day.

3 tablespoons green tea pearls or 4 green tea bags

1 cup packed fresh mint leaves and stems

4 cups hot water

4 cups ice

1 Place tea and mint in a large heatproof glass bowl or pitcher. Add hot water and set aside for 15 minutes.

2 Place ice in a 2-quart pitcher. Pour tea through a strainer over ice. Let cool for 5 minutes, then top up with cold water to bring the total volume to 8 cups.

3 Serve immediately, or keep in the refrigerator in an airtight container for up to 5 days.

SERVES 8

Per Serving

Calories	5
Fat	0g
Sodium	0mg
Carbohydrates	1g
Fiber	0g
Sugar	0g
Protein	0g

GREEN TEA

One of the main active ingredients in green tea is a catechin called epigallocatechin gallate (EGCG). Catechins are natural antioxidants that help prevent cell damage and provide other benefits like reducing inflammation and helping to fight cancer. These substances can reduce the formation of free radicals in your body, protecting LDL cholesterol particles from oxidation, which is one of the key ways you can use your food strategically to prevent heart disease.

Hibiscus Ginger Iced Tea

SERVES 8

Per Serving

Calories	5
Fat	0g
Sodium	0mg
Carbohydrates	1g
Fiber	0g
Sugar	0g
Protein	0g

RED ROOIBOS

Red rooibos tea has a sweet nutty taste and alluring color. The research on rooibos is quite extensive as scientists began to study early claims from a book published in the 1960s about the tea's amazing health benefits. The studies uncovered a wonderfully diverse array of antioxidants and minerals in rooibos that protect our bodies from free radicals; boost our immune system; fight diseases like cancer, heart disease, and Parkinson's disease; and increase energy and overall vitality.

Several studies show that the brilliantly red hibiscus tea has many benefits, including blood pressure reduction and a cholesterol lowering effect. Ginger is loaded with antioxidants and promotes healthy aging.

3 tablespoons loose leaf hibiscus tea

2 organic rooibos tea bags

½ cup chopped unpeeled ginger

4 cups hot water

4 cups ice

1 Place hibiscus tea, rooibos tea bags, and ginger in a large heatproof glass bowl or pitcher. Add hot water and set aside for 15 minutes.

2 Place ice in a 2-quart pitcher. Pour tea through a strainer over ice. Let cool for 5 minutes, then top up with cold water to bring the total volume to 8 cups.

3 Serve immediately, or keep in the refrigerator in an airtight container for up to 5 days.

Matcha Collagen Latte

The L-theanine amino acid in matcha green tea is great for keeping you relaxed yet focused. The collagen gives you an essential burst of morning protein and amino acids to keep your skin, bones, and joints healthy. The amount of protein in collagen powder brands varies widely. Check your label and add enough collagen powder to get 20 grams of protein.

1½ cups unsweetened almond milk, steamed

1 teaspoon matcha green tea powder

2 (¼-cup) scoops collagen powder (20 grams protein)

1 teaspoon organic virgin coconut oil

Place all ingredients in a large mug and blend with a frother. Serve immediately.

SERVES 1

Per Serving

Calories	190
Fat	10g
Sodium	310mg
Carbohydrates	5g
Fiber	0g
Sugar	2g
Protein	22g

COLLAGEN FOR MUSCLES

Consuming about 30 grams of protein in the first hour after you wake up is important for blood sugar control. It's also important for maintaining muscles and youthfulness (good-bye, wrinkles!). Studies suggest that collagen supplements also help boost muscle mass in people with sarcopenia, which is the loss of muscle mass that can happen with age.

Get Better Faster Tea

SERVES 2

Per Serving

Calories	15
Fat	0g
Sodium	20mg
Carbohydrates	2g
Fiber	0g
Sugar	2g
Protein	0g

IMMUNE-BOOSTING FOODS

Boosting your immune system, particularly since the global COVID-19 pandemic, is more important than ever. One simple way is to incorporate more lemon, garlic, ginger, and cayenne pepper into your diet. These ingredients have long been known for their immune-boosting properties and have been used medicinally for centuries. Recent studies have also shown that they can help to improve heart health and reduce cholesterol levels too.

The immune-boosting, antibacterial, and antiviral properties in this tea will help you defend against invaders at the first sign of a tickly throat. For a fruitier flavor, add a rooibos or hibiscus tea bag, or add a couple drops of liquid stevia if you want sweetness. Sip the tea throughout the day.

1 clove garlic, peeled and smashed

1 tablespoon grated fresh ginger

⅛ teaspoon cayenne pepper

1 medium lemon, halved

4 cups hot water

1 Place garlic, ginger, and cayenne in a large teapot. Squeeze lemon halves into the teapot and add lemon halves as well.

2 Add hot water and set aside to steep for at least 15 minutes. Pour through a strainer into a mug and drink hot or cold.

CHAPTER 3

Breakfast and Brunch

Pumpernickel Toast with Cream Cheese

SERVES 2

Per Serving

Calories	300
Fat	22g
Sodium	1,410mg
Carbohydrates	29g
Fiber	4g
Sugar	6g
Protein	7g

RADISHES FOR RADIANCE

Raw radishes are the ultimate beauty food. They contain a powerful combination of vitamins, minerals, and phytonutrients that help nourish, hydrate, and protect the skin from the environment. Studies have shown that radishes can also help to improve heart health by reducing cholesterol and improving blood circulation. They are a good source of fiber, which is essential for keeping the digestive system healthy. In addition, radishes contain antioxidants that can help to protect cells from damage and boost the immune system.

Pumpernickel bread is packed with fiber, which keeps blood sugar even and produces less inflammation than other types of bread. The exceptionally yummy, quick-pickled radishes take only a few minutes to make, and they beautifully complement the creaminess of the avocado and cream cheese.

4 medium radishes, trimmed and thinly sliced

1 tablespoon apple cider vinegar

½ teaspoon sea salt

1 teaspoon fennel seeds, rubbed between your fingers

2 (1-ounce) slices pumpernickel bread, toasted

4 tablespoons full-fat cream cheese

1 medium avocado, peeled, pitted, and thinly sliced

2 tablespoons roughly chopped fresh dill

1 Place radishes, vinegar, salt, and fennel seeds in a small bowl and toss to coat. Set bowl aside for 5 minutes.

2 Place toasted bread on a flat surface and spread each slice with 2 tablespoons cream cheese. Top with avocado slices.

3 Drain radish pickles and divide between toasted bread slices. Garnish with dill and serve immediately.

Avocado Toast

Put this quick, easy, and delectable breakfast toast on repeat several times a week. Top it with crushed red pepper flakes, halved cherry tomatoes, sunflower seeds, or chopped arugula. Add more protein by adding chunks of feta cheese or two small canned sardines on top.

½ medium avocado, peeled and pitted

½ tablespoon lime juice

1 teaspoon extra-virgin olive oil

¼ teaspoon sea salt

½ teaspoon minced garlic

1 (1-ounce) slice rye and flax protein bread, lightly toasted

1 Place avocado, lime juice, oil, salt, and garlic in a small bowl and mash together with a fork until smooth.

2 Spread mixture over toasted bread and serve immediately.

SERVES 1

Per Serving

Calories	180
Fat	16g
Sodium	580mg
Carbohydrates	8g
Fiber	3g
Sugar	0g
Protein	3g

PROTEIN BREAD

Most types of bread are not great for heart health because they can cause a spike in blood sugar levels. However, protein breads contain added fiber and protein to slow the release of starches in the bloodstream. If you can't find protein bread in your local supermarket or health food store, search online for "protein bread" and you'll find hundreds of options. You can also try a 100% whole rye sourdough bread, sliced very thinly, or make Easy Protein Bread (see recipe in Chapter 5).

Salmon Shakshuka

This dish is an easy, nourishing, beautiful one-pot wonder. And it's versatile, so you can use whatever you have on hand. Try chickpeas or black beans instead of cannellini beans. Replace the salmon with mackerel or sardines. For a vegetarian meal, omit the fish and add one more can of beans. If you don't have bird's eye chili, use a sprinkle of crushed red pepper flakes.

1 tablespoon extra-virgin olive oil

1 large red onion, peeled and diced

1 medium red bell pepper, seeded and diced

1 small red bird's eye chili, seeded and minced

2 cloves garlic, peeled and minced

2 tablespoons tomato paste

2 teaspoons sweet smoked paprika

1 teaspoon ground cumin

1 (14.5-ounce) can petite diced tomatoes

1 (15-ounce) can cannellini beans, drained and rinsed

1 (5-ounce) can red salmon, drained and flaked

1 teaspoon sea salt

4 large free-range eggs

2 tablespoons chopped fresh parsley

2 tablespoons chopped fresh cilantro

½ cup crumbled feta cheese (preferably sheep's milk feta)

1 Heat oil in a large deep skillet over medium heat. Sauté onion, bell pepper, and bird's eye chili until softened, 3–5 minutes. Add garlic, tomato paste, paprika, and cumin. Cook, stirring continuously, until fragrant, about 1 minute.

2 Stir in tomatoes, beans, salmon, and salt. Reduce heat to medium-low and bring to a low simmer. Use the back of a large spoon to make 4 hollows in the tomato mixture. Crack 1 egg into each hollow and cover skillet.

3 Maintain a gentle simmer for 2–3 minutes until eggs are lightly poached but yolks are still runny.

4 Remove from heat and top with parsley, cilantro, and feta. Serve immediately.

SERVES 4

Per Serving

Calories	370
Fat	15g
Sodium	1,310mg
Carbohydrates	32g
Fiber	4g
Sugar	8g
Protein	27g

USE ONE POT

Cooking a meal with only one pot, skillet, or baking sheet is perfect for busy weeknights and sleepy mornings when you don't have a lot of time, or mental bandwidth, to cook. And they can be good for you too. Choose one-pot dishes that are packed with vegetables and protein, making them an excellent choice when you're trying to lose weight or maintain a healthy weight. Using up odds and ends from the refrigerator in a one-pot dish means you're reducing food waste. And, best of all, there is only one pot to clean!

Protein Scramble

SERVES 1

Per Serving

Calories	420
Fat	23g
Sodium	790mg
Carbohydrates	23g
Fiber	9g
Sugar	4g
Protein	29g

PRIORITIZE PROTEIN

Start your day with 30 to 40 grams of protein within thirty to sixty minutes of waking up. Studies at the University of Michigan have shown that high-protein foods in the morning provide mental clarity and focus. They also reduce hunger so you won't be tempted to eat junk food later on. High-sugar breakfast foods, such as cereals and granolas, fruit juice, wheat toast, bagels, and pastries, can hijack your energy and fuel weight gain.

These quick eggs are packed with protein and will provide you with energy while keeping brain fog and hunger at bay. If you don't have edamame, you can use lentils or large white beans instead. Add 1 cup each of shiitake mushrooms and spinach if you want a bulkier meal.

2 large free-range eggs

1 teaspoon dried Greek oregano

¼ teaspoon salt

½ tablespoon extra-virgin olive oil

¼ cup minced red onion

1 cup frozen shelled edamame, thawed

1. In a small bowl, whisk eggs, oregano, and salt. Set aside.
2. Heat oil in a medium skillet over medium heat. Sauté onion and edamame for 3–4 minutes until onion is softened. Push mixture to the edges of the skillet.
3. Pour egg mixture into the center of the skillet and cook without stirring for 20 seconds. Use a wooden spoon to move the cooked bits from the middle of the pan toward the edges. Do this a few times to let any still-runny bits come in contact with the bottom of the pan.
4. Remove pan from heat. Keep stirring for another 15–30 seconds until eggs are very lightly cooked and glossy (not dry). Serve immediately.

Broccoli and Feta Egg Bake

You can make this beautiful, crowd-pleasing egg bake for a group, or make it on the weekend and pack individual servings to enjoy throughout the week. This tasty, nutrient-filled breakfast has a good amount of protein and will set your day up right for steady energy and weight loss!

SERVES 6

Per Serving	
Calories	320
Fat	22g
Sodium	650mg
Carbohydrates	11g
Fiber	3g
Sugar	5g
Protein	19g

3 tablespoons extra-virgin olive oil

1 tablespoon dried thyme

2 cloves garlic, peeled and minced

2 tablespoons capers

½ teaspoon crushed red pepper flakes

½ teaspoon salt

3 tablespoons lemon juice

1 tablespoon grated lemon zest

6 cups chopped broccoli florets

2 cups diced red bell peppers

1 medium red onion, peeled and minced

12 large free-range eggs

1 cup crumbled feta cheese (preferably sheep's milk feta)

1 Preheat oven to 375°F and line a 13" × 9" baking dish with parchment paper.

2 Place oil, thyme, garlic, capers, red pepper flakes, salt, lemon juice, and lemon zest in a large bowl. Whisk until combined.

3 Add broccoli, bell pepper, and onion and toss to coat. Pour mixture into the prepared baking dish. Press down with your hands or a spoon to create a flat layer in the bottom of the dish.

4 In a large measuring cup, whisk eggs and add in enough water (about 1 cup) to bring the total liquid volume up to 4 cups. Pour over vegetable mixture.

5 Sprinkle feta cubes over casserole and press down to submerge in the egg mixture.

6 Bake for 30–35 minutes until the middle is no longer jiggly and the surface is light brown and slightly puffy.

7 Cool on a wire rack for 10 minutes before serving.

ENERGIZING EGG BAKES

When it comes to breakfast, few things are more satisfying than a hearty egg bake. An egg bake is a nutrient-dense food that can help you feel energized through the morning. And thanks to their versatility, they can be customized to suit your taste (as well as whatever you have in the refrigerator). Whether you prefer a classic combination of eggs, bacon, cheese, and broccoli or like to go more gourmet with lemon zest, ricotta, and zucchini, there's an egg bake out there for you.

Cherry Tomato Egg Bake

SMOKED PAPRIKA

Smoked paprika, which comes in sweet and hot varieties, is commonly used as a spice in Spanish, Portuguese, and Hungarian cuisine. Regular paprika can be used instead of smoked and will provide the beautiful color, but you will lose the delicious smoky flavor. A 2013 study by Hirosaki University showed that capsaicin, which is found in paprika, helped to reduce LDL cholesterol levels and inflammation markers in people with high cholesterol and contributed to the partial prevention and improvement of obesity-related insulin resistance.

This is a flavor-rich, nutrient-dense breakfast. It features smoked paprika and cholesterol-lowering, immune-boosting nigella seeds, which are also called black cumin or kalonji seeds. Egg bake recipes are great for Saturday brunch or as part of your weekly meal prep. Before you put the dish in the oven, sprinkle a few more nigella seeds on top.

1 tablespoon extra-virgin olive oil

1 medium red onion, peeled and thinly sliced

4 cups sliced button mushrooms

2 cloves garlic, peeled and chopped

1 medium potato, diced into ¼" cubes

1 tablespoon dried Italian seasoning

2 cups packed baby spinach

1 cup chopped fresh cilantro

12 large free-range eggs

1 teaspoon salt

1 teaspoon sweet smoked paprika

1 teaspoon nigella seeds (black cumin seeds)

1½ cups halved cherry tomatoes

1 Preheat oven to 350°F. Line a 13" × 9" baking dish with parchment paper.

2 Heat oil in a large skillet over medium heat. Sauté onion for 3–4 minutes until softened. Add mushrooms, garlic, and potato and sauté for another 5 minutes.

3 Remove pan from heat, then stir in Italian seasoning, spinach, and cilantro. Transfer mixture to the prepared baking dish.

4 In a large bowl, beat eggs with salt, paprika, and nigella seeds. Pour egg mixture over the vegetable mixture.

5 Arrange tomatoes, cut sides up, on top of egg mixture. Press gently to partially submerge tomatoes.

6 Bake for 30–35 minutes until lightly browned on top and the middle is set. Serve warm.

Egg-Stuffed Mushrooms with Feta

Place the mushrooms on an arugula-lined platter for a pretty way to serve this impressive but easy dish. To make a stunning brunch for a group, serve with Fresh Salsa (see recipe in Chapter 12) and Refried Black Beans (see recipe in Chapter 8).

8 large portobello mushrooms

2 tablespoons extra-virgin olive oil

½ teaspoon salt

8 large free-range eggs

2 medium avocados, peeled, pitted, and chopped

1 cup crumbled feta cheese (preferably sheep's milk feta)

1 teaspoon ground black pepper

4 tablespoons fresh thyme leaves

1. Preheat oven to 375°F and line two large baking sheets with parchment paper.
2. Remove stems from mushrooms and carefully scoop out gills to create a bowl shape in each mushroom cap. Add 4 caps to each baking sheet. Brush the insides of caps with oil and sprinkle with salt. Bake for 7 minutes.
3. Crack an egg into each mushroom cap and return pans to the oven. Bake for 7 minutes or until whites appear set but yolks are still runny.
4. Top with avocado, feta, pepper, and thyme. Serve immediately.

SERVES 4

Per Serving

Calories	490
Fat	36g
Sodium	790mg
Carbohydrates	21g
Fiber	6g
Sugar	5g
Protein	25g

FANTASTIC FETA CHEESE

Feta cheese is a delicious, tangy cheese that is an excellent source of protein, calcium, and phosphorus. It also contains conjugated linoleic acid, which has been shown to help prevent cancer and heart disease, as well as probiotics, which can help to prevent gastrointestinal diseases. And the fatty acids in feta cheese can help to improve heart health by reducing cholesterol levels.

Sweet Potato Latkes Benedict

SWEET POTATOES

Sweet potatoes are an excellent source of fiber and antioxidants. They have anti-inflammatory properties, which can help to lower cholesterol and promote heart health. They're also a good source of vitamins A and C, which are important for boosting immunity and maintaining healthy skin. If you're trying to lose weight, eat them in smaller quantities to obtain the valuable nutrients without spiking your blood sugar too much.

These are incredibly tasty with a sprinkle of chopped arugula or fresh herbs, slices of avocado, and cherry tomatoes cut in half.

1 medium yellow onion, peeled and grated

1 large sweet potato, peeled and grated (2 cups)

2 cloves garlic, peeled and minced

1 tablespoon ground cumin

1 teaspoon sea salt

5 large free-range eggs, divided

1 tablespoon organic virgin coconut oil (or grass-fed butter)

1 (8-ounce) package wild smoked salmon

1 cup Hemp Hollandaise (see recipe in Chapter 12)

1 Wrap grated onion in paper towels and squeeze to remove excess moisture. Place onion in a large bowl, then add sweet potato, garlic, cumin, salt, and 1 egg. Stir until thoroughly mixed.

2 Form mixture into four (4") patties.

3 Line a large plate with paper towels. Melt oil in a large skillet over low heat. Cook patties for 15 minutes until edges are brown. Flip and cook the second side for another 15 minutes. Drain on paper towel–lined plate.

4 Heat a medium skillet with 1½" water over medium heat until it's simmering gently. Working close to the water, crack one egg into a small bowl, then ease egg into the water. Repeat until all 4 eggs are in the water. Remove from heat, cover with a lid, and let sit for 3–5 minutes, depending on how runny you like the yolks. Use a slotted spoon to remove an egg from the water. Blot the spoon on a paper towel to remove water and set egg aside on a plate. Repeat for all eggs.

5 To assemble, place 1 latke on a small plate, then top with 2 ounces salmon, 1 poached egg, and 2 tablespoons Hemp Hollandaise. Repeat with remaining ingredients and serve immediately.

Poached Eggs on Beet Quinoa

SERVES 2

Per Serving

Calories	790
Fat	45g
Sodium	960mg
Carbohydrates	56g
Fiber	6g
Sugar	5g
Protein	36g

BEAUTIFUL BEETS

Beets are an excellent source of niacin, a nutrient that helps to keep the skin, nervous system, and endothelial lining of your blood vessels healthy. They're also a good source of fiber, minerals, and vitamins A and C. Studies have shown that eating beets can help to reduce LDL cholesterol and increase HDL cholesterol, as well as lower blood pressure and reduce the risk of stroke.

Beets make a lovely and nutritious addition to cooked quinoa, oats, and other grains. Check the package label for the correct amount of water. Some brands suggest 1³/4 cups of water for every 1 cup quinoa. You can substitute the fresh dill with 4 tablespoons dried dill.

1 cup quinoa, rinsed and drained

1 organic chicken bouillon cube

2 cups water

2 small beets, trimmed and finely grated (about 1 cup)

4 tablespoons extra-virgin olive oil

1 cup chopped fresh dill

4 large free-range eggs

4 (1-ounce) slices wild smoked salmon

1. Place quinoa, bouillon cube, and 1 cup water in a medium saucepan. Bring to a boil over high heat. Reduce heat to low and simmer for 15 minutes or until all liquid is absorbed. Remove from heat and stir in beets, oil, and dill. Set aside.

2. Crack each egg into its own small bowl.

3. Heat a medium skillet with 1½" water over medium heat until it's simmering gently. Working close to the water, ease each egg into the water one at a time. Remove from heat, cover with a lid, and let sit for 3–5 minutes, depending on how runny you like the yolks.

4. Remove each egg from the water with a slotted spoon, blot the bottom of the spoon on a paper towel to remove excess liquid, and set on a plate.

5. Divide quinoa mixture between two plates. Top each serving with 2 poached eggs and 2 slices salmon. Serve immediately.

Vanilla Overnight Oats

To make these oats more satiating, mix in a scoop of grass-fed whey protein powder (equivalent to 20 grams of protein). Try these topping ideas: Greek yogurt, pomegranate seeds, blueberries, raspberries, kiwis, pumpkin or sunflower seeds, or toasted coconut.

½ medium banana, peeled and mashed

⅓ cup full-fat coconut milk

⅓ cup water

⅓ cup rolled oats

2 tablespoons chia seeds

1 teaspoon vanilla extract

1 teaspoon ground cinnamon

1 Place all ingredients in a pint-sized Mason jar and cover tightly with a screw-top lid.

2 Shake for 30 seconds and then refrigerate for at least 3 hours (up to overnight).

3 Serve cold, or remove lid and microwave on high for 90 seconds to warm.

SERVES 1

Per Serving

Calories	480
Fat	28g
Sodium	100mg
Carbohydrates	52g
Fiber	18g
Sugar	8g
Protein	12g

WHY OVERNIGHT OATS?

Overnight oats make a fantastic time-saving breakfast. You prepare them the night before by placing oats, a liquid, and some flavorings in a jar with a lid. Close the jar, shake it, and refrigerate it overnight. In the morning, all you need to do is top the oatmeal with fresh berries, nuts, or some yogurt, and you have a great breakfast to take with you for the office or post-workout. The list of possible toppings and flavors is endless, and as long as you keep the sugar low, the nutrition profile of overnight oats is excellent.

Strawberry Walnut Oatmeal

SERVES 1

Per Serving

Calories	550
Fat	25g
Sodium	0mg
Carbohydrates	71g
Fiber	13g
Sugar	10g
Protein	12g

WONDERFUL WALNUTS

Did you know that walnuts are one of the most nutritious nuts you can eat? They're packed with antioxidants which help to protect cells from damage. They're also a good source of omega-3 fatty acids, which have been linked to a host of health benefits, including heart health, reduced inflammation, and improved cognitive function. Additionally, research has shown that eating walnuts can help to improve cholesterol levels by reducing LDL cholesterol and increasing HDL cholesterol.

Oatmeal is a comforting breakfast food that can be relied upon to reduce inflammation and provide steady energy for hours. This version is made without milk or sugar. Try stirring in a scoop of grass-fed whey protein powder (to add 20 grams of protein), before you add your fruit and nut toppings.

½ cup steel cut oats

1¼ cups water

1 teaspoon ground cinnamon

1 tablespoon organic virgin coconut oil

¼ medium banana, peeled and sliced

½ cup sliced strawberries

5 walnut halves, roughly chopped

1 Combine oats and water in a small saucepan over high heat. Bring to a boil, then reduce heat to low. Simmer for 15 minutes.

2 Remove from heat and stir in cinnamon and coconut oil. Transfer to a serving bowl and top with banana slices, strawberries, and walnuts.

Baked Carrot Oatmeal

Baked oatmeal is so easy to make. Throw it together before jumping in the shower, and while you're getting ready, it's baking away in the oven. Typical oatmeal ingredients magically turn into a cake of sorts in the oven, except there is no refined sugar or flour to weigh you down.

2 cups shredded carrots

2 cups full-fat coconut milk

2 large free-range eggs

8 large Medjool dates, pitted

2 tablespoons minced fresh ginger

2 teaspoons vanilla extract

2½ cups whole oats

1 tablespoon ground cinnamon

1 teaspoon baking powder

2 teaspoons ground cardamom

¼ teaspoon sea salt

½ cup chopped walnuts

¼ cup raisins

1 Preheat oven to 350°F and line a 13" × 9" baking dish with parchment paper.

2 Spread carrots evenly on the bottom of the prepared baking dish.

3 Combine coconut milk, eggs, dates, ginger, and vanilla in a food processor and pulse once. Add oats, cinnamon, baking powder, cardamom, and salt and process for 30 seconds.

4 Pour oat mixture over carrots and smooth the surface with a spatula.

5 Sprinkle walnuts and raisins across the top, then press them down gently so they are partially submerged in the mixture.

6 Bake for 30–35 minutes until lightly browned and set in the middle. Serve warm or at room temperature.

SERVES 8

Per Serving

Calories	390
Fat	20g
Sodium	110mg
Carbohydrates	48g
Fiber	6g
Sugar	21g
Protein	9g

CARDAMOM

Cardamom has been used for centuries in Asian cooking. In recent years, it has gained popularity in the West as a flavor enhancer and health booster. Cardamom is high in antioxidants, which means it helps protect cells from damage. These nutrients also help to reduce LDL cholesterol and inflammation. Additionally, cardamom has been shown to improve blood sugar control and boost weight loss.

Blueberry Buckwheat Bowl

Per Serving

Calories	530
Fat	16g
Sodium	230mg
Carbohydrates	88g
Fiber	22g
Sugar	8g
Protein	18g

ANTIOXIDANT-RICH CINNAMON

Ceylon cinnamon (not cassia cinnamon, which is more commonly found in supermarkets) ranks in the top ten of all foods, spices, and herbs highest in antioxidants. Even ½ teaspoon of cinnamon daily can have positive effects on blood sugar levels, digestion, and immunity.

This is a beautiful purple breakfast bowl that looks stunning topped with a sprinkle of bee pollen, banana slices, blueberries, and sunflower seeds. Add a scoop of grass-fed whey protein powder into the blender with the other ingredients for a high-protein bowl.

½ cup raw buckwheat groats, soaked overnight, then rinsed and drained

1 cup blueberries

1 cup unsweetened almond milk

¼ large banana, peeled

2 tablespoons chia seeds

1 teaspoon ground cinnamon

Place all ingredients in a high-speed blender and process for 1 minute on high. Pour into a serving bowl and serve.

Creamy Berry Parfait

Change up the berries, then add additional nuts, seeds, and other toppings each time you make this super-easy, nutrition-packed (and beautiful) breakfast. It works equally well as a snack or dessert.

½ cup sliced strawberries

½ cup blueberries

¼ cup rolled oats

2 tablespoons shelled raw pumpkin seeds

1 teaspoon ground cinnamon

1 cup whole-milk plain Greek yogurt

½ teaspoon raw honey

1 In a large tall glass, layer ¼ cup strawberries, ¼ cup blueberries, 2 tablespoons oats, 1 tablespoon pumpkin seeds, ½ teaspoon cinnamon, and ½ cup yogurt. Repeat the layers with the remaining berries, oats, pumpkin seeds, cinnamon, and yogurt.

2 Drizzle with honey and serve immediately.

SERVES 1

Per Serving

Calories	530
Fat	23g
Sodium	100mg
Carbohydrates	52g
Fiber	9g
Sugar	26g
Protein	34g

A PROTEIN AND PROBIOTIC POWERHOUSE

Look for a Greek yogurt with live cultures, which provide gut-healthy probiotic bacteria. Make sure to choose a plain, no-sugar yogurt to avoid the detrimental effects that sugar can have on gut diversity and inflammation.

Easy Chia Breakfast Pudding

This chia breakfast pudding tastes like a Creamsicle Ice Cream Bar. For extra deliciousness, top it with finely chopped walnuts or cacao nibs. Make a batch on the weekend for effortless breakfasts all week. It will keep for 5 days in the refrigerator.

2 medium oranges

⅔ cup full-fat coconut milk

1⅓ cups water

2 teaspoons vanilla extract

10 tablespoons chia seeds

1   Using a zester or a box grater, remove zest from orange. Peel and roughly chop orange.

2   Add orange zest and fruit, coconut milk, water, and vanilla to a blender and mix on high for 1 minute.

3   Pour mixture into a small bowl or jar with a lid. Stir in chia seeds and set aside for 5 minutes. Stir again, then cover and refrigerate for at least 2 hours (up to overnight). Serve cold.

SERVES 2

Per Serving

Calories	570
Fat	41g
Sodium	240mg
Carbohydrates	48g
Fiber	33g
Sugar	13g
Protein	18g

CHIA SEEDS

Chia seeds contain 35 percent fiber by weight, and they're loaded with omega-3 fatty acids, protein, and antioxidants. The soluble fiber in chia seeds can help with weight loss by keeping you feeling full and can ease constipation. Chia seeds are believed to help lower LDL cholesterol and decrease the risk of chronic heart disease. Try adding 1–2 tablespoons chia seeds or ground flaxseed into at least three meals per week.

Spinach Pancakes

Here's a tasty way to sneak extra nutrients into a healthy breakfast. You can't really taste the spinach, but the pancakes have a lovely green hue! Quick Strawberry Syrup (see recipe in Chapter 12) is a delicious topper, along with coconut, yogurt, pomegranate seeds, nuts, and assorted berries. Use more than one skillet so everyone can enjoy hot pancakes at the same time.

(see recipe in Chapter 12)

MAKES 12 PANCAKES

Per Serving (4 pancakes)

Calories	100
Fat	3g
Sodium	230mg
Carbohydrates	14g
Fiber	2g
Sugar	2g
Protein	3g

SPINACH SUPERHERO

Popeye was onto something! Spinach is packed with nutrients that offer a host of health benefits, including improved heart health and lower cholesterol levels. It's an excellent source of vitamins A, C, and K, as well as folate, iron, and calcium. It also contains antioxidants and nitrates, which have been shown to promote heart health by reducing inflammation and improving blood flow. In addition, spinach is a low-calorie, high-fiber food, making it an ideal choice if you are trying to lose weight or maintain a healthy weight.

2 cups rolled oats

1 teaspoon baking soda

½ teaspoon salt

2 cups packed baby spinach

1½ cups unsweetened almond milk

1 large free-range egg

1 medium banana, peeled and cut into chunks

1 tablespoon grated lemon zest

1 medium lemon, peeled

1 tablespoon organic virgin coconut oil, melted

1 Place oats, baking soda, and salt in a high-speed blender. Process for 10 seconds or until oats are finely ground.

2 Add spinach, almond milk, egg, banana, lemon zest, and lemon and blend for 20 seconds, stopping once to scrape the sides and bottom of the blender.

3 Heat a large skillet over medium heat and brush with coconut oil.

4 Pour batter into three or four (3") circles in the hot skillet. Cook for 3 minutes or until a few bubbles appear at the edges. Flip and cook for 2 minutes. Remove from skillet and keep warm.

5 Repeat with remaining coconut oil and batter. Serve warm.

Puffed Apple Pancake

This puffy masterpiece is a breakfast that looks like a dessert! Serve it with a spoonful of thick Greek yogurt and a drizzle of Quick Strawberry Syrup (see recipe in Chapter 12). Enjoy great taste and sweetness without excessively spiking your blood sugar levels.

2 tablespoons grass-fed butter or ghee, melted

4 large apples, cored and thinly sliced

1 cup rolled oats, ground

1 cup unsweetened almond milk

8 large free-range eggs

3 large Medjool dates, pitted

2 teaspoons vanilla extract

1 tablespoon ground cinnamon

¼ teaspoon sea salt

½ teaspoon baking powder

1 Preheat oven to 425°F. Place butter in a 13" × 9" glass baking dish. Place in oven until butter melts, about 1 minute.

2 Arrange apple slices in overlapping rows over butter. Return to oven and bake until apples begin to soften and butter is bubbling and beginning to brown around edges of dish, about 8 minutes.

3 Meanwhile, process oats in a high-speed blender on high for 30 seconds until finely ground. Add almond milk, eggs, dates, vanilla, cinnamon, salt, and baking powder to blender. Blend for 15 seconds. Set aside.

4 Remove baking dish from the oven and reduce heat to 350°F.

5 Pour oat mixture over apples. Bake for 15–20 minutes until top is lightly browned and eggs are set. Cool on a wire rack for 10 minutes.

6 Run a spatula around the outside edge of the dish and cut pancake into 4 pieces. Turn pieces over and serve with apples facing up.

SERVES 4

Per Serving

Calories	480
Fat	19g
Sodium	320mg
Carbohydrates	61g
Fiber	7g
Sugar	35g
Protein	17g

WHICH NONDAIRY MILK IS BEST?

While you can find pure nut milks in the store, you can also make your own nondairy milk easily at home (see recipe for Fast Homemade Nut Milk in Chapter 2). It requires only a high-speed blender and a few ingredients. When out at a coffee shop, look for unsweetened nut milks with the least amount of ingredients. Oat and soy milk are usually highly processed and can cause a spike in blood sugar, so it's best to avoid those.

Almond Breakfast Cake

This is a great replacement for regular bread at breakfast. It's full of protein, with almost 10 grams of protein per slice. If you don't have rhubarb, fresh cranberries or tart apples will work. Eat it right out of the oven, or toast it and serve with an array of topping options, such as butter, almond butter, berries, sliced bananas, and Greek yogurt.

SERVES 8

Per Serving

Calories	240
Fat	13g
Sodium	570mg
Carbohydrates	18g
Fiber	5g
Sugar	9g
Protein	12g

2 cups chopped rhubarb stalks (½" pieces)

2 tablespoons grated orange zest

¼ cup orange juice

1 tablespoon maple syrup

2 teaspoons ground cinnamon

12 large free-range eggs

2 teaspoons vanilla extract

½ cup full-fat coconut milk

½ cup coconut flour

1 teaspoon sea salt

1 teaspoon baking soda

2 cups frozen blueberries

4 tablespoons sliced almonds

1 Preheat oven to 350°F. Line a 13" × 9" baking dish with parchment paper.

2 In a medium bowl, mix together rhubarb, orange zest, orange juice, maple syrup, and cinnamon. Pour into the prepared baking dish and spread evenly across the bottom. Bake for 10 minutes.

3 Meanwhile, whisk eggs, vanilla, and coconut milk together in a medium bowl.

4 In a small bowl, combine coconut flour, salt, and baking soda. Add flour mixture slowly to egg mixture while whisking until smooth.

5 Remove baking dish from the oven. Sprinkle blueberries over rhubarb mixture and top with egg mixture. Sprinkle almonds evenly across the top.

6 Return to the oven and bake for 40 minutes or until the edges are brown and a toothpick inserted in the center comes out clean.

7 Cool on a wire rack for at least 15 minutes before serving.

EAT MORE RHUBARB!

Rhubarb is an antioxidant powerhouse and an excellent source of fiber. It also helps with firming and brightening skin. Rhubarb stalks are full of tannins, which improve digestion and gut health as well as a healthy amount of vitamin K which improves bone density. Studies also show that rhubarb helps lower LDL cholesterol levels. Avoid rhubarb leaves; they are poisonous in large quantities.

CHAPTER 4

Handy Snacks on the Go

Roasted Chickpeas

SERVES 6

Per Serving

Calories	220
Fat	6g
Sodium	490mg
Carbohydrates	33g
Fiber	9g
Sugar	6g
Protein	10g

CHICKPEAS ARE POWERFUL

Studies have shown that eating chickpeas can help lower cholesterol levels and improve heart health. One cup of cooked chickpeas provides about 12 grams of fiber, which is essential for keeping the digestive system healthy. Chickpeas are a versatile food and can be eaten alone or added to soups, salads, and rice dishes. They can also be ground into a flour that's used in baked goods.

When you want a crispy, salty, crunchy snack, these chickpeas deliver! Switch up the seasonings for endless variations.

2 (15-ounce) cans chickpeas, drained, rinsed, and dried
1 tablespoon extra-virgin olive oil
1 teaspoon sweet smoked paprika
½ teaspoon garlic powder
½ teaspoon onion powder
½ teaspoon sea salt

1 Preheat oven to 400°F. Line a large baking sheet with parchment paper.
2 Place all ingredients in a large bowl. Mix well until combined. Use your hands to massage seasonings into chickpeas. Transfer to the prepared baking sheet.
3 Bake for 30–35 minutes until crispy. Let cool for 15 minutes.
4 Serve warm, or store in a tightly covered container at room temperature for up to 3 days.

Ranch Almonds

Almonds are great for you, but they're high in calories, so it's a good idea to portion them out in $1/4$-cup containers. Eat these savory nuts alongside an apple for a quick hit of nutrients.

4 cups whole raw almonds

4 tablespoons extra-virgin olive oil

1 tablespoon nutritional yeast

1 teaspoon sea salt

1 teaspoon garlic powder

1 teaspoon onion powder

1 teaspoon dried dill

1 teaspoon dried chives

1 teaspoon dried parsley

$1/4$ teaspoon paprika

1 Preheat oven to 335°F. Line a large baking sheet with parchment paper.
2 In a large bowl, toss all ingredients together. Pour onto the prepared baking sheet and spread out so almonds don't overlap.
3 Bake for 20 minutes, stirring occasionally.
4 Let cool for at least 15 minutes before serving. Store leftovers in a covered container in the refrigerator for up to 3 months.

MAKES 4 CUPS

Per Serving ($1/4$ cup)

Calories	180
Fat	16g
Sodium	125mg
Carbohydrates	6g
Fiber	4g
Sugar	1g
Protein	5g

AMAZING ALMONDS

In 2019, researchers at Tufts University analyzed controlled trials looking at the impact of almond consumption on heart disease risk factors. They summarized that people who ate at least 2 ounces of almonds daily for periods of between three to six weeks lowered both their total and LDL cholesterol significantly. The review noted that almonds helped to decrease other heart disease risk factors such as body weight. Almonds are also known to reduce blood pressure and blood sugar levels, making them a versatile tool in promoting heart health.

Spiced Edamame and Nut Mix

SERVES 10

Per Serving

Calories	210
Fat	16g
Sodium	480mg
Carbohydrates	9g
Fiber	5g
Sugar	1g
Protein	8g

STEVIA SWEETENER

Stevia is derived from a plant indigenous to South America, and depending on the brand, it's two hundred to four hundred times sweeter than regular sugar! Intake of stevia sweetener does not affect blood glucose levels, which means it doesn't drive inflammation like regular sugar. Stevia also contains no calories, which is helpful if you're watching your weight. Choose a pure stevia extract without glucose-spiking fillers. You can find both powder and liquid forms of pure stevia online and in health food stores.

This nut mix features a combination of nuts, seeds, and sweet and salty flavors. The edamame adds protein to help you feel full longer, and the spices provide antioxidants.

2 cups frozen shelled edamame, thawed and patted dry

½ cup nutritional yeast

2 teaspoons sweet smoked paprika

2 teaspoons cumin seeds

2 teaspoons fennel seeds

2 teaspoons nigella seeds (black cumin seeds)

2 teaspoons minced fresh rosemary

1 tablespoon sesame seeds

2 teaspoons sea salt

½ teaspoon stevia powder

3 tablespoons extra-virgin olive oil

½ cup whole raw cashews

½ cup whole raw almonds

½ cup walnut halves

1. Preheat oven to 375°F. Line a large baking sheet with parchment paper.
2. Distribute edamame evenly on the prepared baking sheet and bake for 15 minutes. Remove from oven and stir. Bake another 10 minutes or until edamame are slightly brown and dry. Remove from oven and set aside to cool.
3. In a large bowl, combine nutritional yeast, paprika, cumin seeds, fennel seeds, nigella seeds, rosemary, sesame seeds, salt, stevia and oil. Toss to combine. Stir in edamame, cashews, almonds, and walnuts. Stir well, then spread mixture evenly onto baking sheet.
4. Bake for 10 minutes or until nuts are lightly browned. Let cool completely before serving. Store leftovers in an airtight glass jar or plastic container for up to 3 weeks.

Savory Quinoa Muffins

Making these delicious, protein-rich muffins is an excellent way to use up leftover quinoa. Add feta cheese or diced cooked chicken to the batter to make these muffins even more satisfying.

2 cups cooked quinoa

6 large free-range eggs, beaten

1 small red onion, peeled and minced

1 cup roughly chopped spinach

1 cup halved cherry tomatoes

1 tablespoon extra-virgin olive oil

1 teaspoon salt

½ teaspoon cumin seeds

½ teaspoon crushed red pepper flakes

1 Preheat oven to 350°F. Grease a twelve-cup muffin tin or line the cups with paper liners.
2 In a large bowl, stir together all ingredients.
3 Divide the batter evenly among the muffin cups.
4 Bake for 15–20 minutes until eggs are set and muffins are lightly golden. Serve immediately, or store in an airtight container in the refrigerator for up to 5 days.

SERVES 12

Per Serving

Calories	90
Fat	4g
Sodium	200mg
Carbohydrates	8g
Fiber	1g
Sugar	1g
Protein	5g

SAVORY MUFFINS

You can take any cooked whole grain like quinoa or buckwheat, mix it with some eggs and vegetables, and create a baked egg muffin that is delicious and full of protein to go. Try quinoa, eggs, feta, broccoli, garlic, and crushed red pepper flakes. Or how about buckwheat, eggs, Cheddar cheese (or nutritional yeast), mushrooms, red onion, and a bit of diced red pepper? These muffins are versatile, lending themselves to many combinations of ingredients.

Rosemary Olive Bread

If you love focaccia with olive oil, this recipe is for you. It's full of protein to keep your blood sugar steady. Enjoy it with savory toppings like olive oil or spreads like tapenade or hummus.

SERVES 8

Per Serving

Calories	270
Fat	20g
Sodium	1,110mg
Carbohydrates	9g
Fiber	4g
Sugar	2g
Protein	12g

ROSEMARY

Rosemary contains antioxidant and anti-inflammatory compounds that can improve blood circulation and boost your immune system. Studies have shown that the carnosic and rosmarinic acids in rosemary have powerful antibacterial, antiviral, and antifungal properties. Consuming it regularly could help your immune system by protecting you better from existing infections and fighting off infections before they take hold.

1½ cups pitted green olives

2 cups thinly sliced red onion

1 tablespoon extra-virgin olive oil

12 large free-range eggs

½ cup full-fat coconut milk

½ cup coconut flour

3 tablespoons chopped fresh rosemary

1 teaspoon sea salt

1 teaspoon baking soda

16 walnut halves

1 Preheat oven to 350°F. Line a 13" × 9" baking dish with parchment paper.
2 Mix olives, onion, and oil in a medium bowl. Spread mixture evenly in the prepared baking dish.
3 Whisk eggs and coconut milk together in a medium bowl.
4 In a small bowl, mix coconut flour, rosemary, salt, and baking soda together. Sprinkle the flour mixture into the egg mixture while whisking continuously. Mix until combined. Spread dough over the olive mixture in the baking dish.
5 Top with walnut halves in a decorative pattern.
6 Bake for 40 minutes or until the edges are brown and a toothpick inserted in the center comes out clean.
7 Cool for at least 1 hour before serving.

Buckwheat Olive Crackers

SERVES 8

Per Serving

Calories	120
Fat	8g
Sodium	330mg
Carbohydrates	10g
Fiber	4g
Sugar	1g
Protein	4g

KALAMATA OLIVES

One key ingredient in Kalamata olives, oleuropein, has been shown to reduce the risk of coronary heart disease. Studies suggest that it may protect against acute Adriamycin cardiotoxicity (damage to the heart muscle). It was also found to inhibit the oxidation of LDL cholesterol.

Try these hearty crackers with Red Chili Hummus (see recipe in Chapter 8). You can swap out the olives and oregano for other flavors like caraway, fennel, rosemary, or thyme.

1 cup buckwheat flour

¾ cup finely ground, unsalted, and roasted almonds

1 tablespoon nutritional yeast

2 teaspoons dried oregano

1 teaspoon salt

½ teaspoon baking powder

10 Kalamata olives, pitted and minced

1 clove garlic, peeled and minced

1 tablespoon extra-virgin olive oil

1 large free-range egg, beaten

1. Preheat oven to 350°F.
2. Combine buckwheat flour, almonds, nutritional yeast, oregano, salt, and baking powder in a large bowl. Mix well to combine. Stir in olives and garlic.
3. Add oil and egg, then rub it into the flour mixture with your hands. Add a small amount of water, in 1-teaspoon increments, and continue mixing with your hands until the mixture forms a smooth dough. You should only need 1–3 teaspoons water.
4. Transfer dough to a large sheet of parchment paper. Flatten dough with your fingers and cover with another sheet of parchment paper. Use a rolling pin to press dough into a very thin (⅛"-thick) sheet that measures approximately 12" × 16". Use your hands to straighten the edges.
5. Carefully transfer the dough on parchment paper to a large baking sheet. Remove the top piece of the parchment paper. Use a pizza cutter or a sharp knife to score dough into 1½" squares, but don't break into individual pieces; leave dough in one piece to bake.
6. Bake for 12–19 minutes until golden and crisp. The edge pieces may be ready 5 minutes sooner than the center pieces. Carefully remove the crackers with a thin metal spatula and transfer to a wire cooling rack.
7. Let cool for 10 minutes and carefully break into square crackers along the score lines. Store in an airtight container for up to 2 weeks.

Rosemary Garlic Crackers

Enjoy these crunchy crackers with a slice of goat cheese on top. They can also be served with dips, such as hummus, or spread with a rich mackerel pâté.

1½ cups packed fine almond flour

2 large free-range eggs, divided

1 tablespoon chia seeds

1 teaspoon sea salt

1 tablespoon dried rosemary

½ teaspoon garlic powder

1 teaspoon water

1 Preheat oven to 350°F.

2 In a large bowl, stir together almond flour, 1 egg, chia seeds, salt, rosemary, and garlic powder. Use your hands to squeeze and press mixture into a dough that has the texture of wet sand.

3 Transfer dough to a large sheet of parchment paper. Flatten dough with your fingers and cover with another sheet of parchment paper. Use a rolling pin to press dough into a very thin (⅛"-thick) sheet that measures approximately 12" × 16". Use your hands to straighten the edges.

4 Carefully transfer the dough on parchment paper to a large baking sheet. Remove the top piece of the parchment paper. Use a pizza cutter or a sharp knife to score dough into 1½" squares, but don't break into individual pieces; leave dough in one piece to bake.

5 In a small bowl, whisk the remaining egg with water. Lightly brush the top of the cracker dough with egg mixture.

6 Bake for 12–19 minutes until crackers are very brown and crisp. The edge pieces may be ready 5 minutes sooner than the center pieces. Carefully remove the crackers with a thin metal spatula and transfer to a wire cooling rack

7 Let cool for 10 minutes, then carefully break into square crackers along the score lines. Store in an airtight container for up to 2 weeks.

SERVES 8

Per Serving

Calories	130
Fat	11g
Sodium	310mg
Carbohydrates	4g
Fiber	3g
Sugar	1g
Protein	6g

GARLIC POWDER

While fresh garlic is more potent for health, garlic powder is a convenient way to add garlic flavor to food and reap its many benefits. Garlic powder has been shown to regulate blood pressure, lower cholesterol levels, improve the immune system, reduce the risk of cancer, and aid in digestion. In addition, garlic powder is a good source of the amino acid glutamate, which is responsible for imparting umami (the savory fifth taste).

Protein Goji Bee Bars

For a picture worthy treat, sprinkle a few bits of bee pollen, goji berries, pumpkin seeds, or oats over these bars right after you drizzle the hot chocolate on top, and before you put them in the refrigerator to set.

8 medium Medjool dates, pitted

½ cup flaxseeds

2 tablespoons cacao powder

1 tablespoon no-sugar-added almond butter

1 tablespoon ground cinnamon

1 teaspoon salt

1 cup gluten-free organic rolled oats

½ cup goji berries

1 cup grass-fed whey protein powder

½ cup bee pollen

½ cup raw cacao nibs

¼ cup hot water

2 ounces 85% dark chocolate

SERVES 12

Per Serving

Calories	260
Fat	9g
Sodium	220mg
Carbohydrates	32g
Fiber	6g
Sugar	14g
Protein	12g

1 Line an 8" × 8" baking dish with parchment paper.

2 Blend together dates, flaxseeds, cacao powder, almond butter, cinnamon, and salt in a food processor for 30 seconds. Add oats and goji berries and pulse for another 10 seconds. Pour into a large bowl.

3 Add protein powder, bee pollen, and cacao nibs to bowl and mix well to combine. Pour in hot water and mix with a wooden spoon until the mixture comes together in a firm batter.

4 Transfer mixture to the prepared pan and use your fingers or the back of a spoon to press it firmly into pan.

5 Place chocolate in a small microwave-safe bowl. Microwave on high in 30-second increments until almost completely melted. Stir until smooth. Drizzle chocolate over the top of the bars. Refrigerate for at least 1 hour (up to overnight).

6 Cut into 12 squares and serve, or store in a tightly covered container for up to 1 week.

BEE POLLEN

Bee pollen is often touted as a superfood, and for good reason. It's packed with nutrients that can support skin health, longevity, and heart health. Bee pollen contains high levels of skin-loving vitamins A, C, and E, as well as B vitamins that can help to reduce inflammation. Bee pollen also is a rich source of antioxidants and minerals like selenium and zinc. Studies have shown that bee pollen can help to lower LDL cholesterol levels and reduce inflammation throughout the body. Look for bee pollen granules at local health food shops or online stores.

Energizing Breakfast Bars

SERVES 12

Per Serving

Calories	240
Fat	14g
Sodium	105mg
Carbohydrates	25g
Fiber	5g
Sugar	8g
Protein	7g

FUELING FOR EXERCISE

How you fuel and refuel before and after exercise helps determine the actual fitness-building benefit of the session. That's true whether you're lifting weights, running miles, or swimming laps. Eat 25 to 40 grams of protein within one to two hours both pre- and post-workout, as part of a well-rounded meal that includes both carbs and fats. Munching before exercising provides your body with the energy it needs to power through the session. Chowing down afterward helps with recovery and muscle growth.

These are a great breakfast option for workout days. Enjoy a bar with a large glass of water to go along with all the healthy fiber. Add a few stevia drops for more sweetness if desired.

4 tablespoons water

½ cup no-sugar-added creamy peanut butter

2 tablespoons maple syrup

1 medium banana, peeled and mashed (½ cup)

2 cups rolled oats

1 cup unsweetened shredded coconut

2 tablespoons psyllium husk powder

½ teaspoon salt

5 tablespoons shelled raw pumpkin seeds

3 tablespoons shelled raw sunflower seeds

2 tablespoons minced dried cranberries

2 tablespoons minced dried apricots

1 tablespoon ground cinnamon

1 Preheat oven to 350°F. Line an 8" × 8" baking dish with parchment paper.

2 In a large saucepan, heat water over medium-low heat. Add peanut butter, maple syrup, and banana. Cook, stirring occasionally, until well mixed and melted together, 2–3 minutes. Remove from heat.

3 Stir in oats, coconut, psyllium husk powder, salt, pumpkin seeds, sunflower seeds, dried cranberries, dried apricots, and cinnamon and mix until well combined. If mixture is dry, add an additional 1–2 tablespoons water and mix well. Transfer mixture to the prepared pan and use your fingers to press it firmly into pan.

4 Bake for 10–15 minutes until lightly golden brown.

5 Let cool in pan and then refrigerate for at least 1 hour before cutting into 12 bars. Store in an airtight container in the refrigerator for up to 1 week.

Lemon Coconut Bliss Balls

The lemon and goji berries create a magical flavor combination in these satisfying bliss balls. Pack them two at a time in small plastic containers and you'll be ready if hunger strikes.

1 cup goji berries

1 cup shelled raw pumpkin seeds

1 tablespoon organic virgin coconut oil

6 medium Medjool dates, pitted

1½ teaspoons grated lemon zest

1. Place goji berries and pumpkin seeds in a food processor and blend for 1 minute or until the mixture has a coarsely ground texture.
2. Add coconut oil, dates, and lemon zest and blend for 1 minute.
3. Divide mixture into 10 portions and roll each portion into a ball. Place balls on a large ungreased baking sheet or plate and refrigerate for at least 1 hour.
4. Store in an airtight container in the refrigerator for up to 1 week.

MAKES 10 BALLS

Per Serving (2 balls)

Calories	310
Fat	14g
Sodium	60mg
Carbohydrates	39g
Fiber	7g
Sugar	28g
Protein	10g

BLISS BALLS

Bliss balls, also called energy balls, protein balls, or energy bites, are an ingenious way of enjoying tasty little bites of deliciousness that are also nutrient dense. The key here is density—just a couple of them will fill you up. Bliss balls turn off your hunger drive and help you feel satisfied much more quickly than regular snacks.

Five-Minute Protein Balls

Per Serving (1 ball)

Calories	150
Fat	11g
Sodium	50mg
Carbohydrates	13g
Fiber	3g
Sugar	9g
Protein	4g

POST-WORKOUT PROTEIN

Eating protein after exercise has health benefits beyond muscle building. It can also help with heart health and cholesterol levels. Studies show that eating protein after exercise can help improve lipid metabolism, help reduce LDL cholesterol levels and increase HDL cholesterol levels.

You probably know protein is important, but finding an easy way to get it right after your workout can be tricky when you're in a hurry. These balls offer protein in the peanuts, protein powder, and coconut and you can make them in a few minutes so you're prepared for your next post-workout snack.

⅓ cup no-sugar-added chunky peanut butter

1 cup unsweetened desiccated coconut

4 large Medjool dates, pitted

2 tablespoons grass-fed whey protein powder

1 teaspoon ground cinnamon

1 teaspoon vanilla extract

1 Place all ingredients in a food processor and blend for 2–3 minutes until very well combined.

2 Divide mixture into 9 portions and roll each portion into a ball. Place balls on a large ungreased baking sheet or plate and refrigerate for at least 1 hour.

3 Store in an airtight container in the refrigerator for up to 2 weeks.

Carrot Cake Energy Balls

These high-protein energy balls taste great, and they'll keep your blood sugar stable for hours. If you don't have protein powder, use an extra 1/2 cup almond flour (for 1 cup total).

1/3 cup unsweetened finely shredded coconut

3 tablespoons maple syrup

1 teaspoon vanilla extract

1/2 teaspoon apple cider vinegar

1 tablespoon pumpkin pie spice

1/2 teaspoon sea salt

1 1/2 cups grass-fed whey protein powder, divided

1/2 cup almond flour

3/4 cup finely shredded carrot

1 cup shelled raw sunflower seeds

1/2 cup finely chopped pecans

1 tablespoon organic virgin coconut oil

MAKES 12 BALLS

Per Serving (1 ball)

Calories	220
Fat	14g
Sodium	130mg
Carbohydrates	10g
Fiber	2g
Sugar	5g
Protein	16g

1 Sprinkle coconut on a large plate. Line another large plate with parchment paper.

2 In a large bowl, whisk together maple syrup, vanilla, vinegar, pumpkin pie spice, and salt.

3 Add 1 cup protein powder, almond flour, carrot, sunflower seeds, and pecans to the bowl. Gently stir with a wooden spoon until combined.

4 Add coconut oil and stir until incorporated and a dough starts to form. Add the remaining 1/2 cup protein powder and stir until the mixture dries out a bit. Add extra 1–2 tablespoons protein powder if dough is too sticky or 1 tablespoon coconut oil if it's too dry.

5 Using your hands, divide the dough into 12 portions. Take one portion and roll into a ball, then roll the ball in coconut. Place on the parchment-lined plate. Repeat with the remaining dough and coconut.

6 Refrigerate for at least 3 hours (up to overnight). Store in an airtight container in the refrigerator for up to 1 week, or in a freezer-safe container in the freezer for up to 3 months.

A CARROT A DAY

It turns out that carrots aren't just good for your eyesight—they can also help to keep your heart healthy. Numerous studies have shown that carrots can reduce the risk of coronary heart disease, and for every 25 grams of carrots eaten daily, the risk decreases by 32 percent! The health benefits of carrots come from their high content of fiber, vitamin A, and beta-carotene. Carrots can help to lower cholesterol levels and blood sugar levels too.

Matcha Protein Balls

MAKES 12 BALLS

Per Serving (1 ball)

Calories	130
Fat	7g
Sodium	80mg
Carbohydrates	6g
Fiber	1g
Sugar	4g
Protein	14g

COCONUT OIL

Surprisingly, countries with the highest intakes of coconut oil have the lowest rates of heart disease. While research shows coconut oil contains higher amounts of saturated fat and does increase total cholesterol, those amounts do not increase your heart attack or stroke risk. The saturated fat in coconut is the good kind that increases the large buoyant LDL particles, which is the non-dangerous type.

Enjoy the calming yet energizing impact of matcha in a tasty high-protein snack. Keep these on hand for when you need to focus for long periods.

1 tablespoon matcha green tea powder

3 tablespoons maple syrup, divided

1 teaspoon vanilla extract

1½ cups collagen powder, divided

1 cup unsweetened shredded coconut

4 tablespoons almond flour

1 tablespoon organic virgin coconut oil

1. In a large bowl, whisk together matcha and 1 tablespoon maple syrup until smooth. Stir in vanilla, and remaining 2 tablespoons maple syrup. Add coconut and almond flour to the bowl. Gently stir with a wooden spoon until combined. Stir in 1 cup collagen powder.
2. Line a large, airtight container with parchment paper.
3. Add coconut oil and stir until incorporated and a dough starts to form. Add the remaining ½ cup collagen powder and stir until the mixture dries out a bit. Add extra 1–2 tablespoons collagen powder if dough is too sticky or 1 tablespoon coconut oil if it's too dry.
4. Using your hands, divide the dough into 12 portions and roll each portion into a ball. Place in the prepared container. Repeat with the remaining dough.
5. Cover container and refrigerate for at least 3 hours (up to overnight). Store balls in an airtight container in the refrigerator for up to 1 week.

Spirulina Protein Balls

MAKES 10 BALLS

Per Serving (1 ball)

Calories	250
Fat	14g
Sodium	30mg
Carbohydrates	18g
Fiber	3g
Sugar	12g
Protein	16g

HOW TO SOFTEN DATES

To work well in energy balls, dates must be very soft and gooey so they can help bind everything together. If they are on the drier side, soak them in hot water for a few minutes, then drain well before using. Reserve the soaking liquid, so if the mixture is a tiny bit dry, you can slowly add water, 1 scant tablespoon at a time, to get the dough to the right consistency.

Spirulina is an excellent tool to have in your heart-healthy tool kit, and these protein balls are a great way to get more of this amazing green powder in your life!

1 cup whole raw cashews

1 cup shelled raw pumpkin seeds

6 large Medjool dates, pitted

1 teaspoon ground cinnamon

1 teaspoon spirulina powder

2 teaspoons grated orange zest

1 cup grass-fed whey protein powder

2 tablespoons organic virgin coconut oil

1 Place cashews and pumpkin seeds in a food processor and blend for 1 minute or until a coarsely ground texture is reached. Add dates, cinnamon, spirulina, and orange zest, and blend for 30–60 seconds until well combined. Add protein powder and blend for 30 seconds or until a thick dough forms. Transfer to a large bowl.

2 Add coconut oil and mix with your hands until incorporated.

3 Divide mixture into 10 portions and roll each portion into a ball. Place balls on a large ungreased baking sheet or plate and refrigerate for at least 1 hour.

4 Store in an airtight container in the refrigerator for up to 1 week.

Salted Chocolate Chili Bites

Enjoy these ultra-tasty, protein-rich bites for an anytime snack. Grab a couple on your way out the door to enjoy on a tea or coffee break. They're great for both your heart and your skin.

1 cup chopped walnuts

⅓ cup shelled raw pumpkin seeds

⅓ cup shelled raw sunflower seeds

⅓ cup sesame seeds

6 medium Medjool dates, pitted

3 tablespoons organic virgin coconut oil

8 tablespoons raw cacao powder

1 teaspoon vanilla extract

2 teaspoons grated lime zest

½ teaspoon sea salt

⅛ teaspoon chili powder

1. Place all ingredients in a food processor and blend for 3–4 minutes until nuts have broken down and a sticky dough is formed. If the mixture is dry and too crumbly to form a ball, add 1 more tablespoon coconut oil.
2. Divide mixture into 10 portions and roll each portion into a ball. Place balls on a large ungreased baking sheet or plate and refrigerate for at least 1 hour.
3. Store in an airtight container in the refrigerator for up to 1 week.

MAKES 10 BALLS

Per Serving (2 balls)

Calories	490
Fat	37g
Sodium	250mg
Carbohydrates	33g
Fiber	6g
Sugar	20g
Protein	10g

CHILI POWDER

Chili powder is particularly high in capsaicin, the compound that gives chili peppers their heat. A 2020 chili pepper study released by the American Heart Association analyzed more than 4,700 previous studies from five leading global health databases and found that people who ate chili peppers had 26 percent less risk of dying from heart disease (and a 25 percent drop in all causes of death!), 23 percent less risk of dying from cancer, and 25 percent less risk of dying from any cause compared to people who rarely or never ate chili peppers.

Chocolate Peanut Protein Cookies

MAKES 12 COOKIES

Per Serving (2 cookies)

Calories	350
Fat	17g
Sodium	100mg
Carbohydrates	28g
Fiber	4g
Sugar	20g
Protein	25g

WHY PROTEIN COOKIES?

There is evidence to suggest that eating more protein can help you achieve your weight loss goals. Protein is an essential nutrient that helps to keep your body feeling satisfied and fueled. It also has a number of health benefits, including helping to maintain heart health and cholesterol levels. Eating enough protein, however, can be a challenge for busy people. Protein bars, cookies, balls, shakes, and powders can help you get the nutrients you need without having to spend hours in the kitchen.

These delicious cookies, full of blood sugar–stabilizing protein, make an amazing sweet treat to take with you when you're on the go.

2 tablespoons dark chocolate chips

2 tablespoons raw peanuts

½ cup no-sugar-added extra-chunky peanut butter

4 medium Medjool dates, pitted

2 large free-range eggs

2 tablespoons maple syrup

1 teaspoon vanilla extract

½ teaspoon baking soda

2 tablespoons coconut flour

1 cup grass-fed whey protein powder

1. Preheat oven to 350°F. Line a large baking sheet with parchment paper.
2. Place chocolate chips and peanuts on a cutting board and roughly chop. Set aside.
3. Place peanut butter, dates, eggs, maple syrup, and vanilla in a high-speed blender or food processor and blend for 30 seconds or until dates are finely minced.
4. Transfer the mixture to a medium bowl. Sprinkle baking soda over the top of the batter. Add coconut flour and protein powder and stir with a spatula until well combined. Fold in chopped chocolate chips and peanuts.
5. The dough should be slightly sticky but firm. If it's too dry, sprinkle it with a few drops of water, then mix. If it's too wet, add a bit more protein powder.
6. Use a large spoon to scoop a ball of dough. Use another spoon to push the ball onto the prepared baking sheet. Repeat with the remaining dough until you have 12 balls of dough on the baking sheet. Use a fork to gently flatten the balls.
7. Bake for 5–6 minutes until the edges are lightly browned and dry to the touch, but cookies are still soft in the middle. Let cool on the baking sheet for 3 minutes. Transfer cookies to a wire rack to cool for at least 15 minutes before serving.
8. Store in an airtight container in the refrigerator for up to 4 days, or in a freezer-safe container in the freezer for up to 3 months.

Chocolate Turmeric Fudge Bites

Try sprinkling the top of these with a dusting of cacao, crushed pistachios, finely chopped dried apricots, or raw cacao nibs. Press the toppings into the top of the fudge before you place the pan in the refrigerator.

1 cup chopped walnuts

1 ounce 70% dark chocolate

8 medium Medjool dates, pitted

3 tablespoons raw cacao powder

1 tablespoon ground turmeric

1 tablespoon extra-virgin olive oil

1 teaspoon vanilla extract

¼ teaspoon sea salt

⅛ teaspoon ground black pepper

1 Line an 8" × 8" pan with parchment paper.

2 Place walnuts and chocolate in a food processor and pulse until finely chopped into a powder, 10–20 seconds. Add dates, cacao powder, turmeric, oil, vanilla, salt, and pepper and blend for 30 seconds or until the mixture forms a ball.

3 Use your hands to squeeze the dough together. It should feel like smooth taffy. If the mixture does not come together, add 1 tablespoon cold water and knead the dough.

4 Transfer dough to one side of the prepared pan. Fold the parchment over onto the dough, and use your fingers to press the dough between the parchment, squeezing it into an even layer that covers about ½ the bottom of the pan. Refrigerate for at least 1 hour or up to overnight.

5 Cut into 12 squares and serve, or store in the refrigerator in a tightly covered container for up to 1 week.

SERVES 12

Per Serving

Calories	140
Fat	9g
Sodium	50mg
Carbohydrates	16g
Fiber	2g
Sugar	12g
Protein	2g

NO-BAKE FUDGE BROWNIES

Because of the high levels of antioxidant flavanols, raw cacao has been shown to lower blood pressure and improve overall heart function and circulation, and it is also associated with anti-aging and longevity. No-bake brownies are great because they retain the beneficial properties of the antioxidants and fats in cacao and nuts. Include some no-bake chocolate bars, bites, balls, and brownies in your repertoire to take full advantage of the power of cacao flavanols.

CHAPTER 5

Weekday Lunches

Easy Protein Bread

Most breads can spike the level of blood sugar in your bloodstream, but the protein, fat, and fiber in this delicious nutty loaf work together to slow down the release of sugar. It's super easy to make—just mix everything in one pan, set it aside for a while, and bake. It's excellent toasted.

PSYLLIUM HUSK POWDER

Psyllium husk powder is a type of soluble fiber that helps baked goods bind together without gluten. When psyllium husk comes into contact with water, it forms a gel-like substance that can help to promote regularity. Studies have shown that psyllium husk can help to reduce LDL cholesterol levels while also increasing HDL cholesterol levels, and reduce inflammation.

½ cup buckwheat flour

1 cup rolled oats

1 cup whole raw, almonds

1 cup shelled raw sunflower seeds

3 tablespoons psyllium husk powder (or 4 tablespoons whole psyllium seed husks)

2 tablespoons chia seeds

1 teaspoon salt

1 tablespoon maple syrup

2 tablespoons extra-virgin olive oil

1½ cups water

1 In a greased 9" × 4" bread pan, stir together buckwheat flour, oats, almonds, sunflower seeds, psyllium husk powder, chia seeds, and salt. In a small bowl, whisk together maple syrup, oil, and water, then add to bread pan and mix well. If mixture is too thick to stir, add more water 1 teaspoon at a time.

2 Set pan aside at room temperature for at least 2 hours or up to overnight.

3 Preheat oven to 350°F.

4 Bake for 60 minutes. Bread should shrink away from the pan edges and be easy to remove. Turn pan over and put the loaf upside down on a wire rack. When done, it should sound hollow when tapped. If not, place back in the pan and bake another 10 minutes.

5 Cool completely on a wire rack. Cut loaf into 16 slices. Keep a few slices in a tightly sealed container at room temperature. Freeze what you can't use immediately in a freezer-safe container for up to 3 months. Take frozen slices directly from the freezer and toast.

Roasted Orange Veggies

Serve these vegetables with Roasted Salmon Fillets or Baked Teriyaki Tofu (see recipes in this chapter), along with some salad greens, for a satisfying lunch. The orange vegetables are full of the antioxidant beta-carotene which is great for your skin. The feta cheese increases your ability to absorb beta-carotene, leading to a more beautiful you!

1 large sweet potato, cut into 1" chunks

1 large butternut squash, cut into 1" chunks

1 large parsnip, cut into 1" chunks

1 tablespoon extra-virgin olive oil

1 tablespoon dried sage

1 teaspoon cumin seeds

1 teaspoon salt

1 cup cubed feta cheese (preferably sheep's milk feta)

1 Preheat oven to 350°F. Line a large baking sheet with parchment paper.

2 Combine sweet potato, squash, and parsnip in a large bowl. Add oil, sage, cumin seeds, and salt. Toss to combine, then transfer mixture to the prepared baking sheet.

3 Bake for 15–20 minutes until vegetables are soft and lightly browned. Place baking sheet on a wire rack and cool for 5 minutes.

4 Transfer mixture to a large bowl and add feta. Stir to combine. Divide mixture among four glass or plastic containers. Cover and refrigerate for up to 5 days.

5 Serve cold or heat in the microwave for 60–90 seconds on high.

SERVES 4

Per Serving

Calories	360
Fat	12g
Sodium	1,000mg
Carbohydrates	27g
Fiber	4g
Sugar	23g
Protein	11g

ENERGY LUNCH FORMULA

One of the best things you can do for your energy levels and health is to eat a good lunch. Here's the formula for lunch prep: Roast a few different types (and colors) of vegetables each weekend. Prepare protein, like chicken, salmon, or tofu. Package vegetables with 20–30 grams of protein into individual containers and keep a big bag of salad greens and a jar of healthy dressing at work. Voilà! You've got a week's worth of nutrient-rich lunches.

Whirlpool Crustless Quiche

For easy make-ahead lunches, cut the quiche into 6 portions, wrap tightly in foil, and freeze for up to 1 month. Defrost a piece in the refrigerator overnight and reheat it for a minute or so in the microwave. It's great with a toasted slice of Easy Protein Bread (see recipe in this chapter) and Best Basic Salad (see recipe in Chapter 9).

1 tablespoon organic virgin coconut oil (or grass-fed butter)

12 large free-range eggs, beaten

1 tablespoon dried oregano

1 teaspoon sea salt

1 large zucchini, trimmed and shredded

2 large carrots, peeled and shredded

1 Preheat oven to 350°F.
2 Grease a 13" × 9" baking dish with coconut oil.
3 In a large bowl, whisk together eggs, oregano, and salt until light and frothy. Stir in zucchini and carrots. Pour mixture into the prepared baking dish.
4 Using a fork, create six circular "whirlpool" patterns on the surface of the quiche. Bake for 45 minutes or until edges are lightly browned.
5 Cool on a wire rack for 5 minutes. Cut quiche into 6 pieces and serve.

SERVES 6

Per Serving

Calories	180
Fat	12g
Sodium	550mg
Carbohydrates	4g
Fiber	1g
Sugar	2g
Protein	13g

CRUSTLESS QUICHE

A good quiche or egg bake should have a nutrient-rich variety of textures, flavors, and colors. A great way to achieve this is by including green vegetables like spinach, kale, or broccoli; orange sweet potatoes, winter squash, or shredded carrots; and red options like cherry tomatoes or beets. Add organic, free-range meats, nuts, or a bit of cheese for healthy fats and even more protein.

Roasted Beets and Red Cabbage

SERVES 4

Per Serving

Calories	140
Fat	7g
Sodium	650mg
Carbohydrates	14g
Fiber	4g
Sugar	9g
Protein	3g

AVOID AFTERNOON SLUMPS

You know what it's like to feel an afternoon slump. You're tired, your energy is low, and all you can think about is grabbing some junk food to get you through the rest of the day. To avoid that slump, eat a high-protein, low-sugar, nutritious lunch. It will provide your body with the energy it needs to make it through the afternoon without crashing.

Both beets and red cabbage are excellent sources of antioxidants. These vibrant roasted vegetables can be added to a green salad, or to a filling lunch bowl with a protein and spinach or kale. Or top them with chopped walnuts and fresh dill for a delicious side dish.

4 large beets, trimmed and cut into 8 wedges each

1 small red cabbage, cored and cut into 16 wedges

1 large red onion, peeled and cut into 8 wedges

2 tablespoons extra-virgin olive oil

1 tablespoon dried dill

1 teaspoon salt

1 Preheat oven to 350°F. Line two large baking sheets with parchment paper.

2 Place beets, cabbage, and onion in a large bowl. Add oil, dill, and salt and toss to coat. Divide mixture between the prepared baking sheets and spread out in a single layer.

3 Bake for 25–30 minutes until vegetables are soft and lightly browned. Place baking sheet on a wire rack and cool for 5 minutes.

4 Divide mixture among four glass or plastic containers. Cover and refrigerate for up to 5 days.

5 Serve cold or heat in the microwave for 60–90 seconds on high.

Cabbage Steaks

These caramelized planks of roasted cabbage are easy to make and taste so good, they'll convert even the most hard-core cabbage hater! Use the steaks as a base for an easy lunch. Top them with hummus and canned salmon or Roasted Orange Veggies (see recipe in this chapter) and baked chicken thighs for a well-rounded lunch.

2 tablespoons extra-virgin olive oil

1 tablespoon grated lemon zest

3 tablespoons lemon juice

½ teaspoon salt

2 cloves garlic, peeled and minced

2 medium savoy cabbages, cored and cut into ¾" steaks

¼ cup grated Parmesan cheese

1 Preheat oven to 425°F and line two large baking sheets with parchment paper.
2 In a small bowl, whisk together oil, lemon zest, lemon juice, salt, and garlic.
3 Place cabbage steaks on the prepared baking sheets. Brush the tops with half of the oil mixture and bake for 18–22 minutes until lightly browned, swapping the baking sheets from the top to bottom oven shelves halfway through.
4 Brush cabbage steaks with the remaining oil mixture and sprinkle with Parmesan.
5 Divide steaks among four glass or plastic containers. Cover and refrigerate for up to 5 days.
6 Serve cold or heat in the microwave for 60–90 seconds on high.

SERVES 4

Per Serving

Calories	200
Fat	9g
Sodium	460mg
Carbohydrates	29g
Fiber	12g
Sugar	15g
Protein	7g

BOOST LUNCH PROTEIN

If you're trying to lose weight or keep your weight stable, aim for 20–30 grams of protein at lunchtime. Adequate protein at lunch will also help you maintain high energy levels. A boiled egg has around 6 grams of protein, while a 5-ounce can of fish has around 20 grams. Chicken and tofu are also good options, with 30 grams and 20 grams of protein per serving, respectively. Add the protein to a colorful vegetable base and you'll have a healthy, satisfying meal.

Baked Teriyaki Tofu

SERVES 4

Per Serving

Calories	220
Fat	17g
Sodium	510mg
Carbohydrates	6g
Fiber	1g
Sugar	2g
Protein	13g

SOY IS SAFE

Researchers in Asia have reported that soy consumption can reduce the risk of cardiovascular disease by 16 percent. Women used to avoid soy, as there was a widespread misconception, based on previous studies in rats, that the natural plant phytoestrogens in soy might cause breast cancer. In 2014, a meta-analysis of multiple studies in the journal *PLOS One* found that soy was marginally protective against breast cancer in postmenopausal people from Western countries. So, benefit from the heart and cancer protective benefits of soy in your weekly diet.

This is a great recipe to double so you can have a delicious protein source to add to any meal. Pack some of these tofu bites with raw or roasted vegetables for an outstanding lunch. Or add them to your favorite salad for an extra hit of protein and flavor.

1 (14-ounce) package firm tofu, drained and patted dry

2 tablespoons tamari

2 tablespoons extra-virgin olive oil

1 tablespoon sesame oil

2 tablespoons apple cider vinegar

1 tablespoon minced ginger

1 teaspoon raw honey

⅛ teaspoon crushed red pepper flakes

1 clove garlic, peeled and minced

1 Preheat oven to 375°F. Line a large baking sheet with parchment paper.

2 Cut tofu into 1" × 2" rectangles about ⅓" thick.

3 In a shallow bowl, whisk together tamari, olive oil, sesame oil, vinegar, ginger, honey, red pepper flakes, and garlic. Dip tofu pieces into mixture, coating both sides, and place on the prepared baking sheet.

4 Bake for 7–10 minutes until edges are light brown. Place baking sheet on a wire rack and cool for 5 minutes.

5 Store covered in the refrigerator for up to 7 days.

Red Lentil Lunch Curry

This delicious curry is a snap to make, and it's full of skin-beautifying ingredients. Try adding some protein on top, like cooked shrimp or canned fish.

1 cup dried red lentils, rinsed

½ cup steel cut oats

1 (28-ounce can) crushed tomatoes

½ cup full-fat coconut milk

1 large red onion, peeled and chopped

1 tablespoon ground turmeric

1 tablespoon dried Greek oregano

1 teaspoon sea salt

½ teaspoon ground black pepper

¼ teaspoon crushed red pepper flakes

¼ cup sliced almonds

¼ cup chopped fresh cilantro

1. Place lentils, oats, tomatoes, coconut milk, onion, turmeric, oregano, salt, and black pepper in a medium saucepan. Bring to a boil over medium-high heat. Reduce heat to low, partially cover, and simmer for 15 minutes.
2. Uncover and stir well. If mixture is dry, add about ½ cup water.
3. Simmer uncovered for another 10–15 minutes until lentils are tender.
4. Top curry with red pepper flakes, almonds, and cilantro. Serve hot.

SERVES 4

Per Serving

Calories	430
Fat	13g
Sodium	960mg
Carbohydrates	63g
Fiber	15g
Sugar	12g
Protein	22g

SWAP RICE FOR OATS

Did you know you an use steel cut oats to make an almost risotto-like dish? Steel cut oats, also called pinhead oats, coarse oatmeal, or Irish oatmeal, are more nutrient dense and contain fewer calories than rice, making them a good choice for people who are trying to lose weight. The grainy texture is fairly similar to rice, and oats contain more fiber, which helps to lower cholesterol. A slower rise in blood sugar can also lead to lower inflammation in the body.

Grapefruit and Avocado Salad

This juicy salad is energizing and full of protein and healthy fats. If you don't have shrimp, use canned salmon, tuna, sardines, or mackerel.

SERVES 2

Per Serving

Calories	450
Fat	27g
Sodium	840mg
Carbohydrates	31g
Fiber	6g
Sugar	19g
Protein	27g

CITRUS SUPRÊMES

To make individual grapefruit segments, or suprêmes, first use a sharp knife to cut the ends off the grapefruit. Rest the grapefruit on a cut side. Cut off the remaining rind and pith by cutting in small sections from top to bottom, following the curve of the grapefruit. Once the fruit is peeled, gently slice in between each segment to free the fruit from the membrane. This creates individual suprêmes of grapefruit (or oranges, lemons, and limes).

1 extra-large ruby red grapefruit, cut into suprêmes

4 cups arugula

1 medium avocado, peeled, pitted, and sliced

1 small red onion, peeled and very thinly sliced

6 ounces cooked large shrimp, peeled and deveined

2 tablespoons extra-virgin olive oil

2 tablespoons apple cider vinegar

1 teaspoon raw honey

½ teaspoon salt

1 Place grapefruit, arugula, avocado, onion, and shrimp in a large bowl.

2 In a small bowl, whisk oil, vinegar, honey, and salt together. Pour over salad and toss gently to coat. Serve immediately.

Energizing Pesto Zoodles

Zucchini noodles are a great way to avoid the harmful blood sugar spikes that pasta can cause. You can find inexpensive spiralizers online, in kitchen stores, and even at your local supermarket. If you don't have a spiralizer, cut the zucchini into thin strips with a sharp knife or use a vegetable peeler to make wide slices.

3 large zucchini, trimmed and spiralized

1 cup chopped fresh dill

1 cup chopped fresh parsley

¼ cup shelled hemp seeds

¼ cup feta cheese (preferably sheep's milk feta)

1 clove garlic, peeled

1 tablespoon nutritional yeast

½ teaspoon salt

1 Place zucchini in a large bowl and set aside.

2 Combine dill, parsley, hemp seeds, feta, garlic, nutritional yeast, and salt in a food processor or high-speed blender. Process until very smooth, scraping down the sides of the bowl a few times. If mixture is too thick, add water 1 teaspoon at a time until it reaches a sauce consistency.

3 Pour sauce over zucchini and stir to coat. Serve immediately.

SERVES 4

Per Serving

Calories	130
Fat	7g
Sodium	410mg
Carbohydrates	10g
Fiber	4g
Sugar	6g
Protein	9g

HEMP SEEDS

Shelled hemp seeds (hemp hearts) are packed with nutrients and are excellent energy boosters due to high levels of protein and essential nutrients like omega-3 fatty acids, magnesium, potassium, and iron. The high protein and fiber content of hemp hearts keeps you feeling full and satisfied, and can help to lower cholesterol and keep the digestive system running smoothly. Try sprinkling a tablespoon on oatmeal, or adding some to your favorite smoothie, salad dressing, or vegetable side dish.

Strawberry Sweet Potato Bowl

SERVES 1

Per Serving

Calories	270
Fat	7g
Sodium	270mg
Carbohydrates	45g
Fiber	11g
Sugar	19g
Protein	11g

STUFFED SWEET POTATOES

Stuffed sweet potatoes are a versatile and delicious option for a quick meal or snack. There are a variety of ways to stuff a sweet potato. Good fillings include protein to flatten the glucose spike (as sweet potatoes themselves are higher in carbohydrates). Try hummus, tuna, cheese, vegetables, or ground meat.

Sweet potato, hummus, and scallions are a fantastic combination. This bowl goes further by adding the goodness of strawberries and arugula.

1 small sweet potato

3½ ounces arugula

½ cup Basil Protein Hummus (see recipe in Chapter 8)

1 scallion, trimmed and chopped

1 tablespoon unsalted, roasted, and shelled pumpkin seeds

1 cup sliced strawberries

1 tablespoon balsamic vinegar

1 Preheat oven to 425°F. Line a small baking sheet with foil.
2 Place sweet potato on prepared baking sheet and prick all over with a fork. Bake until tender, 35–40 minutes. Set potato on a wire rack and cool for 10 minutes.
3 Line a shallow bowl with arugula and place sweet potato on top. Cut a slit in the top of sweet potato and open slightly.
4 Top sweet potato with hummus and sprinkle with scallion and pumpkin seeds. Place strawberries on arugula around sweet potato, and drizzle with vinegar.
5 Serve warm.

Open-Faced Tomato Basil Sandwiches

SERVES 2

Per Serving

Calories	450
Fat	32g
Sodium	900mg
Carbohydrates	32g
Fiber	11g
Sugar	5g
Protein	12g

CHERRY TOMATOES

Lycopene is a powerful antioxidant found in tomatoes. This bright red pigment is responsible for the health benefits associated with eating tomatoes, including a reduced risk of cancer and heart disease. While lycopene is found in both large and small tomatoes, it is more concentrated and bioavailable in cherry tomatoes. In fact, one cherry tomato has the same amount of lycopene as one large tomato!

These sandwiches are divine during the cherry tomato season of summer and early fall, but you can use any type of tomatoes that are available. For a filling lunch, top the sandwiches with canned tuna or salmon.

2 tablespoons extra-virgin olive oil

1 tablespoon apple cider vinegar

2 cups finely chopped cherry tomatoes

1 cup chopped fresh basil

1 clove garlic, peeled and minced

½ teaspoon salt

4 slices Easy Protein Bread (see recipe in this chapter), lightly toasted

1 In a small bowl, stir together oil, vinegar, tomatoes, basil, garlic, and salt.

2 Place 2 slices bread on two separate plates. Top with tomato mixture and serve.

Roasted Salmon Fillets

Cooking salmon, which is loaded with omega-3s, is very hard to mess up. It tastes great baked in the oven with very little seasoning. If you like a little heat, add a sprinkle of crushed red pepper flakes. Make a batch at the beginning of the week, and you'll have plenty of heart-healthy protein to add to salads, bowls, and wraps for easy lunches.

4 (5-ounce) salmon fillets

1 tablespoon extra-virgin olive oil

1 teaspoon dried thyme

½ teaspoon salt

1 Preheat oven to 350°F. Line a large baking sheet with parchment paper.
2 Brush tops of salmon with oil and place on prepared baking sheet, skin side down. Sprinkle with thyme and salt.
3 Bake for 15–20 minutes until salmon is opaque all the way through. Remove from oven and let cool before storing.
4 Divide fillets among four glass or plastic containers. Cover and refrigerate for up to 5 days.
5 Serve cold or heat in the microwave for 60–90 seconds on high.

SERVES 4

Per Serving

Calories	210
Fat	10g
Sodium	400mg
Carbohydrates	0g
Fiber	0g
Sugar	0g
Protein	29g

CHOOSE WILD SALMON

Wild-caught salmon tends to have a much higher omega-3 content than farmed salmon. This is because wild salmon eat a diet of small fish and other marine life that are high in omega-3s. In contrast, farmed salmon are fed pellets, which tends to lead to lower omega-3s and higher fat content. Look for fresh, frozen, or canned fish that has been caught in the United States or Canada.

Mango, Shrimp, and Cilantro Salad

SERVES 4

Per Serving

Calories	320
Fat	8g
Sodium	670mg
Carbohydrates	35g
Fiber	4g
Sugar	14g
Protein	31g

CILANTRO

Cilantro boosts the immune system, lowers cholesterol, inhibits lipid oxidization, and offers significant blood sugar–lowering effects. It is best known for its role in detoxifying the body of neurotoxic heavy metals, which are associated with adverse cardiac outcomes. You accumulate heavy metals through eating, breathing, and absorbing them through the skin. Heavy metals like arsenic, cadmium, chromium, lead, and mercury are classified as human carcinogens. Cilantro binds to heavy metals and toxins in your body and helps to remove them.

This protein-packed salad has an amazingly zesty lime-cilantro dressing. This salad keeps well in the refrigerator, so it makes a great meal-prep lunch.

1 (15-ounce) can black beans, drained and rinsed

1 medium red bell pepper, seeded and cut into ½" cubes

1 large mango, peeled, pitted, and cut into ½" cubes

12 ounces cooked large shrimp, peeled and deveined

2 cups roughly chopped fresh cilantro

1 medium avocado, peeled, pitted, and cut into ½" cubes

1½ teaspoons grated lime zest

2 tablespoons lime juice

½ teaspoon salt

⅛ teaspoon crushed red pepper flakes

1. Place all ingredients in a large bowl and stir to combine.
2. Divide mixture among four serving bowls and serve immediately, or store in refrigerator for up to 2 days.

Sardines on Avocado Toast

A slice of this hearty toast will keep you full for hours. This quick protein-filled meal is overflowing with heart-healthy, skin-friendly fat to help you look and feel great. Crushed red pepper flakes and nigella seeds sprinkled on top are fantastic additions.

1 medium avocado, peeled and pitted

1 tablespoon lime juice

2 teaspoons extra-virgin olive oil

½ teaspoon sea salt

1 teaspoon minced garlic

2 (1-ounce) slices rye and flax protein bread, lightly toasted

½ cup minced fresh cilantro

6 cherry tomatoes, halved

1 (4.5-ounce) can oil-packed sardines, drained

1 Place avocado, lime juice, oil, salt, and garlic in a small bowl and mash together with a fork until smooth.

2 Spread mixture over toasted bread. Top with cilantro, tomatoes (cut side up), and sardines.

3 Serve immediately.

SERVES 2

Per Serving

Calories	400
Fat	26g
Sodium	1,101mg
Carbohydrates	25g
Fiber	3g
Sugar	3g
Protein	21g

SKIN-FRIENDLY SARDINES

Packed with phosphorus, protein, vitamins D and B_{12}, calcium, and omega-3 fatty acids, sardines play an important role in keeping your skin hydrated and glowing. According to the University of Maryland Medical Center, they also help increase HDL levels and decrease triglyceride levels. The American Heart Association recommends that people eat one to two meals of non-fried fish or shellfish per week for better cardiovascular health.

Asian Lunch Bowl

SERVES 1

Per Serving

Calories	750
Fat	26g
Sodium	2,130mg
Carbohydrates	60g
Fiber	10g
Sugar	10g
Protein	74g

MACKEREL

Adding canned mackerel to your lunchtime routine is an easy way to boost your protein intake. You'll also get a healthy dose of omega-3 fatty acids to help lower cholesterol levels and reduce inflammation. Mackerel is a rich source of other nutrients, including selenium and vitamin B_{12}, and it has a meaty, dense texture that can keep you feeling full and satisfied all afternoon.

This quick, satisfying lunch bowl can be made in about 5 minutes. It's adaptable, too—swap shiitakes for button mushrooms and use whatever canned fish you have on hand.

1 cup sliced shiitake mushrooms

1½ teaspoons grated lime zest

2 tablespoons lime juice

2 cups loosely packed spinach leaves

½ (15-ounce) can black beans or adzuki beans, drained and rinsed

1 tablespoon tamari

¼ teaspoon crushed red pepper flakes

1½ tablespoons tahini, divided

1 (7-ounce) can mackerel fillets in brine, drained

1 In a medium bowl, combine mushrooms, lime zest, and lime juice. Stir until mushrooms are coated. Set aside for 5 minutes.

2 Stir in spinach, beans, tamari, red pepper flakes, and 1 tablespoon tahini. Transfer mixture to a plate or shallow salad bowl.

3 Top with mackerel and drizzle with remaining ½ tablespoon tahini. Serve immediately.

Tahini Sweet Potatoes with Chicken and Broccoli

Spending a little weekend time on meal prep will provide you with days of easy lunches. Enjoy this colorful meal as is or drizzle it with some Amazing Salad Dressing (see recipe in Chapter 12).

4 small sweet potatoes

4 (6-ounce) free-range, bone-in chicken thighs

1 teaspoon salt

2 cups chopped broccoli

2 cups shiitake mushrooms

4 tablespoons tahini

4 scallions, trimmed and chopped

8 cups baby arugula

SERVES 4

Per Serving

Calories	300
Fat	13g
Sodium	750mg
Carbohydrates	21g
Fiber	6g
Sugar	6g
Protein	28g

1 Preheat oven to 350°F. Line two large baking sheets with parchment paper.

2 Use a fork to poke a few holes in each potato and place on one side of a prepared baking sheet. Place chicken on the other side. Sprinkle tops of chicken with salt. Bake for 40–45 minutes until sweet potatoes are tender and the internal temperature of chicken is at least 165°F.

3 Place broccoli and mushrooms on the second baking sheet and add to the oven for the final 15 minutes of baking time. Stir broccoli mixture once halfway through.

4 Set aside both baking sheets to cool for at least 15 minutes.

5 Place 1 sweet potato and 1 chicken thigh in each of four glass or plastic containers. Spread 1 tablespoon tahini over each sweet potato.

6 Divide broccoli mixture evenly among containers. Top each with scallions and arugula and cover containers tightly. Refrigerate for up to 5 days.

7 Serve at room temperature.

WEEKEND MEAL PREP

If you're like most people, lunchtime during the week can be a rushed affair. Taking a few minutes to prepare weekday lunches over the weekend can save you time and help you make better food choices during the week. Simply choose a few recipes that you can make ahead of time, do the chopping and cooking on the weekend, then package up lunches in individual containers so you can grab and go.

Meatballs and Roasted Cauliflower

SERVES 4

Per Serving

Calories	280
Fat	20g
Sodium	1,100mg
Carbohydrates	17g
Fiber	4g
Sugar	6g
Protein	12g

WHY GRASS-FED BEEF?

Grass-fed beef is higher in omega-3 fatty acids and other nutrients, making it a heart-healthy choice (comparable to the omega-3s in salmon!) that can lower cholesterol levels. In contrast, factory-farmed beef is raised on an industrial diet of grains (mostly corn and soy), rather than grass, along with antibiotics and hormones, all of which have been linked to health problems.

This easy meal-prep lunch can be served over a bed of arugula or spinach with a drizzle of Amazing Salad Dressing (see recipe in Chapter 12). For even more flavor, add a few pitted green olives and some chopped fresh parsley.

12 frozen, raw grass-fed beef meatballs (10% fat, no-sugar-added), thawed

1 medium head cauliflower, cored and cut into florets

1 large red onion, peeled and roughly chopped

3 cloves garlic, peeled and thickly sliced

2 tablespoons capers

2 tablespoons extra-virgin olive oil

1 teaspoon salt

1 teaspoon ground black pepper

1. Preheat oven to 350°F. Line two large baking sheets with parchment paper.
2. Place meatballs on one prepared baking sheet. Bake for 20–25 minutes until well browned. Place baking sheet on a wire rack to cool.
3. While meatballs are cooking, combine cauliflower, onion, garlic, capers, oil, salt, and pepper in a large bowl. Toss to combine, then transfer mixture to the second prepared baking sheet. Bake for 15–20 minutes, stirring once during cooking time, until vegetables are lightly browned. Place baking sheet on a wire rack to cool.
4. Place 3 meatballs in each of four glass or plastic containers. Divide even amounts cauliflower mixture to each container. Cover and refrigerate for up to 5 days.
5. Before serving, heat container in the microwave for 1½–2 minutes until hot.

CHAPTER 6

Quick Dinners

Magical Kale and Cannellini

SERVES 4

Per Serving

Calories	330
Fat	5g
Sodium	810mg
Carbohydrates	52g
Fiber	5g
Sugar	9g
Protein	20g

BLACK TUSCAN KALE

Black Tuscan kale, also known as cavolo nero, lacinato kale, dinosaur kale, or nero di toscana, is one of the world's most antioxidant-rich foods and one that you should eat often. A cup of cooked kale provides almost five times your daily need for vitamin K, around 15–18 percent of the daily recommended amount of calcium, and about 7 percent of your daily phosphorus requirement. Regular consumption of kale is believed to help reduce cholesterol levels as well.

This warm kale meal is remarkably tasty and packed with immune-boosting nutrition. If you don't like anchovies, you can omit them. Or substitute with 1 tablespoon each of nutritional yeast flakes and tamari. Add a sprinkle of sesame seeds for a light, nutty crunch.

1 tablespoon organic virgin coconut oil

2 large red onions, peeled and thinly sliced

1 teaspoon crushed red pepper flakes

2 cups sliced shiitake mushrooms

8 cups stemmed and chopped Tuscan kale

2 (15-ounce) cans cannellini beans, drained and rinsed

4 cloves garlic, peeled and minced

1 (1.5-ounce) jar olive oil–packed anchovy fillets, drained and chopped

16 cherry tomatoes, halved

1. Heat coconut oil in a large saucepan or Dutch oven over medium heat. Sauté onions until softened, 3–4 minutes. Stir in red pepper flakes and mushrooms; sauté for 2 minutes.
2. Reduce heat to low and stir in kale and beans. Cover and cook for 2–3 minutes until kale is softened. If the mixture seems dry, add 1–2 tablespoons water.
3. Remove from heat and add garlic and anchovies. Stir until combined.
4. Divide mixture among four plates, then top with tomatoes. Serve immediately.

Lemon Asparagus Tomato Bake

This is a flavorful, fiber-packed dish that makes use of a spring favorite—asparagus. If it's not available, you can use green beans or broccoli instead. In the last 10 minutes of baking, add a few salmon (or other fish) fillets for a kick of protein.

1 large bunch asparagus (about 2 pounds), trimmed and cut into thirds

1 (15-ounce) can cannellini beans, drained and rinsed

1 (14.5-ounce) can petite-diced tomatoes

4 tablespoons tomato paste

1½ cups cherry tomatoes

2 medium red onions, peeled, halved, and sliced into thin half circles

3 cloves garlic, peeled and minced

1 small bird's eye chili, seeded and minced

3 tablespoons lemon juice

1 tablespoon grated lemon zest

1 teaspoon salt

1 teaspoon cumin seeds

1 teaspoon dried thyme

1 tablespoon extra-virgin olive oil

1 Preheat oven to 350°F. Line a 13" × 9" baking dish with parchment paper.
2 Place all ingredients except oil in the prepared baking dish and stir until well combined.
3 Bake for 15–20 minutes until asparagus is easy to pierce with a fork.
4 Drizzle oil over the top and serve immediately.

SERVES 4

Per Serving

Calories	210
Fat	3.5g
Sodium	940mg
Carbohydrates	35g
Fiber	5g
Sugar	8g
Protein	10g

SPRING ASPARAGUS

Asparagus contains insoluble fiber which binds to cholesterol and carries it out of your body as waste before you have a chance to absorb it. The folate in asparagus helps to lower homocysteine which, if elevated, increases your risks for dementia, heart disease, and stroke. While historical advice has been to snap each stem to remove the woody tip, this has been shown to waste a lot of asparagus. The best way to remove the woody tips is to use a chef's knife to cut a bunch of asparagus where most stalks' green color starts to fade to white.

Pineapple Ginger Lentils

SERVES 4

Per Serving

Calories	210
Fat	16g
Sodium	490mg
Carbohydrates	16g
Fiber	3g
Sugar	7g
Protein	4g

POWERFUL PINEAPPLE

Pineapple has long been hailed as a superfood. This tropical fruit is packed with nutrients and antioxidants that can promote a reduced risk of heart disease. Pineapple contains a compound called bromelain, which has been shown to lower inflammation and cholesterol and improve sugar control. It's also a good source of fiber, vitamins C and B₁, and manganese.

Garnish this easy, tasty dinner with chopped parsley and extra pineapple chunks. It's excellent with some canned fish like mackerel or tuna mixed in before serving.

1 tablespoon organic virgin coconut oil

1 large red onion, peeled and chopped

1 medium jalapeño pepper, seeded and minced

1 teaspoon cumin seeds

1 (3") piece ginger, peeled and minced

2 cups cherry tomatoes

4 tablespoons tomato paste

1 tablespoon ground turmeric

2 cups dried red lentils, rinsed

1 vegetable bouillon cube

1 cup full-fat coconut milk

½ cup diced fresh pineapple

1 In a large saucepan, melt coconut oil over medium-high heat. Sauté onion, jalapeño pepper, and cumin seeds for 3–4 minutes until softened.

2 Add ginger, tomatoes, tomato paste, and turmeric and cook, stirring frequently, for 3–4 minutes until tomatoes soften.

3 Add lentils, bouillon cube, coconut milk, and enough water to just cover lentils. Mix well. Bring to a boil, then reduce heat to low and simmer for 20 minutes or until lentils are tender.

4 Top with pineapple and serve.

Easy Seared Tofu with Satay Sauce

Both the peanut satay sauce and the seared tofu in this dish are deeply flavorful and extremely satisfying. Add a side of quickly grated carrots tossed with a splash of Amazing Salad Dressing (see recipe in Chapter 12) for more nutrients.

2 tablespoons organic virgin coconut oil, divided

20 ounces extra-firm tofu, cut into 1" squares that are ½" high

2 tablespoons tamari, divided

1 large red onion, peeled and chopped

2 cloves garlic, peeled and minced

½ small bird's eye chili, seeded and minced

4 small bok choy, trimmed and quartered lengthwise

2 cups roughly chopped green beans

2 cups broccoli florets

1 cup diced red bell pepper

2 tablespoons water

2 tablespoons no-sugar-added chunky peanut butter

½ tablespoon raw honey

1 teaspoon Chinese five-spice powder

CHINESE FIVE-SPICE POWDER

Studies show that Chinese five-spice powder lowers cholesterol and can help control blood sugar levels. The spice blend ingredients vary depending on the brand, but typically include the antioxidant superstars cloves and cinnamon, as well as fennel, star anise, and Sichuan pepper. Researchers from the Miguel Hernández University have identified cloves (*Syzygium aromaticum*) as the best antioxidant spice for their potent anti-inflammatory effects.

1 Heat 1 tablespoon coconut oil in a large nonstick skillet over medium-high heat and swirl to coat pan. Add tofu chunks and let sit for 2 minutes without moving until lightly browned. Flip tofu and repeat.

2 Add 1 tablespoon tamari and stir to coat tofu. Remove tofu from skillet and set aside.

3 In the same skillet, heat remaining 1 tablespoon coconut oil over medium-high heat. Sauté onion, garlic, and chili until slightly softened, about 3 minutes. Add bok choy, green beans, broccoli, and bell pepper; stir-fry for another 3 minutes. Add water, cover skillet, and cook for 3 minutes.

4 Remove lid and stir in peanut butter, honey, five-spice powder and remaining 1 tablespoon tamari. Add tofu and stir-fry until sauce bubbles and thickens slightly and tofu is warmed up, about 2 minutes. Serve warm.

Eggplant and Chickpea Platter

This dinner is great to double or triple for a crowd. It looks beautiful spread out on a large serving platter, sprinkled with sesame seeds and drizzled with tahini.

2 medium eggplants, trimmed and cut into ¼" rounds

3 tablespoons extra-virgin olive oil, divided

½ teaspoon sea salt

2 tablespoons lemon juice

1 (15-ounce) can chickpeas, drained and rinsed

4 cups arugula

½ cup chopped fresh mint

½ cup chopped fresh cilantro

¼ cup crumbled feta cheese (preferably sheep's milk feta)

½ cup pomegranate seeds

¼ cup raw pine nuts

1 Preheat oven to 375°F. Line two large baking sheets with parchment paper.

2 Lightly brush 1 tablespoon oil on both sides of eggplant slices and sprinkle with salt. Place on prepared baking sheets and bake for 20 minutes or until lightly browned and fork-tender.

3 Whisk lemon juice and remaining 2 tablespoons oil in a large bowl. Add chickpeas, arugula, mint, and cilantro to the bowl and toss to coat.

4 Arrange eggplant across a large serving platter, then scatter chickpea mixture over the top.

5 Top with feta, pomegranate seeds, and pine nuts. Serve warm or cold.

SERVES 2

Per Serving

Calories	760
Fat	44g
Sodium	1,230mg
Carbohydrates	64g
Fiber	17g
Sugar	26g
Protein	26g

EFFICIENT EGGPLANT

Eggplant is filling yet calorie efficient, so it's a great choice if you're trying to lose weight. One cup of eggplant has only 21 calories but gives you 2 grams of fiber. It's rich in antioxidants, including anthocyanins and nasunin, which help to protect cells from damage, lower cholesterol, and keep the heart functioning properly. Additionally, eggplant has been shown to lower blood pressure and improve blood sugar control.

Mushroom Oat Risotto

SERVES 2

Per Serving

Calories	690
Fat	32g
Sodium	630mg
Carbohydrates	77g
Fiber	13g
Sugar	9g
Protein	26g

MUSHROOM MAGIC

Full of vitamins, antioxidants, and phytochemicals, mushrooms can make a positive impact on your skin, future risk of cognitive decline, and overall heart health. Studies have shown that mushrooms, even regular button mushrooms, can help to control blood sugar levels and lower cholesterol. Shiitake and chestnut mushrooms are also great for your immune system.

Steel cut oats are featured in this surprising twist on risotto. For a vegetarian version, omit the bacon and use vegetable stock. Top the risotto with grated Parmesan cheese and extra crushed red pepper flakes and serve it with Best Basic Salad (see recipe in Chapter 9).

2 tablespoons extra-virgin olive oil, divided

4 cups sliced mixed mushrooms (shiitake, chestnut, button, and/or portobello)

2 slices organic bacon, finely chopped

2 medium leeks, peeled, trimmed, and minced

2 cloves garlic, peeled and minced

¼ teaspoon crushed red pepper flakes

1 cup steel cut oats

2 cups chicken stock

2 tablespoons minced fresh thyme or 2 teaspoons dried thyme

1 Heat 1½ tablespoons oil in a large saucepan or Dutch oven over medium heat. Sauté mushrooms for 5 minutes or until golden. Remove from pan and set aside.

2 In the same saucepan, fry bacon for 1 minute over medium heat. Add the remaining ½ tablespoon oil, leeks, garlic, and red pepper flakes. Stir until leeks and garlic are soft, about 1 minute. Stir in oats.

3 Add stock and bring to a boil. Reduce heat to medium-low and simmer for 20 minutes or until a thick consistency is reached.

4 Divide mixture between two serving bowls, sprinkle with thyme, and serve.

Creamy Pasta Alfredo

Top this creamy pasta dish with freshly ground black pepper, grated Parmesan cheese, and minced parsley. You can add some protein by stirring in a can or two of tuna, salmon, or mackerel, along with a sprinkle of capers.

1 large (12-ounce) head cauliflower, cored and cut into florets

5 cloves garlic, peeled

1 medium red onion, peeled and sliced

3 tablespoons extra-virgin olive oil, divided

4 teaspoons sea salt, divided

11 ounces 100% red lentil fusilli or penne

2 cups unsweetened almond milk

2 tablespoons lemon juice

1 Preheat oven to 375°F. Line a large baking sheet with parchment paper.

2 Place cauliflower, garlic cloves, and onion on the prepared baking sheet. Drizzle with 1 tablespoon oil and sprinkle with ½ teaspoon salt. Bake for 20–25 minutes until cauliflower is fork-tender.

3 Bring a large pot of water to a boil over high heat. Add pasta and 3 teaspoons salt, stir, and return to a low boil. Cook for 6–8 minutes until al dente. Drain and set aside.

4 Place roasted cauliflower mixture in a high-speed blender or food processor. Add almond milk, lemon juice, and the remaining 2 tablespoons oil and ½ teaspoon salt. Blend or process on high speed until creamy and smooth.

5 In a large shallow bowl, mix pasta and sauce together. Serve immediately.

SERVES 4

Per Serving

Calories	480
Fat	14g
Sodium	562mg
Carbohydrates	65g
Fiber	5g
Sugar	9g
Protein	23g

RED LENTIL PASTA

One of the best grain-free pastas to hit the market is red lentil pasta. It's high in protein, lower in carbohydrates and calories, and full of nutrition compared to wheat-based pastas. The best part is that red lentil pasta tastes fantastic! It has the texture and firmness most similar to wheat pasta (unlike some grain-free pastas that become somewhat gummy and soft after cooking).

Sweet Potato and Spinach Curry

SERVES 4

Per Serving

Calories	510
Fat	11g
Sodium	1,270mg
Carbohydrates	87g
Fiber	20g
Sugar	19g
Protein	20g

OUTSTANDING CURRY POWDER

Curry powders are full of life-giving antioxidants. The fresher the spice mix, the healthier and more authentic your dish will be. For this recipe, you can swap out regular curry powder and replace it with 1 teaspoon each black mustard seeds, turmeric, coriander, and cumin.

This is a delicious, surprisingly quick curry, despite the long ingredient list! You could add a few fish fillets to the broth when the sweet potatoes are cooking, cover the skillet, and steam them for 8 minutes. For heat, add 1 or 2 chopped fresh green chilis or some crushed red pepper flakes with the onions. If the dish is too spicy, add a little Greek yogurt to cool it down.

1 tablespoon extra-virgin olive oil

2 large red onions, peeled and thinly sliced

2 cloves garlic, peeled and minced

1 tablespoon grated ginger

1 tablespoon medium or hot curry powder

4 cups diced sweet potatoes

2 cups vegetable stock

4 cups packed chopped spinach

2 (15-ounce) cans chickpeas, drained and rinsed

1 teaspoon sea salt

1 cup chopped fresh cilantro

2 tablespoons sliced almonds

1 Heat oil in a large skillet over medium-high heat. Sauté onions, garlic, and ginger for 3–4 minutes until softened. Stir in curry powder.

2 Add sweet potatoes and stock and bring to a boil. Reduce heat to medium-low and simmer for 20 minutes or until sweet potatoes are fork-tender.

3 Add spinach, chickpeas, and salt and cook for 2 minutes until just warmed and spinach is wilted.

4 Remove from heat and top with cilantro and almond slices. Serve immediately.

Baked Fish with Tomatoes and Capers

You can make this beautiful, easy, one-pan meal in less than 30 minutes. It delivers a sophisticated dinner party vibe with the beautiful bright tomatoes and green capers contrasting against the white fish. Serve with Best Basic Salad (see recipe in Chapter 9).

1 medium red onion, peeled and very thinly sliced

2 cloves garlic, peeled and minced

2 cups halved cherry tomatoes

¼ cup dry red wine

2 tablespoons tomato paste

2 tablespoons extra-virgin olive oil

2 tablespoons capers

1 tablespoon apple cider vinegar

4 (4-ounce) cod, hake, halibut or other fish fillets

½ teaspoon salt

¼ cup chopped fresh parsley

1 Preheat oven to 400°F. Line a 13" × 9" baking dish with parchment paper.

2 In a large bowl, combine onion, garlic, tomatoes, wine, tomato paste, oil, capers, and vinegar and stir well. Transfer to the prepared baking dish and spread evenly. Bake for 5 minutes.

3 Remove baking dish from oven and arrange fillets on top of the sauce, leaving space between each fillet. Return to the oven and bake for another 10 minutes.

4 Sprinkle salt and parsley across the top of the dish and serve immediately.

SERVES 4

Per Serving

Calories	200
Fat	8g
Sodium	490mg
Carbohydrates	9g
Fiber	2g
Sugar	4g
Protein	22g

CAPERS

Though they are often considered a garnish, capers are actually quite nutritious. Studies have shown that consuming capers can help to lower cholesterol levels, decrease triglycerides, and increase weight loss. They contain high levels of quercetin, which has antioxidant and anti-inflammatory properties to help reduce swelling, kill cancer cells, control blood sugar, and prevent heart disease.

Garlic Shrimp with Zucchini Pasta

ZOODLES

Consuming pasta can produce a large glucose spike in your bloodstream, followed by a sugar crash. Creating noodles out of zucchini means you can enjoy pasta sauces like pesto, tomato-basil, or Bolognese without carb-heavy pasta. Zucchini noodles will leave you feeling energized rather than heavy, and you'll avoid the post-pasta need for a nap created by a sugar crash.

Serve this light dish with Best Basic Salad (see recipe in Chapter 9) as a starter, and the Chocolate Pudding Heaven (see recipe in Chapter 11) for dessert.

2 large zucchini, trimmed and spiralized

1 tablespoon grated lemon zest

2 tablespoons extra-virgin olive oil, divided

1 medium red bell pepper, seeded and chopped

2 cloves garlic, peeled and minced

¼ teaspoon crushed red pepper flakes

3 tablespoons lemon juice

1 teaspoon salt

6 ounces cooked jumbo shrimp, peeled and deveined

3 tablespoons whole-milk plain Greek yogurt

1 Place zucchini, lemon zest, and 1 tablespoon oil in a large bowl. Mix until well combined.

2 Heat remaining 1 tablespoon oil in a large skillet over medium heat. Sauté bell pepper, garlic, and red pepper flakes for 1 minute or until softened. Add lemon juice and salt, stir to deglaze the pan, then add shrimp. Stir to combine, cover, and cook for 1 minute. Remove from heat and stir in yogurt.

3 Add zucchini mixture to the pan, mix well, and cover skillet. Set aside for 3 minutes or until noodles are gently warmed. Serve immediately.

Salmon with Creamy Kale

Don't let the longish ingredient list throw you—this is a very fast one-pot meal, and it's incredibly tasty. No salmon? Use a couple cans of your favorite beans or Baked Teriyaki Tofu (see recipe in Chapter 5). You can use fresh lemons instead of preserved lemons, but you may need to add more salt.

2 tablespoons extra-virgin olive oil

1 large red onion, peeled and chopped

3 cloves garlic, peeled and thinly sliced

1 teaspoon sweet smoked paprika

6 cups chopped Tuscan kale

1 cup chopped red bell pepper

½ cup water

4 (5-ounce) salmon fillets

¼ teaspoon sea salt

2 small preserved lemons, finely chopped

1 teaspoon lemon juice

½ cup whole-milk plain Greek yogurt

1 Heat oil in a large stockpot over medium-high heat. Sauté onion and garlic for 3–4 minutes until softened. Stir in paprika. Add kale and bell pepper; stir well.

2 Add water and bring to a boil. Place fillets on top of kale mixture and cover pot.

3 Steam for 7–10 minutes until salmon is white and opaque on the outside, but still reddish-pink on the inside. Remove salmon from pot and set aside.

4 Cook kale mixture 3–5 minutes until liquid evaporates. Add salt, preserved lemons, and lemon juice and stir for 1 minute, just until warm.

5 Remove from heat and stir in yogurt. Transfer mixture to a large serving platter and top with salmon. Serve immediately.

SERVES 4

Per Serving

Calories	360
Fat	17g
Sodium	290mg
Carbohydrates	14g
Fiber	4g
Sugar	8g
Protein	38g

PRESERVED LEMONS

Fermented lemons are a delicious way to add probiotics and a salty, tangy taste that is popular in many cuisines. They are a great source of fiber and can help to control blood sugar levels and lower cholesterol. They will add a tart tang to pilafs, tagines, roast chicken, salad dressings, hummus, and many other dishes. If you don't have access to preserved lemons, you can substitute with half a medium lemon, the rind chopped off and the fruit chopped.

Lemony Tabouleh with Salmon

For extra texture and flavor, stir in 1/4 cup each of raisins and pine nuts into the tabouleh. A roughly chopped cucumber is nice to add too.

4 (5-ounce) salmon fillets

8 cups minced fresh parsley

½ cup chopped fresh mint

1 small red onion, peeled and diced

½ cup shelled hemp seeds

1 cup halved cherry tomatoes

1 tablespoon grated lemon zest

3 tablespoons lemon juice

2 tablespoons extra-virgin olive oil

1 teaspoon sea salt

1 Bring ¼" water to a boil over high heat in a large saucepan fitted with a steaming insert. Add salmon and steam for 6–8 minutes until fish is easily flaked with a fork.

2 Meanwhile, place parsley and mint in a food processor and pulse a few times until finely chopped. Transfer to a medium bowl. Add onion, hemp seeds, tomatoes, lemon zest, lemon juice, oil, and salt. Mix vigorously to work lemon juice and salt through parsley. Use your hands to rub handfuls of the mixture together to soften the parsley a bit.

3 Serve parsley mixture topped with salmon.

SERVES 4

Per Serving

Calories	420
Fat	24g
Sodium	760mg
Carbohydrates	14g
Fiber	6g
Sugar	3g
Protein	40g

PARSLEY POWER

Parsley is sometimes thought of as a simple garnish or an antidote to bad breath, but this humble herb is actually packed with vitamins A and C, as well as essential minerals such as iron and calcium. Parsley contains luteolin, an antioxidant that has been shown to reduce inflammation and promote heart health.

Tzatziki Salmon with Quinoa

Per Serving

Calories	410
Fat	1.5g
Sodium	1,270mg
Carbohydrates	35g
Fiber	6g
Sugar	5g
Protein	38g

QUINOA

Make a big batch of quinoa to use in salads, dinners, and even muffins throughout the week. Quinoa is a nutritional powerhouse, packed with protein, fiber, and a host of other nutrients that are good for your health. It's also a low-glycemic food, which means it helps to control blood sugar levels, and it contains antioxidants that help to protect the heart. For perfect quinoa use 2 parts water (or chicken broth) for every 1 part quinoa, and simmer uncovered for 15 minutes. Fluff with a fork before serving.

This enjoyable dinner is bursting with Mediterranean flavors. Save time by using pre-cooked salmon fillets or canned salmon. Add garlic, crushed red pepper flakes, and extra-virgin olive oil to the tzatziki for more kick.

1 cup whole-milk plain Greek yogurt

½ medium cucumber, diced

1 cup minced fresh mint

1 teaspoon sea salt, divided

½ cup white or red quinoa, rinsed and drained

1 cup chopped fresh parsley

2 (5-ounce) wild-caught Alaskan salmon fillets

1 Make the tzatziki: In a small bowl, stir together yogurt, cucumber, mint, and ½ teaspoon salt. Set aside.

2 Add quinoa to a small saucepan and pour 1 cup boiling water over quinoa. Bring to a boil over high heat. Reduce heat to low and simmer for 15 minutes or until tender. Stir in parsley.

3 Preheat oven to 350°F. Line a 13" × 9" baking dish with parchment paper.

4 Place salmon fillets in prepared baking dish. Bake for 8 minutes.

5 Divide quinoa between two plates. Top with salmon and drizzle tzatziki on top. Serve immediately.

Za'atar Chicken Thighs with Spinach Mash

If you don't have za'atar, you can substitute with a sprinkle each of salt, thyme, oregano, and sesame seeds. Mashed beans are highly nutritious and just as satisfying as mashed potatoes. Use a food processor if you want a smoother texture.

3 tablespoons extra-virgin olive oil, divided

4 (6-ounce) bone-in, skin-on chicken thighs

3 teaspoons za'atar spice, divided

1 cup chicken broth

1 large red onion, peeled and minced

2 cloves garlic, peeled and minced

1 (15-ounce) can cannellini beans, drained and rinsed

1 cup chopped fresh cilantro

2 cups packed chopped spinach

1. Heat 2 tablespoons oil in a large skillet over medium-high heat. Sprinkle the skin side of chicken with 2 teaspoons za'atar. Place chicken in hot oil, skin side down, and sear for 5 minutes untouched until skin is golden, crisp, and no longer sticking to the pan. Flip chicken to the other side and fry for another 5 minutes.
2. Add broth and stir around to deglaze the skillet. Cover and cook for 10–15 minutes until the internal temperature reaches 165°F.
3. Meanwhile, heat the remaining 1 tablespoon oil in a large saucepan over medium heat. Add onion and garlic and sauté until onion is softened, 3–4 minutes.
4. Add beans and cook until hot, stirring frequently, about 5 minutes. Using a potato masher, mash the bean mixture. Add cilantro, spinach, and the remaining 1 teaspoon za'atar. Stir well until greens are evenly distributed and are slighted wilted, 1–2 minutes.
5. Divide bean mixture between two plates. Top each with 2 chicken thighs and drizzle with pan sauce. Serve immediately.

SERVES 2

Per Serving

Calories	680
Fat	30g
Sodium	1,210mg
Carbohydrates	44g
Fiber	2g
Sugar	6g
Protein	55g

DARK MEAT IS HEALTHY

Dark chicken meat from thighs and drumsticks contains vitamin K_2, or menaquinone. Studies show that people who ate more K_2-containing foods were more than 57 percent less likely to die of heart disease, and their risk of severe hardening of the arteries was reduced by 52 percent. Chicken skin is an excellent source of type II collagen, which is known for its anti-aging properties.

Sheet Pan Mediterranean Chicken and Vegetables

This is a delicious and super-easy weeknight dinner that's full of flavor. It presents beautifully for guests, and is excellent topped with chopped parsley and served with a side of quinoa.

4 cups cherry tomatoes

2 cups sliced red onion

2 cups chopped zucchini

1 cup pitted and halved black olives

4 tablespoons chopped rosemary

3 tablespoons extra-virgin olive oil

4 tablespoons tomato paste

1 small bird's eye chili, seeded and minced

4 tablespoons capers

3 tablespoons lemon juice

1 tablespoon grated lemon zest

1 teaspoon salt

8 (6-ounce) bone-in, skin-on chicken thighs

1 Preheat oven to 350°F. Line a large baking sheet with parchment paper.

2 In a large bowl, place tomatoes, onion, zucchini, olives, rosemary, oil, tomato paste, chili, capers, lemon juice, lemon zest, and salt. Toss to combine, then transfer to the prepared baking sheet. Place chicken on top of the tomato mixture.

3 Bake for 40 minutes or until the internal temperature of the chicken reaches at least 165°F.

4 Let rest for at least 10 minutes before serving.

SERVES 4

Per Serving

Calories	460
Fat	23g
Sodium	1,200mg
Carbohydrates	20g
Fiber	5g
Sugar	10g
Protein	44g

ONE-PAN DINNERS

Anyone who has ever tried to stick to a diet knows that cooking regularly can be one of the biggest obstacles. After a long day at work, the last thing you want to do is spend hours in the kitchen preparing a complicated meal. This is where one-pan meals can help with weight loss. Pack all the nutrition you need into one dish, with minimal effort and maximal return.

Hazelnut Pesto Chicken

SERVES 2

Per Serving

Calories	600
Fat	31g
Sodium	1,640mg
Carbohydrates	29g
Fiber	3g
Sugar	2g
Protein	48g

FRESH BASIL

Studies have shown that the antioxidants in fresh basil can help to lower cholesterol, improve heart health, boost the immune system, and fight inflammation. Fresh basil also may help to protect against certain types of cancer. A few tablespoons of fresh basil are not nearly enough. Keep a bunch of basil handy and use it liberally!

Pesto is a delicious way to eat more basil. You can change the nuts you use to make pesto with for nutrient variety. Toasting the nuts adds more flavor depth, but it reduces the nutrition a bit.

½ teaspoon sea salt

1 cup packed fresh basil leaves

¼ cup hazelnuts

2 cloves garlic, peeled and chopped

2 tablespoons extra-virgin olive oil

1 tablespoon water

4 tablespoons nutritional yeast

6 ounces 100% buckwheat pasta

2 cups chicken broth

2 (6-ounce) boneless, skinless chicken breasts, sliced

1 Bring a large pot of water to a boil over high heat. Stir in salt.

2 Place basil, hazelnuts, and garlic in a high-speed blender or food processor. Blend or process for 1–2 minutes until very finely chopped. Add oil, water, and nutritional yeast; pulse until a paste forms. Set aside.

3 Add pasta to boiling water. Boil for 5–6 minutes until al dente. Drain and rinse.

4 Meanwhile, bring broth to a simmer in a small saucepan over medium heat. Add chicken to broth and simmer for 4 minutes. Drain and set chicken aside.

5 Add pasta, chicken, and pesto sauce to a large skillet over medium heat. Cook and stir for about 1 minute until everything is just warmed through. Serve immediately.

One-Pan Chicken, Quinoa, and Brussels Sprouts

This easy one-pan dinner is creamy, delicious, and garlicky. If Brussels sprouts aren't in season, you can replace them with broccoli florets or chunks of green cabbage. Before serving, sprinkle with grated lemon zest and Parmesan cheese.

½ cup white or red quinoa, rinsed and drained

1 cup boiling water

1 teaspoon sea salt

3 cloves garlic, peeled and sliced

4 cups whole button mushrooms

2 cups trimmed and halved Brussels sprouts

2 medium red onions, peeled and cut into 8 wedges each

½ cup frozen peas

8 (4-ounce) chicken drumsticks

1 Preheat oven to 350°F. Line the bottom and up the sides of a 13" × 9" baking dish with parchment paper.

2 Add quinoa, boiling water, and salt to the prepared baking dish. Scatter garlic, mushrooms, Brussels sprouts, onions, and peas over quinoa mixture.

3 Lay chicken over vegetable mixture.

4 Bake for 40 minutes or until chicken is well browned and the internal temperature is at least 165°F.

5 Let rest for a few minutes before serving.

SERVES 4

Per Serving

Calories	300
Fat	7g
Sodium	770mg
Carbohydrates	28g
Fiber	5g
Sugar	7g
Protein	32g

BRILLIANT BRUSSELS SPROUTS

Brussels sprouts are packed with disease-preventing antioxidants, including beta-carotene, vitamin C, and alpha-lipoic acid (ALA), an antioxidant that's exceptionally good at reducing inflammation. These antioxidants have been shown to reduce the risk of cancer, heart disease, and other chronic conditions. In addition, the fiber in Brussels sprouts can help to lower cholesterol levels and promote heart health.

Speedy Burgers

Just press ground beef into a pan, bake it, and you can have tasty burgers ready in 20 minutes. Top the burgers with Quick-Pickled Cucumbers and Onions (see recipe in Chapter 12) and serve them with Sweet Potato Fries with Harissa Dip (see recipe in Chapter 8). Put the sweet potatoes in the oven at the same time as the burgers for a perfectly timed meal. If you can find Mutti tomato paste, give it a try, it's incredibly tasty.

1 pound (80/20) organic grass-fed ground beef

1 teaspoon salt

4 large romaine lettuce leaves, torn

4 tablespoons organic, sugar-free tomato paste

4 teaspoons Dijon mustard

1 large beefsteak tomato, cut into 8 slices

1 medium avocado, peeled, pitted, and mashed with a fork

1 Preheat oven to 375°F.
2 Line an 8" × 8" square baking dish with parchment paper.
3 Spread ground beef in the prepared pan and smooth the surface with the back of a spoon or an offset spatula. Sprinkle with salt. Bake for 20 minutes. Remove from oven and cut into 4 equal pieces.
4 Divide lettuce among four plates and top each with a burger.
5 Top with tomato paste, mustard, tomato slices, and avocado. Serve immediately.

SERVES 4

Per Serving

Calories	390
Fat	29g
Sodium	830mg
Carbohydrates	10g
Fiber	4g
Sugar	4g
Protein	22g

BEEF BEFORE BUN

If you can't imagine a burger without a bun, eat the beef, lettuce, tomatoes, and pickles from your burger before eating the bun. By changing the order in which you eat your meal, you can flatten the impact of the bun carbohydrates by up to 73 percent. If you want to enjoy your burger and bread together and still avoid the glucose spike, use a high-protein bread instead of the typical high-carb buns.

CHAPTER 7

Weekend Wonders

Asian Noodle Bowl

SERVES 4

Per Serving

Calories	430
Fat	19g
Sodium	1,520mg
Carbohydrates	30g
Fiber	5g
Sugar	11g
Protein	39g

SEAWEED NOODLES

Chewy, gluten-free kelp noodles are made from sea vegetables. They are high in fiber, rich in metals, a good source of iodine, low in calories and carbohydrates, and sugar-free. Kelp noodles have a neutral flavor, so they are a great substitute for noodles in a variety of dishes. Swap out higher carbohydrate noodles with kelp noodles so you can enjoy the texture of noodles without the inflammation. If you can't find kelp noodles, you can also use shirataki (konjac) noodles. Both are available online.

The flavor in this bowl is outstanding. If you don't feel like having salmon, try replacing it with Baked Teriyaki Tofu (see recipe in Chapter 5). Serve with a side of Coconut Quinoa (see recipe in Chapter 8).

1 (12-ounce) package kelp noodles

3 tablespoons lemon juice

1½ ounces arame noodles

2 cups packed baby spinach

2 cups shredded napa cabbage

1 cup thinly sliced shiitake mushrooms

½ cup bean sprouts

3 scallions, trimmed and thinly sliced

1 large carrot, peeled and cut into ribbons with a vegetable peeler

1 tablespoon black sesame seeds

5 tablespoons tamari

2 tablespoons apple cider vinegar

1 tablespoon raw honey

1 tablespoon sesame oil

1 tablespoon grated ginger

1 clove garlic, peeled and minced

1 teaspoon salt

½ teaspoon crushed red pepper flakes

1 tablespoon extra-virgin olive oil

4 (5-ounce) salmon fillets

4 tablespoons chopped raw almonds

1 Place kelp noodles in a medium bowl. Drizzle with lemon juice and add water to cover. Soak for 30 minutes. In a small bowl, place arame noodles and cover with water; soak for 10 minutes.

2 Place spinach, cabbage, mushrooms, bean sprouts, scallions, carrot, and sesame seeds in a large bowl. Drain arame and add to bowl.

3 In a small bowl, combine tamari, vinegar, honey, sesame oil, ginger, garlic, salt, and red pepper flakes. Whisk to combine and pour over the spinach mixture.

4 Drain kelp noodles and add to bowl. Toss to combine. Set aside at room temperature for at least 1 hour.

5 Heat olive oil in a large nonstick skillet over medium-high heat. Place salmon in the pan skin side down and cook for 2–3 minutes until skin is golden and crisp. Carefully flip fillets and cook for 2–3 minutes until flesh becomes opaque and is easily flaked with a fork.

6 Divide noodle mixture among four shallow bowls and top each with a salmon fillet. Sprinkle with almonds.

Quinoa and Cranberry–Stuffed Mini Pumpkins

Besides being really cute on the table, these mini pumpkins are powerful immune boosters and pack a mean nutritional punch.

4 small (1-pound) mini pumpkins

2 cups water

1 cup quinoa, rinsed and drained

1 tablespoon extra-virgin olive oil

1 medium red onion, peeled and diced

3 cloves garlic, peeled and minced

½ teaspoon crushed red pepper flakes

4 tablespoons minced fresh sage, divided

1½ cups sliced shiitake mushrooms

½ cup dried cranberries

½ cup pine nuts

½ cup chopped fresh parsley

2 teaspoons grated lime zest

2 tablespoons lime juice

SERVES 4

Per Serving

Calories	380
Fat	18g
Sodium	15mg
Carbohydrates	47g
Fiber	7g
Sugar	8g
Protein	12g

POWERFUL PUMPKINS

Pumpkins are more than just a decoration for your front porch! These gourds are chock-full of nutrients such as vitamins A and C, which help maintain blood sugar levels, eyesight, and cholesterol levels. Pumpkins are also full of antioxidants like phenols and beta-carotene, which help minimize damaging free radicals in the body. Roast the seeds for a healthy snack, or make a pot of pumpkin soup for a hearty meal.

1 Preheat oven to 350°F. Line a 13" × 9" baking dish with foil.

2 Cut the tops off pumpkins, reserving tops, and scoop out the seeds.

3 Pour 3–4 tablespoons hot water in the prepared baking dish, then add pumpkins, cut sides up. Place pumpkin tops in the dish. Bake for 20–30 minutes until soft.

4 Meanwhile place water in a medium saucepan and bring to a boil over high heat. Add quinoa, and reduce heat to medium-low. Simmer for 15 minutes or until all water is absorbed. Remove from heat and set aside, covered, for 5 minutes.

5 In a large saucepan or Dutch oven, heat oil over medium heat and sauté onion for 3–4 minutes until softened. Add garlic, red pepper flakes, and 3 tablespoons sage and cook for 1 minute. Add mushrooms and sauté for 3–4 minutes until softened.

6 Remove from heat and add cranberries, pine nuts, parsley, lime zest, lime juice, cooked quinoa, and the remaining 1 tablespoon sage. Stir to mix well.

7 Spoon quinoa mixture into each pumpkin, mounding slightly. Place tops over stuffing and serve immediately.

Heirloom Tomato Stacks with Cod

SERVES 4

Per Serving

Calories	620
Fat	50g
Sodium	1,700mg
Carbohydrates	8g
Fiber	3g
Sugar	2g
Protein	35g

HEIRLOOM TOMATOES

There's nothing quite like a ripe, juicy heirloom tomato. The seeds from heirloom tomatoes (also called heritage tomatoes) have been lovingly selected over many years for desirable traits, such as size, color, and taste. Heirlooms typically have more locules—the cavities with the seeds—than hybrid tomatoes. These locules are the flavor centers, full of volatile compounds that give heirloom tomatoes their signature taste. So, the next time you see these rare tomatoes at your farmer's market, be sure to snatch them up as a special treat!

Drizzle this beautiful dish with a bit of extra-virgin olive oil and sprinkle with salt and pepper. Serve it with the Best Kale Salad (see recipe in Chapter 9).

½ cup finely chopped sun-dried tomatoes packed in extra-virgin olive oil

½ cup crumbled feta cheese (preferably sheep's milk feta)

2 tablespoons extra-virgin olive oil, divided

2 cups thinly sliced basil leaves, divided

4 cups baby spinach

6 large heirloom tomatoes (in different colors), sliced into ¼" thick rounds

1½ cups Cilantro Pesto (see recipe in Chapter 12)

4 (4-ounce) skin-on cod, hake, halibut, or other fish fillets

1 In a small bowl, mix sun-dried tomatoes, feta, 1 tablespoon oil, and 1 cup basil until well combined.

2 Place 1 cup spinach on a plate. Top with 1 tomato slice. Spread Cilantro Pesto on slice and sprinkle with a few strips of basil. Place a second tomato slice on top, followed by a small spoonful of sun-dried tomato mixture. Repeat steps twice.

3 Repeat on three other plates with the remaining spinach, tomato slices, pesto, basil, and sun-dried tomato mixture.

4 Heat the remaining 1 tablespoon oil in a large nonstick skillet over medium-high heat. Place fish in the pan skin side down and cook for 2–3 minutes until skin is golden and crisp. Carefully flip fillets and cook for 2–3 minutes more until flesh becomes opaque and is easily flaked with a fork.

5 Transfer fillets to the plates beside tomato stacks and serve immediately.

Green Olive–Roasted Salmon

The green olive salsa in this recipe is delicious, and it's wonderful to add on top of many other types of fish or meats. This salmon entrée is excellent served with Simple Puy Lentils and Sweet Potato Fries with Harissa Dip (see recipes in Chapter 8).

5 tablespoons extra-virgin olive oil, divided

1 cup pitted green olives

1 tablespoon grated lemon zest

3 tablespoons lemon juice

2 cups loosely packed parsley

3 scallions, trimmed and roughly chopped

2 tablespoons capers

1 teaspoon salt, divided

4 (5-ounce) salmon fillets

1 teaspoon ground black pepper

1 Preheat oven to 350°F. Line a 13" × 9" glass baking dish with parchment paper.

2 In a medium mixing bowl, combine 4 tablespoons oil, olives, lemon zest, lemon juice, parsley, scallions, capers, and ½ teaspoon salt. Mix well and set aside.

3 Pour the remaining 1 tablespoon oil into the prepared baking dish and spread it around using the back of a spoon. Place salmon fillets on top of oil, skin side down. Sprinkle with pepper and remaining ½ teaspoon salt. Roast for 10–15 minutes until flesh is opaque and easily flaked with a fork.

4 Let salmon rest for 2 minutes and then top with green olive salsa. Serve immediately.

SERVES 4

Per Serving

Calories	400
Fat	29g
Sodium	1,410mg
Carbohydrates	4g
Fiber	2g
Sugar	1g
Protein	31g

GORGEOUS GREEN OLIVES

The monounsaturated fat in green olives can help to lower cholesterol levels and improve blood circulation. They are also fermented, so they can aid in digestion and help to prevent constipation. Whether you enjoy them as part of a healthy salad or stuffed with cheese, there's no doubt that green olives offer a variety of health benefits.

Tuna Avocado Rolls

Cholesterol-lowering steel cut oats, when mixed with seasonings, tastes surprisingly similar to Japanese sushi rice. Serve the rolls with pickled ginger, soy sauce, and wasabi paste.

SERVES 4

Per Serving

Calories	530
Fat	15g
Sodium	1,550mg
Carbohydrates	69g
Fiber	12g
Sugar	8g
Protein	36g

SUSHI NORI WRAPS

If you're looking for a nutrient-packed food that's low in calories and high in flavor, look no further than nori. This type of seaweed is grown in the waters off of Japan, Korea, and China, and is prized for its mild, sea-like flavor. Nori is an excellent source of iodine and vitamin B_{12}, and can actually contain up to ten times more calcium than milk. And best of all, nori is very low in calories. In addition, nori is packed full of vitamins A, C, D, E, and K, as well as niacin, folic acid, and taurine.

2 cups cooked steel cut oats, cooled

1 teaspoon salt

1 tablespoon rice vinegar or apple cider vinegar

1 tablespoon maple syrup

1 teaspoon sesame oil

2 (5-ounce) cans water-packed tuna, drained

2 tablespoons whole-milk plain Greek yogurt

2 tablespoons tamari, divided

3 teaspoons wasabi paste, divided

4 (8" x 7") sheets sushi nori wraps

1 small English cucumber, cut into matchsticks

1 medium avocado, peeled, pitted, and cut into matchsticks

4 tablespoons alfalfa sprouts

2 scallions, trimmed and cut lengthwise into long strips

2 teaspoons sesame seeds

1 Place oats, salt, vinegar, maple syrup, and sesame oil in a medium bowl and stir until slightly sticky. Set aside.

2 In a small bowl, mix tuna, yogurt, 1 tablespoon tamari, and 2 teaspoons wasabi paste.

3 Place a sheet of nori on a bamboo mat or a work surface with the rough side facing up and the short side facing you. Place about ½ cup oat mixture on the nori and spread evenly across the bottom third of the sheet, leaving 1" of space clear on the bottom. Smooth ¼ tuna mixture across rice. Lay ¼ of cucumbers, avocado, tuna, sprouts, and scallions across the mixture.

4 Roll nori tightly around the filling. Wet the top with a little water to help seal the roll shut. Using a very sharp knife, cut the roll into 6 pieces, wiping the knife clean with a wet towel between cuts. Repeat with the remaining ingredients to make 3 more rolls.

5 Arrange rolls on a plate and sprinkle with sesame seeds. Combine the remaining 1 teaspoon wasabi and 1 tablespoon tamari in a small dipping bowl. Serve rolls immediately with dipping sauce.

Blueberry Hazelnut Salmon

JUNIPER BERRIES

Juniper berries, the lovely spice behind the famous flavor of gin, are high in nutrients and powerful plant compounds. One chemical assessment found that juniper berries have eighty-seven distinct antioxidant compounds. Animal studies have shown they have anti-inflammatory and anti-oxidant effects and may improve heart health by improving HDL cholesterol, and lowering LDL cholesterol and blood pressure.

Berries, nuts, and the surprising addition of juniper berries make a magical topping for omega-3–rich salmon. Serve it with Roasted Whole Carrots (see recipe in Chapter 8).

4 tablespoons extra-virgin olive oil, divided

5 juniper berries, crushed

½ cup chopped red onion

1 cup blueberries

½ cup chopped hazelnuts

¼ cup red wine

1 teaspoon lemon zest

1 teaspoon raw honey

4 (5-ounce) salmon fillets

¼ teaspoon sea salt

⅛ teaspoon ground black pepper

2 cups arugula

1. Preheat a charcoal or gas grill.
2. In a small saucepan, heat 3 tablespoons oil over medium heat. Add juniper berries and onion; sauté for 3 minutes. Add blueberries, hazelnuts, and wine. Gently simmer until the mixture reduces slightly and thickens, about 3 minutes. Remove from heat and stir in lemon zest and honey. Set aside and keep warm.
3. Brush salmon with remaining 1 tablespoon oil and sprinkle with salt and pepper. Grill 6" from heat until salmon flakes when tested with a fork, about 8–10 minutes.
4. Place arugula on a large serving platter and top with salmon. Pour blueberry sauce over everything. Serve immediately.

Pumpkin Seed–Crusted Trout with Lime Salad

You can swap in ¼ cup dried unsweetened cranberries for the goji berries, or leave them out entirely. Use a hotter chili powder if you like more spice.

3 cups finely shredded green cabbage

2 cups minced fresh cilantro, divided

½ cup goji berries

1 tablespoon grated lime zest

¼ cup lime juice

1 teaspoon salt, divided

½ cup shelled raw pumpkin seeds

1 teaspoon mild chili powder

2 (5-ounce) whole boneless, butterflied trout

1 large free-range egg, beaten

1 tablespoon extra-virgin olive oil

1 Mix cabbage, 1½ cups cilantro, goji berries, lime zest, lime juice, and ½ teaspoon salt in a medium bowl. Transfer to a large serving platter and set aside.

2 Place pumpkin seeds in a food processor and pulse until coarsely chopped. Add chili powder, the remaining ½ cup cilantro, and the remaining ½ teaspoon salt. Process for 10 seconds. Set aside.

3 Brush the flesh side of trout with egg, coating generously. Sprinkle half the pumpkin mixture over the flesh side of each trout and press down.

4 Heat oil in two large nonstick skillets over medium-high heat. Add 1 trout to each pan, skin side down. Cook 2 minutes. Flip and cook until browned and opaque in center, about 2 minutes.

5 Place fish on cabbage salad and serve immediately.

SERVES 2

Per Serving

Calories	570
Fat	29g
Sodium	1,400mg
Carbohydrates	31g
Fiber	10g
Sugar	15g
Protein	46g

TROUT

Trout is a good source of omega-3 fatty acids. Omega-3s have been linked to several health benefits, including improved heart health and reduced inflammation. Trout is also a good source of protein. One 5.5-ounce fillet offers 32.6 grams of protein. Another key reason trout is so healthy is its low level of contaminants. So, when you're looking for healthy seafood options, rainbow trout is a great choice.

Beet Buckwheat Risotto with Mackerel

SERVES 4

Per Serving	
Calories	620
Fat	29g
Sodium	410mg
Carbohydrates	50g
Fiber	9g
Sugar	9g
Protein	41g

BUCKWHEAT

Buckwheat contains more protein than rice and has higher essential amino acids, including lysine and arginine. Because rice, wheat, and corn are especially high on the glycemic scale, they provoke a quick spike in blood sugar levels and promote systemic inflammation. Buckwheat contains the phytochemicals rutin and quercetin, which have antioxidant effects and reduce inflammation.

This unique risotto is excellent sprinkled with a lot of fresh thyme and dill, along with pine nuts. Round out the dish with a few large handfuls of arugula topped with olive oil and vinegar, or make the Best Kale Salad (see recipe in Chapter 9).

2 tablespoons extra-virgin olive oil, divided

1 medium red onion, peeled and diced

3 cloves garlic, peeled and minced, divided

2 small beets, trimmed and diced

8 ounces button mushrooms, diced

¼ cup dried porcini mushrooms

1 teaspoon chili powder

4 tablespoons tomato paste

1 cup buckwheat groats

1½ cups chicken stock

1 tablespoon grated lemon zest

3 tablespoons lemon juice

4 (5-ounce) fresh mackerel fillets

1. Heat 1 tablespoon oil in a large saucepan or Dutch oven over medium-high heat. Sauté onion and garlic for 3–4 minutes until softened.
2. Add beets and button mushrooms and cook, stirring occasionally, for 3 minutes. Add porcini, chili powder, tomato paste, and groats. Stir in stock and bring to a boil.
3. Reduce heat to low and simmer for 30 minutes or until all liquid is absorbed into buckwheat.
4. Remove from heat. Stir in lemon zest and lemon juice. Cover and keep warm.
5. Heat the remaining 1 tablespoon oil in a large nonstick skillet over medium-high heat. Place mackerel in the pan skin side down and cook for 2–3 minutes until skin is golden and crisp. Carefully flip mackerel and cook for 2–3 minutes until the flesh becomes opaque and is easily flaked with a fork.
6. Divide buckwheat risotto among four shallow bowls. Top with mackerel and serve immediately.

Baked Haddock and Fennel with Melon Salad

The melon salad with Parmesan and green beans is a fantastic summer salad to make when the produce department is bursting with fresh melons. If the green beans are super fresh, you can skip steaming them.

2 cups green beans, trimmed

1½ tablespoons lemon juice

1 tablespoon grated lemon zest

4 tablespoons extra-virgin olive oil, divided

1 small honeydew melon, peeled, seeded, and cut into ¾" cubes

4 ounces chopped walnuts

2 ounces grated Parmesan cheese, divided

½ teaspoon salt, divided

2 medium bulbs fennel, trimmed and cut into ½" slices

4 (5-ounce) haddock or halibut steaks

⅛ teaspoon ground cayenne pepper

1 teaspoon paprika

1. Preheat oven to 400°F. Line a 13" × 9" baking dish with parchment paper.

2. Place green beans in a steamer basket in a large saucepan and steam over simmering water for 2 minutes. Remove from heat and set aside.

3. In a large bowl, whisk together lemon juice, lemon zest, and 2 tablespoons oil. Add melon, green beans, walnuts, 1 ounce Parmesan, and ¼ teaspoon salt. Mix well until combined. Set salad aside.

4. Place fennel slices in the prepared baking dish. Drizzle with 1 tablespoon oil and sprinkle with the remaining ¼ teaspoon salt. Bake for 15 minutes. Remove from oven and stir.

5. Arrange haddock on fennel, leaving space between each fillet. Drizzle fish with the remaining 1 tablespoon oil and sprinkle with cayenne and paprika. Return to oven and bake for 10 minutes.

6. Divide fish and fennel among four large plates. Add melon salad to the plates and sprinkle with the remaining 1 ounce Parmesan. Serve immediately.

SERVES 4

Per Serving

Calories	640
Fat	38g
Sodium	960mg
Carbohydrates	48g
Fiber	10g
Sugar	33g
Protein	35g

PURCHASING HADDOCK

Haddock has a fine, firm white flesh. Fillets should be translucent; if you notice the fillet has a chalky hue to it, it is old. Refrigerate haddock as soon as possible after purchase, either in the original wrapping from the store or in an airtight container, and use it within 24 hours. If you freeze the fish, it should last 3 months.

Scallop and Cherry Tomato Skewers

SERVES 4

Per Serving

Calories	200
Fat	11g
Sodium	560mg
Carbohydrates	9g
Fiber	1g
Sugar	2g
Protein	15g

FREEZE UNCOOKED SAUCES

The parsley sauce can be stored in the refrigerator for up to 3 days. For longer storage, it can be frozen. Pour about 2 tablespoons into ice cube trays and freeze until solid. Pop the frozen cubes into a heavy-duty freezer-safe resealable bag, label, and freeze up to 6 months. To defrost, let stand in the refrigerator overnight. You can also use this method with other uncooked sauces like Green Herb Pesto (see recipe in Chapter 12).

The sweetness from the roasted tomatoes is a nice contrast to the tart lemon and tang of Dijon mustard. Serve the skewers with Parmesan Truffle Mash (see recipe in Chapter 8) and Best Kale Salad (see recipe in Chapter 9).

1 pound sea scallops

12 cherry tomatoes

4 scallions, trimmed and cut in half crosswise

½ cup chopped fresh parsley

1 tablespoon fresh oregano leaves

3 tablespoons extra-virgin olive oil

1 tablespoon grated lemon zest

3 tablespoons lemon juice

2 cloves garlic, peeled

1 teaspoon Dijon mustard

⅛ teaspoon salt

⅛ teaspoon ground black pepper

1 Preheat broiler.

2 Thread scallops, tomatoes, and scallions alternately on metal skewers.

3 In a high-speed blender or food processor, combine parsley, oregano, oil, lemon zest, lemon juice, garlic, mustard, salt, and pepper. Blend or process until smooth. Set aside ¼ cup sauce.

4 Brush remaining sauce onto the skewers and place skewers on a broiler pan. Broil 6" from heat for 3 minutes per side, turning once during cooking time. Serve with remaining sauce.

Mulled Red Cabbage with Hake

Bacon is optional in this outstanding dish. The flavors develop over time, and it reheats well. Serve it with Parmesan Truffle Mash (see recipe in Chapter 8).

2 tablespoons extra-virgin olive oil, divided

2 large red onions, peeled and thinly sliced

3 slices organic bacon, diced

1 teaspoon crushed red pepper flakes

8 whole cloves

1 (3") cinnamon stick

1 large Granny Smith apple, diced

1½ tablespoons grated orange zest

¼ cup orange juice

1 large red cabbage, cored and finely shredded

2 tablespoons apple cider vinegar

1 cup red wine or chicken stock

1 tablespoon maple syrup

6 (4-ounce) hake, cod, halibut or other fish fillets

1 Heat 1 tablespoon oil in a large saucepan or Dutch oven over medium-high heat. Sauté onions, bacon, red pepper flakes, cloves, and cinnamon stick for 3–4 minutes until onions are softened.

2 Add apple, orange zest, and juice to the pan and cook, stirring for 3 minutes. Stir in cabbage and vinegar. Cover and cook 2 minutes.

3 Add wine and maple syrup, mix well, and reduce heat to medium-low. Cook, covered, for 35 minutes. Uncover the pan once or twice and add a small amount of water if the pan seems dry.

4 Heat the remaining 1 tablespoon oil in a large nonstick skillet over medium-high heat. Place hake in the pan skin side down and cook for 2–3 minutes until skin is golden and crisp. Carefully flip fillets and cook for 2–3 minutes until flesh is opaque and flakes easily with a fork. Remove from heat.

5 Serve fillets over the cabbage mixture.

SERVES 6

Per Serving

Calories	330
Fat	11g
Sodium	210mg
Carbohydrates	29g
Fiber	6g
Sugar	16g
Protein	26g

RED CABBAGE

A growing body of research suggests that diets high in anthocyanins—the pigment that gives red cabbage its color—are linked with lower blood pressure and a reduced risk of cardiovascular disease. One large study found that women who regularly eat foods rich in anthocyanins may benefit from an 11–32 percent lower risk of heart attacks, compared with those who eat fewer of these foods.

Arugula Pesto Pizza with Prosciutto

Use the crust and pizza sauce in this recipe for any variety of toppings. You can freeze several prebaked pizza shells in an airtight container for a quick weeknight dinner.

½ cup coconut flour

¼ cup almond flour

3 tablespoons psyllium husk powder (or 4 tablespoons whole psyllium seed husks)

¼ teaspoon sea salt

½ teaspoon garlic powder

2 teaspoons baking powder

1 teaspoon apple cider vinegar

1 cup lukewarm water (105°F–110°F)

1 tablespoon extra-virgin olive oil

½ cup Speedy Blender Pizza Sauce (see recipe in Chapter 12)

½ cup Arugula Pesto (see recipe in Chapter 12), divided

2 cups arugula, divided

10 cherry tomatoes, halved

8 slices prosciutto, roughly torn

6 ounces fresh buffalo mozzarella cheese, thinly sliced

SERVES 4

Per Serving

Calories	370
Fat	20g
Sodium	1,380mg
Carbohydrates	27g
Fiber	14g
Sugar	6g
Protein	22g

PROSCIUTTO AND IBÉRICO HAM

Many people are surprised to learn that there are two types of processed meat that contain beneficial fats. Nine slices of Italian Parma ham (prosciutto di Parma) or Spanish Ibérico ham (*jamón Ibérico di bellota*) will give you the same amount of omega-3 fatty acids (14 grams) as a 3-ounce serving of salmon. The pigs are fed diets of either acorns (Spain) or chestnuts (Italy), which are high in omega-3s that can help reduce inflammation and lower cholesterol.

1　Preheat oven to 400°F.

2　In a medium bowl, stir together coconut flour, almond flour, psyllium husks, salt, garlic powder, and baking powder.

3　Stir in vinegar and water for 30 seconds, then knead dough for 1 minute. Form into a smooth ball and set aside for 10 minutes.

4　Place a large sheet of parchment paper on a clean work surface. Place dough in the middle and brush with oil. Press down on dough to flatten slightly. Roll dough into a 10" disc.

5　Sightly pinch the outermost edges of the dough back toward the center to form a small crust edge. Slide the parchment paper and dough onto a large baking sheet or pizza pan. Bake for 15 minutes.

6　Remove from oven. Spread sauce over crust and then drizzle with ¼ cup pesto. Top with 1½ cups arugula, then tomatoes, prosciutto, and mozzarella. Return to oven and bake for 8–10 minutes until cheese is melted and golden brown in spots.

7　Top pizza with the remaining ½ cup arugula and spoon the remaining ¼ cup pesto decoratively around the top of the pizza. Serve immediately.

Fish and Walnut Shepherd's Pie

SERVES 6

Per Serving

Calories	540
Fat	32g
Sodium	970mg
Carbohydrates	38g
Fiber	10g
Sugar	10g
Protein	36g

LOW-CARBOHYDRATE THICKENERS

Thickeners are often full of carbohydrates and can be inflammatory. However, some thickeners are low in carbohydrates, such as kudzu, or kuzu, root; psyllium husk powder; and xanthan gum. Kudzu root is a common Japanese root used to thicken dishes, and is rich in antioxidants that protect cells from oxidative stress that can lead to heart disease. Kudzu and other low-carb thickeners are widely available online and in most health food stores.

This pie is easy to make, despite its many ingredients. If you can't find kudzu, use another low-carb thickening agent like xanthan gum.

2 large sweet potatoes, peeled and cut into ½" cubes

1 large cauliflower, cut into bite-sized pieces

4 tablespoons extra-virgin olive oil

3 cloves garlic, peeled and minced, divided

1 teaspoon sea salt

2 large red onions, peeled and diced

2 cups sliced shiitake mushrooms

½ teaspoon crushed red pepper flakes

2 cups chicken stock

½ cup nutritional yeast

4 tablespoons kudzu powder

2 tablespoons chopped fresh dill

1 tablespoon grated lemon zest

3 tablespoons lemon juice

1 cup chopped walnuts

2 (4.5-ounce) cans oil-packed sardines, drained

1 (5-ounce) can red salmon, drained

1 (5-ounce) can oil-packed tuna, drained

4 cups fresh spinach

1 Place sweet potatoes and cauliflower in a large saucepan. Add 1 cup water and cover. Steam over medium-high heat for 15 minutes or until tender. Drain and transfer to a food processor. Add 2 tablespoons oil, 1 clove garlic, and salt. Process until smooth. Set aside.

2 Preheat oven to 375°F.

3 Heat remaining 2 tablespoons oil in a large skillet over medium-high heat. Sauté onions for 4 minutes. Add remaining 2 cloves garlic, mushrooms, and pepper flakes and cook for another 3 minutes. Stir in stock and nutritional yeast. Reduce heat to medium-low.

4 In a small bowl, mix kudzu powder with 1–2 teaspoons cold water until the mixture forms a paste. Add to the skillet and stir to mix. Cook and stir for 1–2 minutes until thickened.

5 Add dill, lemon zest, lemon juice, walnuts, sardines, salmon, tuna, and spinach and toss to coat. Pour into a 13" × 9" baking dish. Spread sweet potato mixture evenly over the top.

6 Bake 15–20 minutes until the top is browned. Remove from oven, let cool for 10 minutes, and serve.

Za'atar Roast Chicken

This is an easy recipe to make on the weekend when you have a bit more time. It's satisfying to have a bronzed bird on your table! Serve it with Parmesan Truffle Mash (see recipe in Chapter 8).

1 (3½-pound) free-range organic chicken

2 tablespoons extra-virgin olive oil

½ teaspoon sea salt

½ teaspoon ground black pepper

1 tablespoon za'atar

1 medium lemon, halved

6 cloves garlic, peeled and smashed

8 large carrots, unpeeled and cut in 2" pieces

1 Preheat oven to 400°F. Line a large roasting pan with parchment paper.

2 Rinse and dry chicken using paper towels. Place in the prepared pan.

3 Drizzle oil over chicken and inside the cavity. Sprinkle salt, pepper, and za'atar on the skin and in the cavity. Place lemon halves and garlic inside the cavity.

4 Roast chicken for 15 minutes.

5 Reduce oven temperature to 350°F and roast for 30 minutes.

6 Remove from oven and spoon the pan juices over chicken. Add carrots to the pan around chicken. Return to oven and roast for 30–40 minutes until the internal temperature reaches 165°F.

7 Remove from oven and tent chicken with foil. Allow chicken to rest for 10 minutes before slicing and serving with carrots.

SERVES 4

Per Serving

Calories	360
Fat	13g
Sodium	540mg
Carbohydrates	17g
Fiber	5g
Sugar	7g
Protein	42g

ZA'ATAR SPICE

Za'atar spice mixtures can vary but they usually contain a tantalizing mixture of oregano, a few varieties of thyme, sumac, sesame seeds, and salt. The sumac gives it a lovely lemony flavor that balances well with the herbs. Ingredients in za'atar have shown the ability to reduce cholesterol, and sumac has been shown to lower the blood sugar of type 2 diabetics. Sumac, thyme, and oregano are all rich sources of flavonoids, powerful antioxidants that can protect cells from damage.

Hazelnut-Crusted Chicken with Raspberries

SERVES 2

Per Serving

Calories	520
Fat	36g
Sodium	1,540mg
Carbohydrates	20g
Fiber	9g
Sugar	8g
Protein	31g

HAZELNUTS

The most abundant anti-oxidants in hazelnuts are known as phenolic compounds, and they've been shown to help decrease blood choles-terol and inflammation. An eight-week study showed that eating hazelnuts, with or with-out the skin, significantly decreased oxidative stress compared to not eating hazelnuts.

You can make this recipe with boneless, skinless chicken thighs, but they don't look as pretty.

3 tablespoons extra-virgin olive oil, divided

1 tablespoon apple cider vinegar

1½ tablespoons Dijon mustard, divided

1 teaspoon raw honey

1¼ cups fresh raspberries, divided

3 cups mixed greens

2 (4-ounce) boneless, skinless chicken breasts

1 teaspoon sea salt, divided

½ teaspoon ground black pepper, divided

1 large free-range egg, beaten

⅓ cup chopped hazelnuts

1 In a small bowl, whisk together 2 tablespoons oil, vinegar, ½ tablespoon mustard, and honey. Add ¼ cup raspberries and use a fork to mash them into the dressing. Set aside.

2 Place chicken between two sheets of waxed paper on a flat surface. Pound, starting at the center, until ¼" thick. Sprinkle chicken with ½ teaspoon salt and ¼ teaspoon pepper. Spread both sides of chicken with the remaining 1 tablespoon mustard.

3 In a shallow bowl, whisk egg. Place hazelnuts in another shallow bowl. Dip chicken into egg, then into hazelnuts, pressing to coat both sides.

4 Heat the remaining 1 tablespoon oil in a medium skillet over medium heat. Add chicken; cook for 3 minutes without moving. Carefully flip and cook for 1–3 minutes until chicken is thoroughly cooked and nuts are toasted.

5 Divide greens between two plates and scatter the remaining 1 cup raspberries on top. Add 1 chicken breast to each plate. Pour salad dressing over greens and sprinkle everything with the remaining ½ teaspoon salt and ¼ teaspoon pepper. Serve immediately.

Burrito Bowls

Serve these flavorful bowls with High-Fiber Guacamole (see recipe in Chapter 8) and Fresh Salsa (see recipe in Chapter 12). Add a scattering of sliced scallions and jalapeños, as well as a sprinkle of nutritional yeast or your favorite cheese.

1 tablespoon extra-virgin olive oil

1 medium red onion, peeled and diced

4 cloves garlic, peeled and minced

1 tablespoon ground cumin

1 tablespoon dried oregano

1 teaspoon chili powder

1 teaspoon sea salt

1 pound 80/20 grass-fed organic ground beef

2 teaspoons grated lime zest

2 tablespoons lime juice

1 (14.5-ounce) can diced tomatoes

1 (15-ounce) can black beans, drained and rinsed

4 cups shredded romaine lettuce

½ cup whole-milk plain Greek yogurt

1 Heat oil in a large saucepan or Dutch oven over medium-high heat. Sauté onion for 3–4 minutes until softened, then add garlic, cumin, oregano, chili powder, and salt and cook for 1 minute. Add ground beef, stir to break it up in the pan, and cook for 5 minutes or until no longer pink.

2 Stir in lime zest, lime juice, tomatoes, and beans and reduce heat to medium-low. Simmer for 20 minutes or until much of the liquid is gone and the sauce is very thick. Remove from heat.

3 Divide romaine among four shallow bowls. Top with the beef mixture and dollops of yogurt. Serve immediately.

SERVES 4

Per Serving

Calories	530
Fat	30g
Sodium	1,070mg
Carbohydrates	30g
Fiber	4g
Sugar	9g
Protein	35g

COCONUT WRAPS

Another way to enjoy burritos is by wrapping them in keto or coconut wraps. Coconut wraps do the same job as a burrito wrap, but they don't spike your blood sugar. There are many options available; look for ones without added sugar, wheat, or corn. You'll find coconut or keto wraps in health food stores, online shops, and maybe even your local supermarket.

Beef Bolognese on Zucchini Noodles

SERVES 4

Per Serving

Calories	180
Fat	9g
Sodium	360mg
Carbohydrates	17g
Fiber	2g
Sugar	10g
Protein	8g

TOMATO PURÉE (PASSATA)

Tomato passata is puréed, strained tomatoes usually sold in glass bottles. It's made out of 100% tomatoes with no additives or flavorings, except added salt in some cases. The consistency is uniform and smooth, unlike crushed or chopped tomatoes, and it makes exceptionally thick tomato-based sauces. You can approximate passata by blending cans of crushed or chopped tomatoes until smooth.

This sauce is great with or without the beef (puy lentils are an excellent substitute). The fresh injection of rosemary, olives, and garlic at the very end ensures maximum nutrition and flavor!

3 tablespoons minced fresh rosemary

20 large Kalamata olives, pitted and chopped

2 tablespoons minced capers

4 cloves garlic, peeled and minced, divided

1 tablespoon extra-virgin olive oil

2 large red onions, peeled and diced

1 large carrot, peeled and diced

1 pound 80/20 grass-fed organic ground beef

½ teaspoon crushed red pepper flakes

2 (24-ounce) bottles tomato passata

4 tablespoons tomato paste

10 medium zucchini, trimmed and spiralized

1 Place rosemary, olives, capers, and 1 minced garlic clove in a small bowl. Mix well and set aside.

2 Heat oil in a large saucepan or Dutch oven over medium-high heat. Add onions and carrot. Sauté until softened, 3–4 minutes.

3 Add the remaining 3 garlic cloves, ground beef, and red pepper flakes. Cook, stirring frequently, until beef is browned throughout, 5–6 minutes.

4 Add passata and tomato paste and bring to a boil. Reduce heat to medium-low and simmer for 10 minutes.

5 Add rosemary mixture and zucchini noodles. Toss to coat. Cook for 3–5 minutes until zucchini is warm and slightly wilted. Serve immediately.

Asian Cucumber Ribbons with Thai Beef

CHOPPED PEANUTS

Peanuts contain a mix of soluble and insoluble fiber, which provides a slew of benefits, one of which is helping lower LDL cholesterol levels. Peanuts also contain niacin (vitamin B₃), which is important for healthy heart function. One study found that consuming just over 1 ounce (42 grams) of peanuts per day for twelve weeks helped participants reduce blood pressure, cholesterol, and triglyceride levels. The combination of protein, fiber, and healthy fats found in peanuts can help keep you feeling full and satisfied between meals.

The lime in this dish unites all the flavors and provides a fresh flavor, along with the mint and cilantro that contrast beautifully with the beef. Sprinkle the final dish with a tiny amount of sesame seeds.

2 medium English cucumbers, cut in half crosswise

¼ cup apple cider vinegar

1 tablespoon grated lime zest

¼ cup lime juice

1 teaspoon raw honey or maple syrup

2 tablespoons tamari

2 teaspoons sesame oil

½ teaspoon crushed red pepper flakes

1 teaspoon organic virgin coconut oil

1 pound organic, pasture-raised beef fillet, cut horizontally into 2 equal pieces

4 medium shallots, peeled and thinly sliced

1 cup fresh cilantro leaves

½ cup fresh mint leaves

½ cup peanuts, toasted and roughly chopped

1 Cut cucumbers lengthwise into ⅛" ribbons using a mandoline or a peeler.

2 In a medium bowl, whisk vinegar, lime zest, lime juice, honey, tamari, sesame oil, and red pepper flakes. Pour half of the mixture into a large bowl. Add cucumbers and toss to coat. Set aside to marinate for 5 minutes.

3 Heat coconut oil in a medium skillet over high heat. Sear beef for 2–3 minutes per side, being careful not to overcook past medium rare. Transfer to a plate and allow to rest for 10 minutes in a warm place.

4 Thinly slice beef and transfer to a large bowl. Add shallots, cilantro, mint, peanuts, and the remaining lime mixture. Toss to combine.

5 To serve, place a mound of beef salad in the middle of each plate and surround each mound with cucumber ribbons.

CHAPTER 8

Dips, Small Plates, and Sides

Red Chili Hummus

SERVES 4

Per Serving

Calories	230
Fat	10g
Sodium	520mg
Carbohydrates	28g
Fiber	8g
Sugar	5g
Protein	9g

HOMEMADE HUMMUS

Homemade hummus tastes much better than the store-bought kind. Make a large batch on the weekend and you'll always have a quick snack. For crunch, top it with sesame seeds or crispy oven-baked chickpeas. Hummus is great as a dip with vegetables or crackers, and a spoonful on top of a salad or vegetable side adds flavor and protein.

If you don't have a fresh chili or you don't like spice, replace it with a slice of red bell pepper and a tiny sprinkle of crushed red pepper flakes. After you drizzle olive oil on top of the hummus, dust it with paprika and a sprinkle of chopped fresh cilantro or parsley.

1 (15-ounce) can chickpeas, drained and rinsed

2 tablespoons tahini (100% Humera sesame seeds)

1 tablespoon grated lemon zest

3 tablespoons lemon juice

1 large clove garlic, peeled

1 small red chili, seeded and chopped

1 teaspoon ground cumin

½ teaspoon sea salt

1 tablespoon extra-virgin olive oil

1 Place chickpeas, tahini, lemon zest, lemon juice, garlic, chili, cumin, and salt in a medium bowl. Mash with a fork until combined but chunky. Alternatively, pulse in a food processor until smooth.

2 Transfer hummus to a small shallow serving bowl and use the back of a spoon to create circular trenches on top. Drizzle oil over hummus. Serve immediately, or cover and store in the refrigerator for up to 5 days.

Beet Horseradish Hummus

If you can't find plain precooked beets, use 4 small raw beets. Rinse and steam them for 30 minutes until tender. Garnish this dip with sesame seeds, parsley, a drizzle of olive oil, and a dollop of horseradish.

1 (8.8-ounce) package precooked red beets

1 (15-ounce) can chickpeas, drained and rinsed

2 tablespoons tahini

1 tablespoon extra-virgin olive oil

1 tablespoon sugar-free horseradish paste

1 clove garlic, peeled

1 tablespoon grated lemon zest

3 tablespoons lemon juice

1 teaspoon ground cumin

1 teaspoon salt

1   Place all ingredients in a food processor and process for 1 minute, stopping once or twice to run a spatula around the edges to push all the ingredients down toward the blade. Add 2–4 tablespoons cold water if hummus is too thick.

2   Transfer to a serving bowl and serve immediately or cover and refrigerate for up to 4 days.

SERVES 4

Per Serving

Calories	270
Fat	11g
Sodium	890mg
Carbohydrates	35g
Fiber	10g
Sugar	10g
Protein	10g

HORSERADISH

The sharp, pungent flavor of horseradish is due to a chemical called allyl isothiocyanate, which is also responsible for its powerful medicinal properties. Allyl isothiocyanate has been shown to have antioxidant, anti-inflammatory, and anticancer effects in test-tube and animal studies. Additionally, horseradish contains mustard oil, a compound that may boost weight loss.

Basil Black Bean Hummus

SERVES 4

Per Serving

Calories	360
Fat	14g
Sodium	960mg
Carbohydrates	46g
Fiber	8g
Sugar	8g
Protein	17g

BASIL HELPS LOWER CHOLESTEROL

Basil contains compounds that can help to lower cholesterol levels. Additionally, basil has anti-inflammatory properties that may help to reduce the risk of heart disease and other inflammatory disorders, such as arthritis.

Basil and tomatoes bring an Italian flavor to this scrumptious, creamy hummus. Eating hummus weekly is a great way to increase your bean intake.

1 (15-ounce) can chickpeas, drained and rinsed

1 (15-ounce) can black beans, drained and rinsed

1 cup packed thinly sliced basil leaves

6 cherry tomatoes

2 tablespoons tomato paste

2 tablespoons tahini

2 cloves garlic, peeled

2 teaspoons grated lime zest

2 tablespoons lime juice

1 teaspoon sea salt

2 tablespoons extra-virgin olive oil, divided

1 Place chickpeas, black beans, basil, tomatoes, tomato paste, tahini, garlic, lime zest, lime juice, salt, and 1 tablespoon oil in a food processor or high-speed blender. Process for 30–60 seconds until smooth.

2 Transfer hummus to a small shallow serving bowl and use the back of a spoon to create circular trenches on top. Drizzle the remaining 1 tablespoon oil over hummus. Serve immediately, or cover and store in the refrigerator for up to 5 days.

Basil Protein Hummus

The addition of protein powder makes this hummus a great lunch box addition. Use it as a dip, or add it to a baked sweet potato with some scallions on top, or spoon it over a bowl of salad greens for a well-rounded meal.

1 tablespoon grated lemon zest

3 tablespoons lemon juice

2 (15-ounce) cans chickpeas, drained and rinsed

2 cups roughly chopped fresh basil

2 cloves garlic, peeled

¼ cup extra-virgin olive oil

2 teaspoons salt

½ cup unflavored whey protein concentrate 80%

1 Place lemon zest, lemon juice, chickpeas, basil, garlic, oil, and salt in a food processor. Process for 30 seconds. Scrape down the sides with a spatula, then process again until very smooth, about 15 seconds. Add protein concentrate and pulse for 10 seconds or just until blended.

2 Serve immediately, or refrigerate in a covered container for up to 5 days.

MAKES 3 CUPS

Per Serving (½ cup)

Calories	240
Fat	11g
Sodium	1,020mg
Carbohydrates	27g
Fiber	8g
Sugar	0g
Protein	11g

HUMMUS

More than just a dip, hummus is delicious and nutritious. It can be a satisfying addition to chicken, salmon, vegetable side dishes, and salads. Add ¼ cup hummus to your next meal for a hit of fiber, which helps to lower cholesterol and keep the digestive system healthy.

Greek Fava Dip

This dip is deeply satisfying and great to double. Although it's called "fava dip," it's made with split yellow peas, not fava beans. (Fáva in Greek refers to yellow split peas.) Serve it with raw vegetables like red bell pepper strips, baby carrots, and celery sticks.

4 tablespoons extra-virgin olive oil, divided

1 large red onion, peeled and thinly sliced

1 medium carrot, peeled and grated

1 cup dried yellow split peas, rinsed and drained

2½ cups chicken stock

1 clove garlic, peeled

2 tablespoons lemon juice

½ teaspoon sea salt

2 teaspoons capers

1 tablespoon minced fresh parsley

1 Heat 1 tablespoon oil in a medium saucepan over medium heat. Sauté onion and carrot for 3–4 minutes until softened. Stir in split peas and cook for 3 minutes.

2 Add stock and bring to a boil. Reduce heat to low, cover, and simmer for 45 minutes or until peas are very soft and tender. Check pan occasionally and add water to almost cover peas if necessary.

3 Transfer pea mixture to a food processor or high-speed blender, along with garlic, lemon juice, salt, and 2 tablespoons oil. Process for 1 minute, stopping once or twice to run a spatula around the edges to push all the ingredients down toward the blade.

4 Transfer dip to a shallow bowl and drizzle with the remaining 1 tablespoon oil. Garnish with capers and parsley. Serve immediately, or store in an airtight container in the refrigerator for up to 1 week, or in a freezer-safe container in the freezer for up to 3 months.

SERVES 6

Per Serving

Calories	340
Fat	10g
Sodium	400mg
Carbohydrates	26g
Fiber	9g
Sugar	2g
Protein	11g

BEAN DIPS AND SPREADS

Hummus is the most famous bean dip, but you can make similarly tasty dips with a variety of beans and peas, such as fava, black, or cannellini beans. Make a large batch and freeze it in small portions so you'll always have a nutritious lunch or snack on hand. Add ¼–½ cup to the top of salads, fish dishes, or lunch bowls.

High-Fiber Guacamole

SERVES 12

Per Serving

Calories	90
Fat	5g
Sodium	220mg
Carbohydrates	10g
Fiber	1g
Sugar	1g
Protein	3g

KEEPING GUACAMOLE GREEN

Guacamole turns brown because compounds in its cells oxidize when exposed to air. This is called enzymatic browning. To prevent this, you can either add an acidic ingredient like lime juice to slow down the enzymes or you can limit air exposure. When covering guacamole, press plastic wrap directly on its surface to limit exposure to air.

Creamy cannellini beans add fiber and stretch your guacamole further. For a more authentic flavor, swap out the crushed red pepper flakes with a minced jalapeño pepper.

2 teaspoons grated lime zest

2 tablespoons lime juice

2 medium avocados, halved, pitted, and peeled

1 (15-ounce) can cannellini beans, drained and rinsed

2 cloves garlic, peeled and minced

1 tablespoon extra-virgin olive oil

1 teaspoon sea salt

½ teaspoon crushed red pepper flakes

8 cherry tomatoes, halved

¼ medium yellow onion, peeled and minced

¼ cup minced fresh cilantro

1 Place lime zest, lime juice, avocados, beans, garlic, oil, salt, and red pepper flakes in a food processor or high-speed blender. Process for 30 seconds until almost smooth. Add tomatoes, onion, and cilantro. Pulse a few times until just mixed, but not smooth.

2 Transfer to a serving bowl and serve immediately, or cover and refrigerate for up to 4 hours.

Awesome Artichoke Dip

This dip is incredibly tasty served with vegetables for scooping. For a fun party appetizer, top oatcakes or whole-wheat crackers with 2 teaspoons artichoke dip and a small basil leaf.

1 (6.5-ounce) jar artichoke hearts, drained (about 1 cup)

1 (5.3-ounce) jar pitted green olives (about 1 cup)

2 cloves garlic, peeled

1 cup packed chopped fresh basil

1 tablespoon grated lemon zest

3 tablespoons lemon juice

2 tablespoons extra-virgin olive oil

¼ teaspoon sea salt

1 Place all ingredients in a food processor and process for 1 minute, stopping once or twice to run a spatula around the edges to push all the ingredients down toward the blade.

2 Serve immediately.

SERVES 4

Per Serving

Calories	130
Fat	11g
Sodium	890mg
Carbohydrates	6g
Fiber	1g
Sugar	0g
Protein	2g

ANTIOXIDANT-RICH ARTICHOKES

Artichokes are thought to impact cholesterol in two primary ways. First, artichokes contain luteolin, an antioxidant that prevents cholesterol formation. Second, artichoke leaf extract (which can be found in supplement form) encourages your body to process cholesterol more efficiently, leading to lower overall levels. One medium artichoke contains almost 7 grams of fiber, which is a whopping 23–28 percent of the reference daily intake (RDI).

Mackerel Pâté with Fennel and Herbs

Pâté is a delicious crowd-pleasing starter spread for seedy crackers, sourdough toast, or red bell pepper strips. Or scoop some on top of a lunch or dinner salad for extra protein.

SERVES 4

Per Serving

Calories	220
Fat	9g
Sodium	730mg
Carbohydrates	19g
Fiber	1g
Sugar	2g
Protein	15g

CANNED FISH DIPS

Canned fish makes an excellent base for a quick dip. You can mix it with beans or Greek yogurt and add your favorite spices and herbs. Salmon, sardines, mackerel, and tuna all make excellent protein-rich dips, protein bread spreads, and salad toppings. Here are a couple combinations to try: salmon with fresh dill, chives, garlic, and cannellini beans; or tuna with capers, dill pickles, and Greek yogurt.

1 (4-ounce) can olive-oil-packed mackerel fillets (sustainably fished)

1 (15-ounce) can black beans, drained and rinsed

1 cup fresh herbs (dill, parsley, chives, and/or cilantro)

2 tablespoons capers

2 cloves garlic, peeled

2 tablespoons extra-virgin olive oil

1 tablespoon grated lemon zest

3 tablespoons lemon juice

1 tablespoon Dijon mustard

1 teaspoon fennel seeds, rubbed between your fingers

1 teaspoon cumin seeds

½ teaspoon sea salt

1 Place all ingredients in a food processor and process for 1 minute, stopping once or twice to run a spatula around the edges to push all the ingredients down toward the blade.

2 Serve immediately.

Smoked Mackerel Cucumber Canapés

These elegant little bites are easy to make, look gorgeous, and taste amazing. In addition to the dill sprigs, you can top these canapés with one or two small thin slices of red onion and a sprinkle of crushed red pepper flakes.

3 (11-ounce) vacuum-packed smoked mackerel fillets

¼ cup whole-milk plain Greek yogurt

1½ teaspoons grated lemon zest

1½ tablespoons lemon juice

1 tablespoon roughly chopped capers

1 large English cucumber, trimmed and cut into ¼" slices

¼ cup fresh dill sprigs

1 In a food processor, combine mackerel, yogurt, lemon zest, lemon juice, and capers. Process for 30–45 seconds until smooth.

2 Arrange cucumber slices on a large serving platter. Top each slice with a spoonful of the mackerel mixture and a tiny piece of dill. Serve immediately, or cover and refrigerate for up to 4 hours.

SERVES 6

Per Serving

Calories	490
Fat	38g
Sodium	1,200mg
Carbohydrates	2g
Fiber	1g
Sugar	1g
Protein	35g

ENGLISH CUCUMBERS

English cucumbers are not waxed, so you can serve them with the peel, which increases the fiber and nutrient content. All cucumbers contain compounds that help to lower blood pressure as well as fight diabetes and cancer. And thanks to their silica content, cucumbers can also be beneficial for the skin. So next time you're looking for a healthy snack, reach for a slice of cucumber!

Burst Tomatoes with Lemon Cream

SERVES 6

Per Serving

Calories	90
Fat	7g
Sodium	55mg
Carbohydrates	6g
Fiber	1g
Sugar	4g
Protein	1g

APPETIZERS AS SIDES

Instead of rice or potatoes, think about choosing small vegetable-focused dishes as the main feature of your meal. Have you ever noticed how appetizers in a restaurant tend to be more fun? Pick an appetizer or something you really like the look of, and then make a quick protein (almost as an afterthought). You could simply open a can of fish, broil a fish fillet, or pop a pan of chicken thighs into the oven before you start making your appetizer. Your protein will be ready about the same time as your side, and you'll have a fun, nutritious plate in front of you.

The combination of oven-hot juicy tomatoes and refrigerator-cold Thick Creamy Lemon Sauce (see recipe in Chapter 12) is magical. Spread the mixture onto oatcakes, whole-wheat crackers, or sourdough rye bread, or use it as a side dish for fish or chicken.

4 cups cherry tomatoes

3 tablespoons extra-virgin olive oil

4 cloves garlic, peeled and thinly sliced

6 thin strips lemon zest

1 teaspoon cumin seeds

1 teaspoon raw honey

5 sprigs fresh oregano

5 sprigs fresh thyme

⅛ teaspoon sea salt

2 cups Thick Creamy Lemon Sauce (see recipe in Chapter 12)

1 Preheat oven to 400°F. Line a 13" × 9" baking dish with parchment paper.

2 Place tomatoes, oil, garlic, lemon zest strips, cumin, honey, oregano, thyme, and salt in the prepared baking dish and stir to combine. Bake for 25 minutes or until mixture is bubbling and tomatoes break open.

3 Spoon Thick Creamy Lemon Sauce onto the middle of a serving plate. Use a large spoon to spread sauce in a small circle in the center of the plate until the circle is roughly ½" high. Make a small indent in the middle of the circle. Fill indent with the tomato mixture.

4 Serve immediately.

Zucchini Antipasti

Finish this fresh-tasting appetizer with freshly ground black pepper and shavings of Parmesan cheese.

⅓ cup sun-dried tomatoes

2 large zucchini, trimmed and cut lengthwise into ⅛" slices

2 tablespoons extra-virgin olive oil

1 cup whole-milk ricotta cheese

1 clove garlic, peeled

3 tablespoons minced fresh chives

3 tablespoons minced capers

2 teaspoons grated lemon zest

1 tablespoon chopped fresh oregano

1 teaspoon sea salt

½ teaspoon ground black pepper

1 Preheat broiler. Line a large baking sheet with foil.
2 Place sun-dried tomatoes in a small bowl and cover with boiling water. Set aside for 10 minutes.
3 Brush both sides of zucchini slices with oil and place on the prepared baking sheet. Broil for 1 minute on each side. Remove from oven and set aside.
4 Drain sun-dried tomatoes and discard soaking liquid. Blot dry, coarsely chop, and transfer to a food processor. Add ricotta, garlic, chives, capers, lemon zest, oregano, salt, and pepper. Pulse until just combined.
5 Spoon 1 tablespoon tomato mixture onto 1 end of a zucchini slice. Roll zucchini around filling and secure with a toothpick. Repeat with remaining zucchini slices and tomato mixture. Serve immediately.

SERVES 4

Per Serving

Calories	230
Fat	16g
Sodium	810mg
Carbohydrates	13g
Fiber	3g
Sugar	7g
Protein	10g

ZUCCHINI

Zucchini is a heart-healthy food that can help to lower cholesterol. Zucchini is rich in vitamin B_6, which studies have shown can help regulate blood glucose. Carotenoids—lutein, zeaxanthin, and beta-carotene—are particularly plentiful in zucchini. Research suggests that eating foods rich in carotenoids could slow or lower your risk of developing cardiovascular disease.

Roasted Asparagus with Sunshine Sauce

Try other green vegetables, such as green beans, broccoli, or zucchini, with this inflammation-busting creamy lemon turmeric sauce.

SERVES 6

Per Serving

Calories	100
Fat	8g
Sodium	200mg
Carbohydrates	6g
Fiber	3g
Sugar	3g
Protein	4g

TURMERIC AND PEPPER

Turmeric is known forits antioxidant and anti-inflammatory effects. To get the most out of turmeric, it is best to consume it with black pepper. Black pepper helps to increase the bioavailability of turmeric, making it more effective. Another way to increase the bioavailability of turmeric is to consume it with a source of fat, such as olive oil, avocado, fish, nuts, or nut butters. This will help the body to absorb the curcumin in turmeric more effectively.

3 tablespoons extra-virgin olive oil, divided

1 tablespoon grated lemon zest

3 tablespoons lemon juice

¼ cup whole-milk plain Greek yogurt

1 teaspoon ground turmeric

½ teaspoon sea salt

⅛ teaspoon ground black pepper

⅛ teaspoon ground cayenne pepper

1½ pounds fresh asparagus, trimmed

1. Preheat oven to 425°F. Line a 13" × 9" baking dish with parchment paper.
2. In a small bowl, whisk together 2 tablespoons olive oil, lemon zest, lemon juice, yogurt, turmeric, salt, black pepper, and cayenne; set aside.
3. Place asparagus in a large bowl and drizzle with remaining 1 tablespoon oil. Toss to coat and transfer to the prepared baking dish. Roast for 12 minutes or until tender.
4. Drizzle asparagus with sauce and serve immediately.

Parmesan Truffle Mash

You need only 15 minutes to make this heavenly side dish. Garnish it with Parmesan, crushed red pepper flakes, and a tiny drizzle of truffle oil. Finely chopped parsley is also a nice topping.

1 large head cauliflower, cored and cut into florets

2 tablespoons grass-fed butter

1 teaspoon truffle oil

1 clove garlic, peeled

½ cup grated Parmesan cheese

½ teaspoon sea salt

⅛ teaspoon ground black pepper

1 Place 1 cup water in a large saucepan. Bring to a boil over high heat. Add cauliflower and reduce heat to medium-low. Cover and simmer for 10 minutes or until fork-tender.

2 Drain cauliflower, reserving cooking water, and transfer to a food processor. Add butter, oil, garlic, Parmesan, salt, and pepper. Process for 1 minute until combined. If the mixture is too thick, add 1–2 tablespoons reserved cooking water and blend again until desired consistency is reached.

3 Serve immediately.

SERVES 4

Per Serving

Calories	160
Fat	10g
Sodium	530mg
Carbohydrates	12g
Fiber	4g
Sugar	4g
Protein	7g

CAULIFLOWER MASH

Cauliflower is a low-calorie, low-carb way to enjoy the texture and feeling of hot mashed potatoes without the blood sugar spike. Potatoes are best eaten cold. If you eat potatoes when they're cold, as in potato salad, you get a nearly 40 percent lower blood sugar spike. Cold potatoes contain resistant starch, which can lower blood sugar levels, reduce appetite, and aid digestion.

Simple Puy Lentils

Lentils make a protein-rich, intensely satisfying side dish. Season it with salt, freshly ground black pepper, some crushed red pepper flakes, and a drizzle of olive oil. Make a double or triple batch and keep in the refrigerator for up to 4 days or the freezer for up to 2 months.

SERVES 4

Per Serving

Calories	140
Fat	4.5g
Sodium	270mg
Carbohydrates	19g
Fiber	1g
Sugar	4g
Protein	6g

FRENCH PUY LENTILS

Puy lentils are a delicious standby side for busy nights. They're inexpensive, easy to make (no soaking required), highly nutritious, high in protein and fiber, and really versatile. Puy lentils are particularly firm and chewy, which makes them a good ground beef substitute in pasta sauces and stews. Use them as the base of a salad with roasted carrots, feta, mint, and tahini.

1 tablespoon extra-virgin olive oil

1 medium red onion, peeled and diced

2 cloves garlic, peeled and crushed

1 teaspoon dried rosemary

1 cup dried puy lentils, rinsed

4 cups vegetable stock

1 Heat oil in a medium saucepan over medium heat. Add onion and sauté for 3–4 minutes until softened. Add garlic and rosemary and sauté for 1 minute or until fragrant.

2 Add lentils and stock and increase heat to high. Bring to a boil, then reduce heat to medium-low and simmer for 20–25 minutes until lentils are tender but still hold their shape.

3 Serve hot or cold.

Roasted Whole Carrots

Pop some whole carrots in the oven when you start making dinner, and they'll be nicely caramelized when you're about to eat.

1½ pounds medium carrots, trimmed

2 tablespoons extra-virgin olive oil

1 tablespoon apple cider vinegar

3 cloves garlic, peeled and smashed

1 tablespoon dried thyme

¼ teaspoon sea salt

⅛ teaspoon ground black pepper

1 Preheat oven to 400°F. Line a large baking sheet with parchment paper or foil.

2 Place carrots in a large bowl. Add oil, vinegar, garlic, thyme, salt, and pepper and turn carrots to coat.

3 Transfer to the prepared baking sheet, cover tightly with foil, and bake for 30–40 minutes until just tender. Uncover and cook for 10 minutes until carrots have browned.

4 Serve hot or cold.

SERVES 4

Per Serving

Calories	140
Fat	7g
Sodium	260mg
Carbohydrates	18g
Fiber	5g
Sugar	8g
Protein	2g

SMASH GARLIC BEFORE COOKING

What does it mean when you see "crushed garlic" or "smashed garlic"? Putting a clove (peeled or unpeeled) under your chef's knife, and hitting the flat of the blade firmly with the heel of your hand smashes the garlic clove. The crushing releases healthful compounds that may lower blood pressure and thin your blood by breaking up potentially harmful clusters of platelets in the bloodstream. So before you chop or mince, make sure to crush the garlic first under your knife.

Sweet Potato Fries with Harissa Dip

Double this incredibly tasty side dish to keep extra portions in the refrigerator to add nutrient density to lunches and dinners. Like spicy food? Add more harissa paste to the dip.

SERVES 6

Per Serving

Calories	180
Fat	7g
Sodium	480mg
Carbohydrates	24g
Fiber	4g
Sugar	8g
Protein	6g

HARISSA

Harissa is a healthy and flavorful option for those who enjoy spice in their food. The North African chili paste is rich in vitamins and minerals, including vitamins E, C, B$_6$, and K, as well as iron and copper. Harissa can help boost metabolism and is rich in antioxidants. While it is spicy, the heat level can vary depending on the brand or recipe, so it is possible to find a variety that suits your heat preference.

1 cup whole-milk plain Greek yogurt
½ teaspoon harissa paste
1 teaspoon grated lemon zest
1 teaspoon salt, divided
4 large sweet potatoes, peeled and cut into ¼" strips
2 tablespoons extra-virgin olive oil
½ teaspoon chili powder
1 teaspoon ground cumin
1 teaspoon sweet smoked paprika
¼ teaspoon ground black pepper

1 Preheat oven to 425°F. Line two large baking sheets with parchment paper.
2 In a small bowl, stir together yogurt, harissa paste, lemon zest, and ½ teaspoon salt. Set aside.
3 Place sweet potatoes in a large bowl and drizzle with oil. Toss to coat.
4 In a separate small bowl, stir together chili powder, cumin, paprika, pepper, and remaining ½ teaspoon salt. Sprinkle over sweet potatoes and toss again. Arrange sweet potatoes in a single layer on the prepared baking sheets.
5 Bake for 25–35 minutes, turning once during cooking time, until potatoes are deep golden brown and crisp.
6 Serve fries immediately with dip.

Citrus-Roasted Beet Platter

Pair this earthy side dish of beets and the delicious, creamy, and sweet mustard sauce with grilled fish or chicken. It's even better sprinkled with crushed red pepper flakes and chopped fresh mint and parsley.

SERVES 4

Per Serving

Calories	150
Fat	8g
Sodium	440mg
Carbohydrates	2g
Fiber	0g
Sugar	13g
Protein	4g

BEET GREENS

Don't toss the beet tops—they are the most nutritious part of the beet! Beet greens can be cooked and served like spinach with a drizzle of olive oil, salt, pepper, and minced garlic.

6 medium red beets, trimmed and cut into 1" cubes

2 tablespoons extra-virgin olive oil

1 tablespoon lemon juice

3 tablespoons orange juice, divided

¼ teaspoon sea salt

¼ cup whole-milk plain Greek yogurt

1½ tablespoons grated orange zest

2 tablespoons Dijon mustard

1 Preheat oven to 425°F. Line a 13" × 9" baking dish with parchment paper.

2 Place beets in a large bowl. Drizzle with oil, lemon juice, and 1 tablespoon orange juice. Sprinkle with salt. Roast for 30 minutes or until beets are tender when pierced with a knife. Set aside to cool.

3 In a small bowl, stir together yogurt, remaining 2 tablespoons orange juice, orange zest, and mustard.

4 Arrange beets on a large serving platter, drizzle with yogurt mixture, and serve.

Artichoke-Stuffed Baby Eggplants

The stuffing is full of heart-friendly fats and fiber, and it tastes like a bread crumb–based stuffing. Use it to stuff other vegetables as well, such as bell peppers, zucchini, or large tomatoes.

4 baby eggplants

1 cup marinated artichoke hearts (in brine)

½ cup shelled hemp seeds

2 cloves garlic, peeled and minced

4 tablespoons extra-virgin olive oil

¼ teaspoon sea salt

1 Preheat oven to 425°F. Line a large baking sheet with parchment paper.

2 Cut each eggplant in half lengthwise. Using the tines of a fork, scrape out some flesh on the cut sides to make a cavity for stuffing. Place cut sides up on prepared baking sheet. Bake for 10 minutes.

3 Meanwhile, place artichoke hearts, hemp seeds, garlic, oil, and salt in a food processor. Process until combined but still coarse, about 1 minute.

4 Remove eggplant from oven. Spoon a small amount of artichoke mixture onto each eggplant half.

5 Return to oven and bake for 8–10 minutes until eggplants are tender and topping is golden brown. Serve immediately.

SERVES 2

Per Serving

Calories	680
Fat	52g
Sodium	780mg
Carbohydrates	39g
Fiber	7g
Sugar	1g
Protein	22g

BABY EGGPLANTS

Eggplants come in all shapes and sizes, from the large, purple globe eggplant to the small, delicate Japanese eggplant. The difference among these various types of eggplants lies in their taste, texture, and use. For example, Italian or baby eggplants have a milder flavor than their larger counterparts. They're also much more tender, making them ideal for use in salads or other dishes where you don't want the eggplant to overpower the other flavors.

Caramelized Brussels Sprouts

SERVES 4

Per Serving

Calories	90
Fat	7g
Sodium	85mg
Carbohydrates	6g
Fiber	2g
Sugar	2g
Protein	2g

BRUSSELS SPROUTS

A 1/2-cup serving of Brussels sprouts contains 3 grams of soluble fiber. Research suggests that upping your soluble fiber intake by just 5–10 grams each day can lower your LDL cholesterol levels by 3–5 percent. Furthermore, Brussels sprouts are a good source of potassium, a mineral that helps to keep your blood pressure in check and reduce your risk of stroke.

This easy side dish will surprise even non-Brussels sprouts lovers with its unexpectedly satisfying flavor. The trick is the high heat that caramelizes the sprouts' sugars.

2 cups trimmed and halved Brussels sprouts

1 medium lemon, sliced

2 tablespoons extra-virgin olive oil

2 tablespoons lemon juice

2 tablespoons water

1/8 teaspoon salt

1/8 teaspoon ground black pepper

1 Preheat oven to 400°F. Line a large baking sheet with parchment paper.

2 Place all ingredients in a large bowl and toss to coat. Transfer to the prepared baking sheet and spread evenly, cut sides down.

3 Roast for 15–19 minutes until browned. Serve immediately.

Ginger Pistachio Snow Peas

Whip up a delicious side dish in less than 5 minutes! Snow peas are excellent served with baked fish, chicken, or Asian tofu dishes.

2 tablespoons extra-virgin olive oil

1 pound sugar snap peas or snow peas

3 cloves garlic, peeled and minced

1 tablespoon grated fresh ginger

⅛ teaspoon salt

⅛ teaspoon ground black pepper

¼ cup chopped, roasted, unsalted pistachios

1　Heat oil in a large skillet over medium heat. Add peas, garlic, and ginger; stir-fry for 3–4 minutes until peas are crisp-tender.

2　Sprinkle with salt, pepper, and pistachios and serve immediately.

SERVES 4

Per Serving

Calories	160
Fat	11g
Sodium	75mg
Carbohydrates	12g
Fiber	4g
Sugar	5g
Protein	4g

SUGAR SNAP AND SNOW PEAS

Sugar snap and snow peas are two varieties of garden peas that are commonly consumed in Asia and Europe. Both sugar snap and snow peas are packed with nutrients like vitamin C, vitamin K, and fiber. Additionally, they contain phytonutrients that have been shown to offer heart-health benefits. Sugar snap and snow peas contain niacin (vitamin B_3), which is known to lower cholesterol in the blood and supports the metabolism, helping the body derive energy from foods after digestion.

Refried Black Beans

SERVES 4

Per Serving

Calories	170
Fat	7g
Sodium	280mg
Carbohydrates	20g
Fiber	1g
Sugar	3g
Protein	8g

BLACK BEANS

Black beans help to regulate blood sugar levels and promote digestive health. Additionally, black beans are a good source of antioxidants, which can help to protect against cell damage and reduce the risk of some chronic diseases. Studies have shown that people who eat a diet rich in black beans may improve their blood pressure and LDL cholesterol levels.

This is a tasty protein-rich side dish to serve alongside brunch eggs and salsa. Or serve it with fish or meat dinners instead of mashed potatoes.

2 tablespoons extra-virgin olive oil

1 cup diced red onion

¼ teaspoon sea salt

1 teaspoon ground cumin

¼ teaspoon crushed red pepper flakes

1 (15-ounce) can black beans, drained and rinsed

¼ cup water

½ tablespoon lime juice

½ teaspoon ground black pepper

1 Heat oil in a medium saucepan over medium-high heat. Add onion and salt and sauté 3–4 minutes until softened. Add cumin and red pepper flakes and stir for 30 seconds.

2 Stir in beans and water. Cover and cook for 5 minutes.

3 Reduce heat to low, uncover pan, and use a fork to mash about half the beans. Continue to cook, stirring often, until thickened, about 2 minutes.

4 Remove from heat and stir in lime juice and black pepper. If beans are too dry, add a splash of water and stir to mix. Serve warm or at room temperature.

Coconut Quinoa

Quinoa has less of a blood sugar impact than rice and other grains. However, it's so tasty, it can be easy to eat too much of it. Keep the serving size to 1/2 cup.

1 cup white or red quinoa, rinsed and drained

1/4 cup full-fat coconut milk

1 3/4 cups chicken stock

2 tablespoons desiccated coconut

1 Place quinoa, coconut milk, and stock in a small saucepan over high heat. Bring to a boil, then reduce heat to medium-low. Simmer for 15–20 minutes until all liquid has been absorbed.

2 Remove from heat, cover, and set aside for 5 minutes. Fluff with a fork, then stir in coconut. Serve immediately.

SERVES 6

Per Serving

Calories	160
Fat	5g
Sodium	130mg
Carbohydrates	21g
Fiber	3g
Sugar	3g
Protein	6g

FLUFFY QUINOA

The secret to avoiding mushy quinoa is less about water quantity and more about technique. No matter the quantity you're cooking, you should cook it uncovered until all the liquid has been absorbed. Then remove it from the heat, pop the lid on to cover it, and let it steam for 5 minutes. Steaming allows the quinoa to become beautifully fluffy.

Quinoa with Spinach and Artichokes

SERVES 6

Per Serving

Calories	210
Fat	7g
Sodium	320mg
Carbohydrates	30g
Fiber	8g
Sugar	5g
Protein	7g

QUINOA AND WHOLE GRAINS

Studies have found that postmenopausal women who ate whole grains like quinoa slowed progression of plaque buildup in the arteries. Quinoa also is a good source of important antioxidants that help reduce inflammation, including one with the tongue-twister name of superoxide dismutase. It's also a good source of folate and magnesium.

For a yummy cheese flavor, add $1/4$ cup nutritional yeast or grated Parmesan cheese when you add the lemon juice. Top the final dish with crushed red pepper flakes and slivered almonds.

2 tablespoons extra-virgin olive oil

1 medium yellow onion, peeled and chopped

4 cloves garlic, peeled and minced

1 (10-ounce) package frozen spinach, thawed and drained

1 (10-ounce) package frozen artichoke hearts, thawed and drained

1 cup white or red quinoa, rinsed and drained

2½ cups chicken broth

2 tablespoons lemon juice

1 teaspoon fresh oregano leaves

1 Heat oil in a large saucepan over medium heat. Add onion and garlic and sauté until onion is softened, 3–4 minutes. Add spinach and artichokes; cook and stir until most of the liquid evaporates, about 5 minutes.

2 Stir in quinoa and broth. Bring to a simmer, then reduce heat to low. Simmer for about 15 minutes or until all liquid has been absorbed. Remove from heat, cover, and set aside for 10 minutes.

3 Uncover pan and fluff quinoa with a fork. Stir in lemon juice and oregano and serve immediately.

CHAPTER 9

Salads

Best Basic Salad

SERVES 1

Per Serving

Calories	160
Fat	14g
Sodium	610mg
Carbohydrates	8g
Fiber	3g
Sugar	3g
Protein	1g

FIBER FIRST

In the US, only 5 percent of people get the recommended 25 grams of fiber per day. Fiber slows down the absorption of food in your intestine, which lessens glucose spikes. It also helps you absorb fewer calories from the food you eat and reduces the glucose impact of everything you eat after the fiber (even sweet treats!).

Enjoy this simple salad before most meals to curb hunger and blunt your glucose curves.

1 tablespoon extra-virgin olive oil

1 tablespoon apple cider vinegar

¼ teaspoon sea salt

¼ teaspoon ground black pepper

2 cups mixed salad greens

1 Place oil, vinegar, salt, and pepper in a small bowl and whisk with a fork.
2 Place salad greens on a plate and drizzle with dressing. Serve immediately.

Best Kale Salad

Learn how to make this simple kale salad, then make it your own depending on your mood and what you have in your pantry. Replace the cranberries with raisins. Add pumpkin or sunflower seeds. Whisk some minced red onion or garlic into the dressing.

2 small bunches curly kale, stems removed and thinly sliced

¼ cup lemon juice

1 teaspoon sea salt

¼ cup unsweetened dried cranberries, minced

2 cups halved cherry tomatoes

¼ cup pine nuts

2 tablespoons extra-virgin olive oil

1 Place kale, lemon juice, and salt in a large bowl. Toss together with your hands, grabbing large handfuls of the kale and vigorously rubbing it against itself for about 1 minute to soften the kale.

2 Add cranberries, tomatoes, pine nuts, and olive oil and toss to combine. Serve immediately.

SERVES 4

Per Serving

Calories	270
Fat	13g
Sodium	680mg
Carbohydrates	34g
Fiber	5g
Sugar	8g
Protein	9g

KALE VERSUS ICEBERG

Iceberg lettuce needs no preparation, but it has almost no nutritional value due to its high water content. Dark green kale, on the other hand, is so good for you, but it takes a little work. Bring out kale's best flavor by removing the tough ribs and stems and massaging or steaming the leaves. Add healthy fats like avocado, nuts, and olive oil. The fiber and antioxidants in kale help to lower cholesterol levels; it deserves at least a weekly spot at your dinner table.

Carrot, Goji, and Mint Salad

This tasty salad lasts in the refrigerator for days, so it's perfect to make ahead of time for a week's worth of packed lunches. Top it with cooked shrimp, a can of fish, or other protein. Add pine nuts or pumpkin seeds for more crunch.

4 cups shredded carrots

½ cup goji berries

½ cup chopped scallions

1 cup chopped fresh mint

1 cup chopped fresh cilantro

3 tablespoons apple cider vinegar

2 tablespoons extra-virgin olive oil

1 teaspoon sea salt

½ teaspoon crushed red pepper flakes

1 Place carrots, goji berries, scallions, mint, and cilantro in a large bowl.

2 In a small bowl, whisk together vinegar, oil, salt, and red pepper flakes. Pour over the carrot mixture and toss together.

3 Serve immediately, or keep covered in the refrigerator for up to 5 days.

SERVES 4

Per Serving

Calories	140
Fat	7g
Sodium	660mg
Carbohydrates	18g
Fiber	4g
Sugar	9g
Protein	3g

POWERFUL ORANGE FOODS

Carrots, sweet potatoes, mangoes, cantaloupes, pumpkins, squash, and other orange foods contain beta-carotene, an antioxidant that is beneficial to your skin. Cooking orange vegetables makes beta-carotene more easily absorbed, especially when served with a small amount of healthy fat, such as a drizzle of olive oil, a sliver of grass-fed butter, or the good fats in nuts.

Toasted Walnut Starter Salad

SERVES 2

Per Serving

Calories	270
Fat	21g
Sodium	790mg
Carbohydrates	16g
Fiber	4g
Sugar	11g
Protein	9g

MAKE SALADS INDIVIDUALLY

Layering a few healthy salad ingredients on a chilled salad plate is a quick way to create healthy (and pretty) individual salads. Try choosing a handful of greens (like arugula), a fruit (like raspberries), a few nuts (like walnuts), and protein or a bit of cheese (like feta). Spoon a quick dressing (olive oil, vinegar, and salt) over the top and your salad is done!

Toasted walnuts make a simple salad something special. It's a crowd-pleasing dinner party starter but easy enough for any day of the week.

10 walnut halves

4 cups torn romaine lettuce

2 cups cherry tomatoes

½ cup crumbled goat cheese

1 tablespoon extra-virgin olive oil

1 tablespoon apple cider vinegar

1 teaspoon Dijon mustard

1 teaspoon raw honey

½ teaspoon sea salt

1 Preheat oven to 375°F. Line a small baking sheet with parchment paper.

2 Place walnuts on prepared baking sheet. Bake for 5–7 minutes, checking frequently in the last couple of minutes to avoid burning. Walnuts should be fragrant and lightly browned. Set aside to cool.

3 Divide lettuce and tomatoes between two salad plates. Top with cheese and walnuts.

4 In a small bowl, whisk oil, vinegar, mustard, honey, and salt. Drizzle over salads and serve immediately.

Blueberry Beet Salad with Walnuts

Try topping this salad with goat cheese slices and fresh dill. Serve it with canned fish such as sardines or mackerel for a quick lunch or dinner.

7 ounces arugula

2 cups blueberries

1 medium beet, trimmed and grated

14 walnut halves

2 tablespoons extra-virgin olive oil

2 tablespoons apple cider vinegar

1 teaspoon raw honey

1 teaspoon Dijon mustard

¼ teaspoon sea salt

1 Place arugula, blueberries, beet, and walnuts in a large bowl.

2 In a small bowl, whisk together oil, vinegar, honey, mustard, and salt. Pour over arugula mixture and toss to coat. Serve immediately.

SERVES 2

Per Serving

Calories	340
Fat	24g
Sodium	370mg
Carbohydrates	29g
Fiber	5g
Sugar	22g
Protein	4g

AWESOME ARUGULA

Also called rocket, roquette, and rucola, arugula is known for its pungent and peppery flavors. It's part of the same family as broccoli, cabbage, kale, mustard, and watercress—the Brassicales. Arugula's slightly bitter taste is due to the presence of glucosinolates, which have been shown to have a strong anticancer and cholesterol-lowering mechanism.

Artichoke, Hazelnut, and Feta Salad

SERVES 4

Per Serving

Calories	450
Fat	39g
Sodium	900mg
Carbohydrates	16g
Fiber	5g
Sugar	5g
Protein	13g

DIJON MUSTARD

Dijon mustard is a type of mustard that originates from the Dijon region of France. Studies have shown that Dijon mustard can help to improve heart health and lower cholesterol levels. The antioxidants in mustard seeds have been shown to reduce inflammation and protect against cell damage. And the vinegar in Dijon can help to prevent blood clots and reduce the risk of heart attack or stroke.

If you have less time, you can skip toasting the hazelnuts in this beautifully fresh and satisfying summer salad. Top it with grilled salmon or tofu to make it a meal.

1 cup hazelnuts

4 cups packed mixed salad greens

½ cup chopped fresh mint

½ cup chopped fresh dill

½ cup chopped fresh basil

½ cup chopped fresh cilantro

1 cup chopped scallions

1 cup chopped oil-packed artichoke hearts

1 cup crumbled feta cheese (preferably sheep's milk feta)

2 tablespoons apple cider vinegar

3 tablespoons extra-virgin olive oil

1 teaspoon Dijon mustard

½ teaspoon sea salt

1. Preheat oven to 350°F. Line a small baking sheet with parchment paper.
2. Place hazelnuts on prepared baking sheet. Bake for 5–7 minutes until lightly toasted. Set aside to cool for 5 minutes.
3. Place salad greens, mint, dill, basil, cilantro, scallions, artichokes, and feta in a large bowl.
4. In a small bowl, whisk together vinegar, oil, mustard, and salt. Pour over salad and toss to coat. Top with toasted hazelnuts and serve immediately.

Cucumber Sesame Salad

This refreshing Japanese fusion salad goes well with fish. Top with chopped scallions and a sprinkle of sesame seeds or crushed red pepper flakes. Use a mandoline or the slicing blade in a food processor to get the thinnest cucumber slices.

4 cups thinly sliced cucumbers

1 (15-ounce) can black beans, drained and rinsed

2 cups packed chopped fresh cilantro

3 tablespoons tahini (100% Humera sesame seeds)

2 tablespoons apple cider vinegar

2 tablespoons tamari

1 tablespoon nutritional yeast flakes

1 Place cucumbers, beans, and cilantro in a large bowl.
2 In a small bowl, whisk together tahini, vinegar, tamari, and nutritional yeast flakes until emulsified. Pour over the cucumber mixture. Toss to coat. Serve immediately.

SERVES 4

Per Serving

Calories	190
Fat	6g
Sodium	640mg
Carbohydrates	24g
Fiber	2g
Sugar	4g
Protein	11g

NUTRITIONAL YEAST FLAKES

Nutritional yeast is a type of deactivated yeast that is often sold in the form of yellow flakes or powder. It's known for its delicious nutty and cheesy flavor, and it's a good source of fiber, protein, and nutrients, including vitamins B_3 (niacin), B_6, and B_{12}; folic acid; selenium; zinc; and copper. A 2017 study by Silla University in Korea found that taking $1^1/_2$ tablespoons of nutritional yeast flakes a day reduced the participants' total cholesterol levels by 6 percent.

Pear, Walnut, and Radish Salad

SERVES 2

Per Serving

Calories	360
Fat	23g
Sodium	370mg
Carbohydrates	50g
Fiber	10g
Sugar	32g
Protein	6g

PEAR PECTIN

Pears are a great source of the soluble fiber pectin. Pectin helps to regulate digestion and promote regularity. It also supports gut health by feeding beneficial gut flora. In addition, pectin can help to lower cholesterol levels by trapping cholesterol in the intestine and preventing it from being reabsorbed into the bloodstream. Pears are a good source of vitamins C and K, both of which are essential for maintaining heart health.

This salad is excellent with a bit of blue cheese on top. If you do add blue cheese, you'll need to use less salt in the salad.

3 cups packed baby spinach

14 walnut halves

2 medium pears (any type), cored, quartered, and cut into thin slices

10 radishes, trimmed and thinly sliced

2 tablespoons extra-virgin olive oil

1 tablespoon grated lemon zest

3 tablespoons lemon juice

2 teaspoons grated ginger

1 teaspoon raw honey

¼ teaspoon sea salt

¼ teaspoon ground black pepper

1 Divide spinach between two wide, shallow bowls. Layer walnuts, pears, and radishes over spinach.

2 In a small bowl, whisk together oil, lemon zest, lemon juice, ginger, and honey. Drizzle dressing over salad. Season with salt and pepper and serve immediately.

Kale and Marinated Mushroom Salad

SERVES 4

Per Serving

Calories	200
Fat	12g
Sodium	610mg
Carbohydrates	20g
Fiber	7g
Sugar	7g
Protein	7g

PROTECTIVE SHIITAKE MUSHROOMS

Studies show that there are powerful health compounds in shiitake mushrooms that can help to boost immune system function and heart health. Powerful polysaccharide sugars called beta-glucans cause an increase in immune function. Shiitakes also contain a substance called eritadenine, which influences the way the liver produces cholesterol, ultimately lowering LDL cholesterol.

Marinating the mushrooms in balsamic vinegar gives them a smooth flavor that combines sweet, sour, and umami tastes. If you don't have Tuscan kale or shiitakes, use regular kale and button mushrooms.

3 cups sliced shiitake mushrooms

2 tablespoons extra-virgin olive oil

2 tablespoons balsamic vinegar

1 clove garlic, peeled and minced

⅛ teaspoon crushed red pepper flakes

8 cups finely chopped Tuscan kale

3 tablespoons lemon juice

1 teaspoon salt

¼ cup sliced almonds, raw unsalted

1 medium yellow bell pepper, seeded and diced

1. Place mushrooms, oil, vinegar, garlic, and red pepper flakes in a medium bowl and stir together. Set aside to marinate for 2 minutes.
2. Place kale, lemon juice, and salt in a large bowl. Toss together with your hands, grabbing large handfuls of the kale and vigorously rubbing it against itself for about 1 minute to soften the kale.
3. Add almonds, bell pepper, and mushroom mixture to kale mixture and mix well. Serve immediately.

Tomato Salsa Salad

This salad combines the tastes of salsa and guacamole in a delicious, healthy dish. For spice, add a minced fresh chili or crushed red pepper flakes. Chickpeas or black beans can be used instead of adzuki beans.

1 small red onion, peeled and thinly sliced

1 tablespoon balsamic vinegar

½ teaspoon sea salt

4 cups halved cherry tomatoes

1 (15-ounce) can adzuki beans, drained and rinsed

1 medium avocado, peeled, pitted, and diced

1 cup chopped fresh cilantro

2 tablespoons shelled raw pumpkin seeds

1 Place onion, vinegar, and salt in a small bowl and toss to combine. Set aside for 2 minutes to pickle and soften onion.

2 Place tomatoes in a large bowl and press them against the bowl with a wooden spoon to release some of the juices. Add beans, avocado, cilantro, and onion mixture and mix until combined.

3 Sprinkle with pumpkin seeds and serve immediately.

SERVES 2

Per Serving

Calories	520
Fat	16g
Sodium	620mg
Carbohydrates	78g
Fiber	23g
Sugar	11g
Protein	24g

ADZUKI OR ADUKI BEANS

Adzuki beans are small red beans that are popular in Japanese and Chinese cuisine. They're a good source of fiber and protein, and they are also high in polyphenols, which are antioxidants that can help to protect against chronic diseases. One of the main health benefits of adzuki beans is that they can help to lower cholesterol levels. The specific nutrients in adzuki beans that are responsible for this effect are saponins, which bind to cholesterol and prevent it from being absorbed by the body.

Fresh Herb and Chickpea Salad

SERVES 2

Per Serving

Calories	540
Fat	26g
Sodium	690mg
Carbohydrates	60g
Fiber	16g
Sugar	12g
Protein	22g

SHEEP'S MILK VERSUS COW'S MILK FETA

Cheese made from sheep's milk has higher levels of CLA (conjugated linoleic acid) than cow's milk cheese. Animal studies suggest this fatty acid can improve your overall body composition by reducing body fat and increasing lean mass.

Fresh green herbs are full of antioxidant nutrients. If you don't like mint or cilantro, you can easily substitute other fresh herbs such as basil, dill, or parsley. Use green herbs liberally to reduce antioxidant stress in your body, soothe inflammation, and benefit your complexion. Consider starting a new healthy habit of buying three or more bunches of different fresh herbs each week!

1 (15-ounce) can chickpeas, drained and rinsed

1 cup chopped fresh mint

1 cup chopped fresh cilantro

½ small red onion, peeled and thinly sliced

1 cup thinly sliced cucumber

⅓ cup crumbled feta cheese (preferably sheep's milk feta)

1 tablespoon extra-virgin olive oil

2 tablespoons lemon juice

2 tablespoons tahini

1 Place chickpeas, mint, cilantro, onion, cucumber, and feta in a medium bowl.

2 In a small bowl, whisk together oil and lemon juice. Pour over salad and toss to coat.

3 Drizzle salad with tahini before serving.

Red Cabbage Salad with Pomegranate and Cilantro

This salad is a beautiful, tasty way to enjoy the powerful nutrients in red cabbage. It's delicious topped with grilled fish, chicken, or tofu.

4 cups finely shredded red cabbage

1 small red onion, peeled and thinly sliced

1½ tablespoons grated orange zest

¼ cup orange juice

1 cup chopped fresh cilantro

1 cup pomegranate seeds

3 tablespoons apple cider vinegar

2 tablespoons extra-virgin olive oil

½ teaspoon sea salt

½ teaspoon crushed red pepper flakes

¼ cup chopped walnuts

1 Place cabbage, onion, orange zest, orange juice, cilantro, and pomegranate seeds in a large bowl and mix together.

2 In a small bowl, whisk together vinegar, oil, salt, and red pepper flakes. Pour over salad and toss to coat. Top with walnuts and serve immediately.

SERVES 4

Per Serving

Calories	190
Fat	12g
Sodium	310mg
Carbohydrates	20g
Fiber	4g
Sugar	11g
Protein	3g

RELEASING POMEGRANATE SEEDS

Getting the juicy seeds (known as arils) out of a pomegranate takes a little time, but it's worth it! The first step is to score the fruit all the way around the middle. Once the fruit is scored, carefully twist it open to reveal the seeds inside. To remove the seeds, hold the pomegranate away from you with the cut side facing down into a bowl. Hold with one hand and use the other to gently nudge the seeds out, section by section. Remove any white membrane that lands in the bowl.

Watermelon Tomato Salad

This salad is a knockout for heart health. Watermelon and feta cheese make a lovely combination. Serve this summertime favorite with any kind of grilled fish.

5 cups chopped watermelon

2 cups halved cherry tomatoes

1 cup diced red onion

1 cup diced cucumber

1 cup chopped fresh mint

¾ cup crumbled feta cheese (preferably sheep's milk feta)

2 tablespoons extra-virgin olive oil

3 tablespoons apple cider vinegar

2 teaspoons nigella seeds (black cumin seeds)

4 cups arugula

1 tablespoon sesame seeds

1 Place watermelon, tomatoes, onion, cucumber, and mint in a large salad bowl. Mix well to release some extra juice from watermelon. Gently stir in feta.

2 In a small bowl, whisk together oil, vinegar, and nigella seeds. Drizzle over watermelon mixture and toss to mix.

3 Divide arugula among four shallow bowls and top with watermelon mixture. Sprinkle with sesame seeds before serving.

SERVES 4

Per Serving

Calories	260
Fat	15g
Sodium	280mg
Carbohydrates	27g
Fiber	4g
Sugar	18g
Protein	8g

BLACK SEEDS

Nigella seeds, also known as nigella sativa, kalonji seeds, black cumin, or black onion seeds, have long been revered for their medicinal properties. Recent studies have shown that nigella seeds can help to improve heart health by reducing cholesterol levels and inflammation. In a 2012 study by the University of Dammam in Saudi Arabia, participants who consumed 2 grams of nigella seeds per day for twelve weeks saw a significant reduction in LDL cholesterol and triglycerides.

Watermelon Mint Salad

SERVES 4

Per Serving

Calories	230
Fat	15g
Sodium	640mg
Carbohydrates	18g
Fiber	2g
Sugar	12g
Protein	7g

WATERMELON IS UNDERRATED

Watermelon is a good source of lycopene, an antioxidant that has been linked to heart health. Studies have shown that lycopene can help to lower cholesterol levels and reduce the risk of developing heart disease. In addition, watermelon is a good source of potassium, vitamin C, and citrulline, which is an amino acid that helps to relax blood vessels and improve blood circulation.

Cut up a watermelon into a square shape by cutting off the top and bottom. Set it on a cutting board and slice off the sides. From there, it's easy to turn it into bite-sized cubes.

4 cups chopped watermelon

1 small red onion, peeled and thinly sliced

1 cup thinly sliced cucumber

1 cup chopped fresh mint

1 cup chopped fresh cilantro

1 cup crumbled feta cheese (preferably sheep's milk feta)

2 tablespoons apple cider vinegar

2 tablespoons extra-virgin olive oil

½ teaspoon salt

½ teaspoon crushed red pepper flakes

1 Place watermelon, onion, cucumber, mint, cilantro, and feta in a large bowl and stir gently.

2 In a small bowl, whisk together vinegar, oil, salt, and red pepper flakes. Pour over watermelon mixture and toss to coat. Serve immediately.

Warm Kale and Halloumi Salad

This super-satisfying warm salad is bursting with a variety of nutrients and loads of fiber. The beans and Halloumi cheese add lovely protein, and you can top the salad with canned fish such as sardines or mackerel for more.

4 cups roughly chopped Tuscan kale

2 cups halved cherry tomatoes

1 cup green olives

5 ounces Halloumi cheese, cut into bite-sized pieces

2 tablespoons extra-virgin olive oil

1 tablespoon apple cider vinegar

1 teaspoon capers

1 small bird's eye chili, seeded and minced

1 (15-ounce) can cannellini beans, drained and rinsed

2 tablespoons chopped olive-oil-packed anchovy fillets

1 clove garlic, peeled and minced

¼ cup whole raw cashews

1 Preheat oven to 350°F. Line a 13" × 9" baking dish with parchment paper.

2 Place kale, tomatoes, olives, Halloumi cheese, oil, vinegar, capers, chili, and beans in a large bowl and stir until combined. Transfer mixture to the prepared baking dish and bake for 10 minutes.

3 Remove from oven and stir in anchovies, garlic, and cashews. Serve immediately.

SERVES 4

Per Serving

Calories	400
Fat	24g
Sodium	1,410mg
Carbohydrates	25g
Fiber	2g
Sugar	4g
Protein	20g

HALLOUMI CHEESE

Halloumi cheese is a delicious source of protein, packing 7 grams into a 1-ounce serving. It's known for its tangy taste and firm, chewy texture. It has a much higher melting point than many other types of cheese, so it can be baked, grilled, or fried while keeping its shape. It's often served cooked, which enhances its signature salty taste.

Seaweed Salad

This is a great salad for beautiful skin, partially from the iodine in seaweed that most people are lacking. Sprinkle the finished salad with black or white sesame seeds and crushed red pepper flakes. If you don't have rice vinegar, use apple cider vinegar instead.

SERVES 2

Per Serving

Calories	340
Fat	8g
Sodium	1,390mg
Carbohydrates	45g
Fiber	27g
Sugar	8g
Protein	21g

EDIBLE SEAWEEDS

Wakame and arame are highly nutritious, edible seaweeds that can add a range of vitamins and minerals to your diet for a low number of calories. Pop the seaweed straight into a salad, add it to a stir-fry, or simply stir it into cooked rice for loads of iodine, fiber, omega-3s, and magnesium to lower cholesterol levels and reduce inflammation.

1 (1.75-ounce) package arame seaweed

1 medium carrot

1 medium cucumber

2 cups frozen shelled edamame, thawed

2 tablespoons tamari

1 tablespoon brown rice vinegar

1 teaspoon honey

1 teaspoon sesame oil

1 teaspoon finely grated ginger

1 Place arame in a large bowl. Cover with cool water and soak for 15 minutes. Drain and rinse. Set aside.

2 Use a vegetable peeler to cut carrot and cucumber into long strips. Place strips in a large bowl and add arame and edamame.

3 In a small bowl, whisk together tamari, vinegar, honey, sesame oil, and ginger. Pour over salad and toss to coat. Serve immediately.

Orange and Fennel Salad

Punch up this salad with pomegranate seeds and chopped scal-lions. You can increase the orange flavor by adding orange zest and orange juice to the dressing.

4 cups baby spinach

2 large navel oranges, peeled and thinly sliced crosswise

1 medium fennel bulb, trimmed and shaved into thin ribbons

3 tablespoons extra-virgin olive oil

2 tablespoons apple cider vinegar

1 teaspoon fennel seeds, rubbed between your fingers

1 tablespoon Dijon mustard

¼ teaspoon crushed red pepper flakes

¼ cup sliced almonds, toasted

1 Arrange spinach leaves on four salad plates. Top with orange slices and fennel.

2 In a small bowl, whisk together oil, vinegar, fennel seeds, mustard, and red pepper flakes until combined.

3 Spoon dressing on salads, sprinkle with almonds, and serve immediately.

SERVES 4

Per Serving

Calories	210
Fat	15g
Sodium	170mg
Carbohydrates	18g
Fiber	6g
Sugar	9g
Protein	5g

FANTASTIC FENNEL

Fennel has a long history of use as both a food and a medicine. This anise-flavored plant is packed with nutrients like potassium, which is important for maintaining healthy blood pressure levels. Fennel has been shown to lower cholesterol levels and improve heart health due to its high level of fiber and polyphenols.

Cucumber, Beet, and Dill Salad

Per Serving

Calories	360
Fat	17g
Sodium	780mg
Carbohydrates	41g
Fiber	11g
Sugar	16g
Protein	13g

DELICIOUS DILL

This fragrant herb is packed with flavonoids, which have been shown to help reduce the risk of heart disease and stroke. But that's not the only reason dill is thought to improve heart health. Research on animals shows that dill can also reduce LDL cholesterol levels, making it a great addition to any heart-healthy diet.

Lightly toss the salad at the very end so the color doesn't bleed into the lighter-colored cucumbers and chickpeas. It's a photo-worthy salad!

3 tablespoons extra-virgin olive oil

2 tablespoons balsamic vinegar

½ teaspoon salt

1 cup minced fresh dill

1 medium red onion, peeled and sliced

1 (15-ounce) can sliced beets

1 large cucumber halved, seeded, and thinly sliced

1 (15-ounce) can chickpeas, drained and rinsed

½ cup crumbled feta cheese (preferably sheep's milk feta)

1 In a large bowl, whisk together oil, vinegar, salt, and dill. Add onion and beets. Toss together until combined. Add cucumber and chickpeas and lightly toss.

2 Divide salad among four plates and scatter feta on top before serving.

CHAPTER 10

Soups and Stews

Spiced Cauliflower Soup

SERVES 4

Per Serving

Calories	220
Fat	9g
Sodium	780mg
Carbohydrates	26g
Fiber	7g
Sugar	8g
Protein	13g

INDIAN SPICES

Common Indian spices, such as cumin, turmeric, cinnamon, peppercorns, cardamom, mustard seeds, coriander seeds, cloves, mace, and nutmeg, can improve your health. Cinnamon is a great source of antioxidants, while mustard seeds have been shown to help lower cholesterol. Mace and nutmeg can help improve circulation and digestion.

This deeply spiced cauliflower soup is full of heart- and skin-friendly nutrients. Top the soup with coconut flakes, pumpkin seeds, or chopped cilantro. Serve it with a side of Easy Protein Bread (see recipe in Chapter 5).

1 medium head cauliflower, cored and cut into florets

2 tablespoons extra-virgin olive oil, divided

1 tablespoon ground cumin

½ teaspoon sea salt

¼ teaspoon ground black pepper

1 large red onion, peeled and chopped

2 cloves garlic, peeled and minced

1 tablespoon ground turmeric

½ tablespoon ground Ceylon cinnamon

1 medium red bell pepper, seeded and chopped

1 large sweet potato, peeled and chopped

4 cups chicken stock

1 Preheat oven to 375°F. Line a large baking sheet with parchment paper.

2 Place cauliflower florets on prepared baking sheet. Drizzle with 1 tablespoon oil and sprinkle with cumin, salt, and black pepper. Toss to coat.

3 Roast for 25 minutes or until lightly browned.

4 Meanwhile, heat the remaining 1 tablespoon oil in a large stockpot or Dutch oven over medium-high heat. Sauté onion, garlic, turmeric, and cinnamon for 3–4 minutes until onion is softened.

5 Add bell pepper, sweet potato, and stock. If necessary, add water so that the liquid just covers vegetables. Bring to a boil, then reduce heat to medium-low and simmer for 10 minutes until vegetables are soft. Stir in roasted cauliflower.

6 Blend until smooth using an immersion blender. Alternatively, transfer the soup in batches to a high-speed blender and purée until smooth. Serve immediately.

Basil Asparagus Soup

Top this vibrant green soup with a dollop of Greek yogurt, crushed red pepper flakes, lemon zest, and Parmesan cheese. You can also use this method to make soup with broccoli, fresh peas, or green beans instead of asparagus.

2 tablespoons extra-virgin olive oil

1 large red onion, peeled and diced

2 teaspoons minced garlic, divided

2 small red potatoes, peeled and chopped

1 pound asparagus, trimmed and cut into 1" pieces

4 cups chicken stock

½ cup packed fresh basil

1 Heat oil in a large stockpot or Dutch oven over medium-high heat. Sauté onion and 1½ teaspoons garlic for 3–4 minutes until softened. Add potatoes and sauté for 5 minutes.

2 Stir in asparagus and stock. Bring to a boil, then reduce heat to low, cover, and simmer for 10 minutes.

3 Add basil and the remaining ½ teaspoon garlic to the soup, then blend until smooth using an immersion blender. Alternatively, transfer the soup in batches to a high-speed blender and purée until smooth. Serve immediately.

SERVES 4

Per Serving

Calories	210
Fat	9g
Sodium	440mg
Carbohydrates	23g
Fiber	4g
Sugar	5g
Protein	13g

SOUP POWER

It's not that you don't like vegetables, but sometimes it feels like there's just not enough time to work them into your meal. That's where soup comes in. By adding a bowl of soup loaded with vegetables, herbs, whole grains, and beans, you can instantly switch the balance of a meal in a healthy direction. Just add a side of protein bread and you've got a complete meal.

Easy Tomato Lentil Soup

SERVES 4

Per Serving

Calories	300
Fat	6g
Sodium	670mg
Carbohydrates	38g
Fiber	10g
Sugar	5g
Protein	22g

SOUP CONTROLS WEIGHT

Soup can be your ally for weight control. Some research suggests that starting a meal with soup may help to reduce portion size. For relatively few calories, soup brings a feeling of fullness and a high level of nutrients.

Top this simple soup with chopped parsley or cilantro and a squeeze of lime. A few pumpkin seeds will add crunch.

1 tablespoon extra-virgin olive oil

1 large red onion, peeled and chopped

1 tablespoon ground cumin

2 teaspoons minced garlic, divided

1 cup dried red lentils, rinsed

1 (14.5-ounce) can diced tomatoes

4 cups chicken stock

1 Heat oil in a medium saucepan over medium-high heat. Sauté onion until softened, 3–4 minutes. Add cumin and 1 teaspoon garlic and sauté for 1 minute or until fragrant.

2 Stir in lentils, tomatoes, and stock. Bring to a boil, then reduce heat to medium-low. Simmer for 20 minutes or until lentils are soft.

3 Remove from heat. Add the remaining 1 teaspoon garlic and blend until smooth using an immersion blender. Alternatively, transfer the soup in batches to a high-speed blender and purée until smooth. Serve immediately.

Artichoke and Lentil Comfort Bowl

SERVES 4

Per Serving

Calories	160
Fat	4.5g
Sodium	1,110mg
Carbohydrates	25g
Fiber	4g
Sugar	6g
Protein	8g

LENTILS REDUCE DISEASE RISKS

High in fiber, folate, and potassium, lentils are a great source of plant-based protein and wonderful for managing blood pressure, blood sugar, and cholesterol. Lentils provide an antioxidant and anti-inflammatory effect, are cardio-protective, and help with appetite control.

Serve this colorful, inviting soup in flat wide bowls for best effect. If you want an extra burst of flavor, take an extra 5 minutes and whip up the zesty Green Herb Pesto (see recipe in Chapter 12) to drizzle on top.

1 tablespoon extra-virgin olive oil

1 large red onion, peeled and chopped

2 cloves garlic, peeled and minced

1 cup dried puy lentils, rinsed

4 cups chicken broth

1 (6.5-ounce) jar artichoke hearts, drained and chopped

2 cups chopped asparagus

2 medium carrots, peeled and diced

1 Heat oil in a large stockpot or Dutch oven over medium heat. Sauté onion and garlic until softened, 3–4 minutes.

2 Add lentils and stir for 30 seconds. Add broth, reduce heat to medium-low, and gently simmer for 20 minutes.

3 Add artichoke hearts, asparagus, and carrots and simmer for 10 minutes.

4 Serve immediately.

Creamy Tomato "Noodle" Soup

This is a tasty way to eat more cabbage. Cabbage is phenomenal for heart health and a great noodle substitute when sliced very thinly.

1 tablespoon extra-virgin olive oil

1 medium yellow onion, peeled and chopped

4 cloves garlic, peeled and minced

3 cups finely shredded green cabbage

1 (14.5-ounce) can diced tomatoes

1 (6-ounce) can tomato paste

2 cups organic chicken stock

1 teaspoon balsamic vinegar

1 (15-ounce) can cannellini beans, drained and rinsed

⅓ cup nonfat plain Greek yogurt

1 Heat oil in a large stockpot or Dutch oven over medium heat. Add onion and garlic; sauté until onion is softened, 3–4 minutes. Add cabbage; sauté for 3 minutes longer.

2 Add tomatoes, tomato paste, stock, and vinegar. Cook and stir until tomato paste dissolves in soup.

3 Stir in beans and bring to a boil over high heat. Reduce heat to medium-low and simmer for 10 minutes. Remove from heat. Stir in yogurt and serve immediately.

SERVES 4

Per Serving

Calories	270
Fat	5g
Sodium	890mg
Carbohydrates	39g
Fiber	4g
Sugar	12g
Protein	17g

VEGGIE NOODLES

Cutting vegetables like cabbage, zucchini, carrots, and sweet potatoes into "veggie noodles" allows you to get a similar mouthfeel that you get from eating high-carb noodles in a soup, without the typical weight gain. Create cabbage noodles by using a sharp chef's knife and cutting through the cabbage with the smallest slivers you can manage.

Carrot and Cauliflower Soup

SERVES 4

Per Serving

Calories	180
Fat	9g
Sodium	500mg
Carbohydrates	17g
Fiber	5g
Sugar	7g
Protein	12g

RAW GARLIC

Adding small amounts of raw garlic to food enhances flavor and adds several health benefits. Crushed raw garlic retains more allicin, which is the sulfur-containing compound responsible for many of garlic's benefits. Recent human and animal studies have shown that garlic can help protect against heart disease, high blood pressure, diabetes, and other chronic conditions.

Add a drizzle of tahini and a sprinkle of crushed red pepper flakes, cilantro, and pumpkin seeds for a tasty bowl topper. You can also poach fish fillets directly in the soup for 7 minutes when the carrots are simmering.

2 tablespoons extra-virgin olive oil

1 medium red onion, peeled and chopped

3 teaspoons minced garlic, divided

1 tablespoon minced ginger

2 teaspoons ground cumin

3 large carrots, peeled and cut into ½" rounds

1 medium head cauliflower, cored and cut into florets

4 cups chicken stock

1 Heat oil in a stockpot or Dutch oven over medium-high heat. Sauté onion, 2 teaspoons garlic, ginger, and cumin for 3–4 minutes until onion is softened.

2 Add carrots, cauliflower, and stock. Bring to a boil, then reduce heat to medium-low. Simmer for 12–15 minutes until carrots are tender but not mushy.

3 Remove from heat and add the remaining 1 teaspoon garlic, then blend until smooth using an immersion blender. Alternatively, transfer the soup in batches to a high-speed blender and purée until smooth. Serve immediately.

Ginger Parsnip Soup

Parsnips contain very potent prebiotics, which can stimulate the growth of good bacteria in your gut, improve your digestion, and make your skin glow. No parsnips? Try using a dozen carrots.

2 tablespoons extra-virgin olive oil

1 large red onion, peeled and chopped

2 large cloves garlic, peeled and minced

1 teaspoon ground cumin

2 tablespoons minced fresh ginger

6 large parsnips, peeled and roughly chopped

4 cups chicken stock

1½ tablespoons grated orange zest

¼ cup freshly squeezed orange juice

1 Heat oil in a large stockpot or Dutch oven over medium heat. Add onion, garlic, and cumin; sauté until onion is softened, 3–4 minutes.

2 Add ginger, parsnips, and stock. If necessary, add water so that the liquid just covers vegetables. Bring to a boil over high heat. Reduce heat to medium-low and simmer for 10–12 minutes until parsnips are soft.

3 Remove from heat and stir in orange zest and orange juice. Blend until smooth using an immersion blender. Alternatively, transfer the soup in batches to a high-speed blender and purée until smooth. Serve immediately.

SERVES 4

Per Serving

Calories	290
Fat	11g
Sodium	450mg
Carbohydrates	49g
Fiber	12g
Sugar	17g
Protein	13g

PARSNIPS

Parsnips are a good source of dietary fiber, with 3–5 grams per serving. They are rich in both soluble and insoluble fiber, which means they can help curb your appetite and improve your mix of beneficial gut microbes. And because they are naturally sweet, parsnips can be a helpful substitute for other sugary foods in the diet.

Pumpkin Sage Soup

SERVES 4

Per Serving

Calories	280
Fat	10g
Sodium	310mg
Carbohydrates	33g
Fiber	1g
Sugar	9g
Protein	15g

SAGE

Sage is an herb with a long history of uses in cooking and medicine. These days, it's gaining popularity for its potential ability to improve heart health, lower inflammation, and boost the immune system. In one small 2009 study at the University of Minho in Portugal, women who drank sage tea twice daily for four weeks had lower levels of total and LDL cholesterol, as well as higher levels of HDL cholesterol.

This pretty soup looks wonderful, and it's great for a dinner party. Pumpkin and sage are a winning flavor combination found in many pasta dishes.

2 tablespoons extra-virgin olive oil

8 large sage leaves

1 large red onion, peeled and diced

2 cloves garlic, peeled and minced

½ teaspoon crushed red pepper flakes

1 (15-ounce) can solid-pack pumpkin

2 cups chicken stock

1 (15-ounce) can cannellini beans, drained and rinsed

½ cup whole-milk plain Greek yogurt

2 teaspoons balsamic vinegar

1 Heat oil in a large stockpot or Dutch oven over medium heat. Add sage leaves and fry for 30 seconds or until crisp. Drain on a paper towel and set aside.

2 Add onion, garlic, and red pepper flakes to the pot and sauté for 3–4 minutes until softened.

3 Reduce heat to low. Add pumpkin, stock, and beans and simmer for 5 minutes or until warmed through.

4 Ladle 1 cup of the soup into a small bowl and add 4 sage leaves. Blend until smooth using an immersion blender. Alternatively, transfer 1 cup soup and 4 sage leaves to a high-speed blender and purée until smooth. Return to pot and stir to blend.

5 Serve soup in wide, shallow soup bowls topped with a dollop of yogurt, a drizzle of vinegar, and a reserved crispy sage leaf.

Feel-Better Soup

At the first sign of a throat tickle, or to help ward off future colds and flu, make this amazing immune-boosting soup. The spices get to work fighting off invaders and help you feel fantastic.

2 tablespoons extra-virgin olive oil

1 large red onion, peeled and diced

4 cloves garlic, peeled and minced

3 tablespoons minced fresh ginger

2 large sweet potatoes, roughly chopped

2 cups sliced shiitake mushrooms

1 cup goji berries

4 cups chicken stock

1 Heat oil in a large stockpot or Dutch oven over medium-high heat. Add onion, garlic, and ginger and cook for 3–4 minutes until soft.

2 Stir in sweet potatoes, mushrooms, and goji berries. Add stock and bring to a boil. Reduce heat to medium-low and simmer for 10–15 minutes until sweet potatoes are soft.

3 Blend until smooth using an immersion blender. Alternatively, transfer the soup in batches to a high-speed blender and purée until smooth. Serve immediately.

SERVES 4

Per Serving

Calories	320
Fat	9g
Sodium	550mg
Carbohydrates	47g
Fiber	9g
Sugar	19g
Protein	16g

GOJI BERRIES

Goji berries have a wide range of health benefits such as antioxidant, anti-inflammatory, antimicrobial, immuno-stimulating, anti-diabetic, neuro-protective, anticancer, prebiotic, and anti-obesogenic effects. As of 2022, there is a lot of scientific research interest in reviewing and applying goji berries in the development of functional food products. Because they are rich in antioxidants, vitamins A and C, and other nutrients that are known to fight free radicals and inflammation, they are a useful tool in your heart-health tool kit.

Broccoli and Walnut Soup

This emerald green soup is a deeply flavorful showstopper. For extra kick, try adding a raw garlic clove and a sprinkle of crushed red pepper flakes when you blend the broccoli. Toast the walnuts gently for a few minutes in the oven or in a dry skillet on the stovetop.

2 teaspoons sea salt, divided

6 cups chopped broccoli

1 teaspoon ground black pepper

4 ounces soft goat cheese, cut into 4 slices

12 walnut halves, toasted

2 tablespoons extra-virgin olive oil

1 Bring 4 cups water to a boil in a large stockpot or Dutch oven over high heat. Add 1 teaspoon salt and broccoli. Reduce heat to medium-low and simmer for 4 minutes or until tender but still bright green. Drain broccoli in a colander over a large bowl. Reserve cooking liquid in the bowl.

2 Transfer broccoli to a large high-speed blender. Add enough cooking liquid to cover half of broccoli. Add pepper and remaining 1 teaspoon salt and blend until thick.

3 Return soup to the stockpot and reheat for 2 minutes over medium heat.

4 Add 1 slice of cheese to each of four wide, shallow soup bowls. Gently pour soup around cheese and top each bowl with 3 walnuts and a drizzle of olive oil. Serve immediately.

SERVES 4

Per Serving

Calories	260
Fat	18g
Sodium	1,320mg
Carbohydrates	18g
Fiber	8g
Sugar	3g
Protein	12g

SUPER-FAST SOUP

Here's how to make an ultra-tasty, easy soup: Add virtually any chopped vegetable to a soup pot along with a couple of flavorings like garlic, crushed red pepper flakes, salt, and pepper. Add enough chicken or vegetable stock to cover the vegetables and simmer for 15 minutes or so until the vegetables are fork-tender. Purée in a high-speed blender and top with a drizzle of olive oil and a sprinkle of herbs or nuts. With almost no effort, you've got a restaurant-quality soup to serve before dinner or as a light lunch.

Tomato and Fennel Soup

SERVES 4

Per Serving

Calories	200
Fat	8g
Sodium	900mg
Carbohydrates	20g
Fiber	6g
Sugar	9g
Protein	11g

FENNEL SEEDS

Fennel seeds are a versatile and flavorful addition to many dishes, and they also offer a variety of health benefits. One benefit is that they can help to freshen breath and improve skin appearance. The seeds contain an essential oil known as anethole, which has potent anti-bacterial properties. Fennel seeds also help to regulate blood pressure and reduce asthma and other respiratory ailments.

This beautiful deep red soup cooks up quickly in about 15 minutes. The taste is divine and you'll be craving it regularly.

2 tablespoons extra-virgin olive oil

1 large red onion, peeled and diced

1 large bulb fennel, trimmed and diced

2 cloves garlic, peeled and minced

2 (14.5-ounce) cans diced tomatoes

4 cups chicken stock

1 tablespoon apple cider vinegar

2 teaspoons fennel seeds, rubbed between your fingers

1 Heat oil in a large stockpot or Dutch oven over medium heat. Sauté onion, fennel, and garlic for 3–4 minutes until softened.

2 Add tomatoes, stock, vinegar, and fennel seeds. If necessary, add water so that the liquid just covers vegetables. Simmer for 10 minutes.

3 Blend until smooth using an immersion blender. Alternatively, transfer the soup in batches to a high-speed blender and purée until smooth. Serve immediately.

Easy Weeknight Ramen

Ready in less than 15 minutes, this ramen is an easy mid-week supper. Sprinkle it liberally with scallions, squeeze in some lime juice, and sprinkle in white or black sesame seeds. If you have some leftover chicken thighs, throw those in too.

1 tablespoon extra-virgin olive oil

2 cloves garlic, peeled and minced

1 tablespoon minced fresh ginger

1 medium red chili, seeded and diced

4 cups chicken stock

2 cups sliced shiitake mushrooms

1 tablespoon tamari

1 tablespoon toasted sesame oil

2 large free-range eggs

1 small bok choy, trimmed and halved

3½ ounces konjac or kelp noodles

1. Heat olive oil in a medium saucepan over medium heat. Add garlic, ginger, and chili and sauté for 3 minutes. Add stock, mushrooms, tamari, and sesame oil.
2. Increase heat to high and bring to a boil. Add eggs (in the shell), reduce heat to medium, and simmer for about 4 minutes.
3. Remove eggs using a slotted spoon and place in a small bowl of cold water to cool.
4. Add bok choy and noodles to the soup. Simmer for 1–2 minutes until warmed through.
5. Divide ramen between two shallow soup bowls. Peel eggs and cut them in half. Place two halves on top of each bowl. Serve immediately.

SERVES 2

Per Serving

Calories	400
Fat	22g
Sodium	1,720mg
Carbohydrates	25g
Fiber	8g
Sugar	9g
Protein	33g

STOCK BROTH AND SALT

If you're using store-bought stock or broth instead of homemade stock, it's a good idea to taste your soup before automatically adding salt. Canned stock contains added salt, so you may not need much, if any, salt. You can buy lower-salt versions of canned stock or broth so that you can control the amount of salt you add to your soups.

Smoky Vegetarian Chili with Lime and Cilantro

SERVES 6

Per Serving

Calories	380
Fat	9g
Sodium	1,410mg
Carbohydrates	57g
Fiber	4g
Sugar	11g
Protein	18g

Top this chili with Greek yogurt, diced avocado, chopped scallions, sliced jalapeños, and Fresh Salsa (see recipe in Chapter 12). If you prefer a nonvegetarian chili, brown some grass-fed ground beef with the onions and garlic.

3 tablespoons extra-virgin olive oil

2 large red onions, peeled and chopped

6 cloves garlic, peeled and minced

1 tablespoon ground cumin

1 tablespoon sweet smoked paprika

1 teaspoon chili powder

2 (14.5-ounce) cans diced tomatoes, undrained

1 (6-ounce) can tomato paste

1 (15-ounce) can black beans, drained and rinsed

1 (15-ounce) can kidney beans, drained and rinsed

1 (15-ounce) can pinto beans, drained and rinsed

2 organic vegetable bouillon cubes

½ cup water

4 teaspoons grated lime zest

¼ cup lime juice

3 cups chopped fresh cilantro

1 Heat oil in a large stockpot or Dutch oven over medium heat. Sauté onions and garlic for 3–4 minutes until softened. Stir in cumin, smoked paprika, and chili powder and cook for 1 minute.

2 Add tomatoes, tomato paste, beans, bouillon cubes, and water. Stir well to combine. If chili seems too thick, add more water, 1 tablespoon at a time until it reaches the desired consistency. Cook, stirring occasionally, for 15 minutes or until warmed through.

3 Remove from heat. Stir in lime zest, lime juice, and cilantro. Serve hot.

Umami Bounty Bowls

This is an amazingly tasty soup with a unique combination of ingredients that results in an explosion of umami flavor.

1 tablespoon extra-virgin olive oil

1 large red onion, peeled and diced

2 cloves garlic, peeled and minced

1 cup sliced Jerusalem artichokes

1 cup dried puy lentils, rinsed

½ tablespoon hot smoked paprika

4 tablespoons tomato paste

6 cups vegetable stock

1 cup Tuscan kale, stems removed and chopped

1 cup chopped fresh parsley

1 cup pitted green olives

1 (4-ounce) can olive-oil-packed mackerel fillets

2 extra-large free-range eggs

1 Heat oil in a large stockpot or Dutch oven over medium-high heat. Sauté onion, garlic, and Jerusalem artichokes for 3–4 minutes until softened.
2 Add lentils, paprika, and tomato paste. Stir for 1 minute.
3 Stir in stock and bring to a boil. Reduce heat to medium-low and simmer for 20 minutes.
4 Add kale, parsley, olives, mackerel, and eggs (still in their shells) into the pot. Simmer for 4 minutes. Remove eggs using a slotted spoon and place in a small bowl of cold water to cool.
5 Ladle soup into four shallow soup bowls. Peel eggs and cut them in half. Place one half on top of each bowl. Serve immediately.

SERVES 4

Per Serving

Calories	320
Fat	14g
Sodium	1,280mg
Carbohydrates	33g
Fiber	2g
Sugar	12g
Protein	18g

JERUSALEM ARTICHOKES

Jerusalem artichokes are knobby little roots that look like a cross between a potato and ginger. This tuber is full of immune-boosting prebiotics to help feed the good bacteria in your gut, as well as a good amount of vitamin C, fiber, and the B vitamin niacin. Cut them into chunks or coin shapes and when cooked, they take on the texture of a soft potato.

Tuscan White Bean and Kale Soup

Per Serving

Calories	300
Fat	11g
Sodium	960mg
Carbohydrates	30g
Fiber	3g
Sugar	6g
Protein	20g

CHOOSE SAUSAGE CAREFULLY

While you should reduce the amount of processed meats, including sausages, in your diet, it's fine to enjoy them in small servings once in a while. You can choose tasty sausages that are gluten-free, nitrate-free, and organic, with minimal ingredients (just meat), no additives, and no sugar or bread crumbs.

You can swap out the sausage for extra-firm tofu (cut into ¹/₂" cubes). Serve this soup with a sprinkling of fresh herbs, like rosemary, thyme, or oregano, and grated Parmesan cheese.

2 tablespoons extra-virgin olive oil

3 cloves garlic, peeled and minced

1 medium red onion, peeled and chopped

3 ounces organic Italian chicken or turkey sausage, cut into ½" slices

1 (14.5-ounce) can diced tomatoes

2 tablespoons tomato paste

1 (15-ounce) can cannellini beans, drained and rinsed

4 cups chicken stock

4 cups chopped kale

1 tablespoon dried oregano

1 Heat oil in large stockpot or Dutch oven over medium heat. Add garlic, onion, and sausage. Sauté until onion is softened and sausage is browned, 3–4 minutes. Stir in tomatoes and tomato paste.

2 Increase heat to medium-high. Add beans, stock, kale, and oregano. Bring to a boil, then reduce heat to medium-low and simmer for 15–20 minutes until kale is tender. Serve immediately.

Thai Salmon Soup

SERVES 2

Per Serving

Calories	800
Fat	47g
Sodium	550mg
Carbohydrates	51g
Fiber	9g
Sugar	4g
Protein	52g

LOVELY LEMONGRASS

One of the most impressive benefits of lemongrass is its ability to reduce inflammation. This is due to the presence of quercetin (also found in red onions), a flavonoid that inhibits cancer cell growth and prevents heart disease. Moreover, quercetin is helpful in managing high cholesterol issues. Lemongrass also stimulates blood circulation and lowers blood pressure.

This soup is so tantalizing, you'll want to make it weekly. Top it with lots of chopped cilantro, crushed red pepper flakes, a tablespoon of Thai fish sauce, and a squeeze of lime.

2 stalks fresh lemongrass

2 tablespoons extra-virgin olive oil

1 large red onion, peeled and diced

2 cloves garlic, peeled and minced

2 tablespoons minced fresh ginger

2 kaffir lime leaves

½ cup dried red lentils, rinsed

1 cup full-fat coconut milk

2 cups chicken stock

2 (5-ounce) salmon fillets

1 Place lemongrass on a flat surface and pound the stalks two or three times with a rolling pin or the side of a large chef's knife.

2 Heat oil in a large stockpot or Dutch oven over medium-high heat. Sauté lemongrass, onion, garlic, ginger, and kaffir lime leaves for 4–5 minutes until softened.

3 Add lentils, coconut milk, and stock and bring to a boil. Reduce heat to low and simmer for 15 minutes.

4 Add salmon to pot and simmer another 8 minutes. Break salmon up into chunks and serve immediately in large bowls.

Chicken Bone Broth

Nutrient-rich chicken broth is inexpensive and simple to make. It adds an amazing flavor to almost everything. Add salt to taste or save the seasoning for your finished dishes.

4 organic chicken carcasses

8 chicken feet or 1 pig's foot

½ cup apple cider vinegar

1 large onion, roughly chopped

2 medium carrots, roughly chopped

3 stalks celery, roughly chopped

1 tablespoon whole black peppercorns

4 bay leaves

1 Place chicken carcasses, chicken feet, and vinegar in a very large stockpot. Add enough water to cover everything by 1". Bring to a boil over high heat, then reduce heat to low.

2 Simmer gently for 10 hours. As the liquid evaporates, add more water so the bones are always covered. If a film or foam forms on top, skim it with a shallow metal spoon.

3 Add onion, carrot, celery, peppercorns, and bay leaves and simmer for 1 hour more.

4 Strain broth into a large bowl. Discard bones and other solids. Let cool for an hour until a layer of fat forms on the surface. Use a shallow spoon to remove the fat, then drag a paper towel through the top of the broth to remove the rest of the fat.

5 Pour broth into 1-quart containers and store in the refrigerator for up to 1 week. Stock can be frozen in freezer-safe plastic containers for up to 3 months.

MAKES 20 CUPS

Per Serving (1 cup)

Calories	30
Fat	1.5g
Sodium	25mg
Carbohydrates	2g
Fiber	0g
Sugar	1g
Protein	2g

WHY BONE BROTH?

Bone broth is simmered for a long time with an added acid ingredient that extracts nutrients from the bones. Bone broth can help to support collagen production, slow down the aging process, boost the immune system, and maintain a healthy gut lining. Consuming 10 ounces of bone broth has been shown to increase plasma levels of the precursor amino acids glycine and proline that the body requires to form collagen.

Beef Bone Broth

A steaming mug of this bone broth is a fabulous source of antiaging minerals including glucosamine, chondroitin, and hyaluronic acid to keep your joints young and flexible. Add salt to taste.

MAKES 15 CUPS

Per Serving (1 cup)

Calories	340
Fat	21g
Sodium	410mg
Carbohydrates	3g
Fiber	1g
Sugar	1g
Protein	32g

BEEF VERSUS CHICKEN

Beef bones are denser than chicken bones, and as a result, they yield a higher concentration of minerals and collagen. This higher concentration of minerals may help boost energy levels and provide extra nourishment. In addition, beef bone broth is better for gut health, sleep, and mood. Chicken bone broth, on the other hand, is better for joint and tendon pain, as well as improved skin appearance. It also can be used in more recipes, due to its milder flavor.

6½ pounds grass-fed beef bones (marrow, joints, and knuckle bones are best)

2½ pounds organic lamb bones

1 pig's foot

½ cup apple cider vinegar

1 large onion, roughly chopped

2 medium carrots, roughly chopped

3 stalks celery, roughly chopped

1 tablespoon whole black peppercorns

4 bay leaves

1 Place bones, pig's foot, and vinegar in a very large stockpot. Add enough water to cover everything by 1". Bring to a boil over high heat, then reduce heat to low.

2 Simmer gently for 22 hours. As the liquid evaporates, add more water so the bones are always covered. If a film or foam forms on top, skim it with a shallow metal spoon.

3 Add onion, carrot, celery, peppercorns, and bay leaves and simmer for 1 hour more.

4 Use tongs to remove the larger bones, then strain broth into a large bowl. Discard bones and other solids. Let cool for an hour until a layer of fat forms on the surface. Use a shallow spoon to remove the fat, then drag 2–3 connected paper towels through the top of the broth to remove the rest of the fat. Repeat until the broth is clear and the fat is mostly gone. (You may need about 20 paper towels.)

5 Pour broth into 1-quart containers and store in the refrigerator for up to 1 week. Stock can be frozen in freezer-safe plastic containers for up to 3 months.

CHAPTER 11

Sweet Treats

Speedy Strawberry Mousse

SERVES 4

Per Serving

Calories	150
Fat	4.5g
Sodium	15mg
Carbohydrates	24g
Fiber	5g
Sugar	13g
Protein	4g

CACAO NIBS

Cacao nibs are little pieces of cacao beans that have been roasted and broken up. They have a slightly bitter taste, but they also have a rich chocolate flavor. Cacao nibs are a great source of fiber and antioxidants. They can help to lower your cholesterol and blood pressure. Cacao nibs are a great way to satisfy your chocolate cravings without all the sugar and calories. You can eat them straight from the bag or add them to your favorite trail mix for a delicious and healthy snack.

Here's an elegant dessert you can mix up in 5 minutes. No strawberries? Try blueberries, blackberries, or raspberries. If you don't have cacao nibs, try topping with berries, peach slices, and mint sprigs.

2½ cups strawberries, hulled
2 medium bananas, peeled and sliced
½ cup whole-milk plain Greek yogurt
2 teaspoons grated orange zest
2 tablespoons cacao nibs

1 Place strawberries, bananas, yogurt, and orange zest in a high-speed blender. Blend until smooth. Transfer to four small dessert bowls or ramekins.
2 Top with cacao nibs and serve immediately, or refrigerate in separate, covered ramekins for up to 5 days.

Strawberries with Basil Ricotta

Strawberries and creamy cheese is a winning combination and keeps your blood sugar stable. This is a quick dessert to make but sophisticated enough to serve to guests.

6 cups sliced strawberries

1½ tablespoons grated orange zest

¼ cup orange juice

1 cup whole-milk ricotta cheese

9 drops liquid stevia

1 teaspoon maple syrup

1 tablespoon grated lemon zest, divided

10 basil leaves, divided

1 Place strawberries, orange zest, and orange juice in a medium bowl. Stir well to combine.

2 In another medium bowl, whisk ricotta, stevia, maple syrup, and ½ tablespoon lemon zest. Mince 6 basil leaves and stir into ricotta mixture.

3 Divide the strawberry mixture among four small plates and top with the ricotta mixture. Sprinkle with the remaining ½ tablespoon lemon zest and garnish with the remaining 4 basil leaves. Serve immediately.

SERVES 4

Per Serving

Calories	200
Fat	9g
Sodium	55mg
Carbohydrates	25g
Fiber	5g
Sugar	15g
Protein	9g

BASIL IN DESSERTS

When used in desserts, basil can help to balance out the sweetness and add a refreshing flavor. It's full of antioxidants and vitamins that can help boost the immune system as well as reduce cholesterol and blood pressure. If you're looking for a new way to enjoy basil, try adding it to your favorite dessert recipe. You may be surprised at how well it complements the other flavors.

Blueberry Banana Nice Cream

Nice cream is a surprisingly delicious 5-minute frozen dessert made with naturally sweet bananas. Omit the blueberries if you want a lovely vanilla nice cream. Or swap out the blueberries and experiment with other berries, chocolate, peanut butter, or any flavor you crave!

2 medium bananas, peeled, sliced, and frozen

1 cup frozen blueberries

1 teaspoon vanilla extract

½ cup unsweetened almond milk

1 Place bananas, blueberries, vanilla, and almond milk in a heavy-duty food processor or high-speed blender.

2 Process for 1 minute or until well mixed. If the texture is too thick and the machine is struggling, slowly add a few drops of almond milk until the mixture forms a very thick paste.

3 Serve immediately, or freeze in a covered freezer-safe container for at least 2 hours to firm up.

SERVES 4

Per Serving

Calories	90
Fat	1g
Sodium	20mg
Carbohydrates	20g
Fiber	3g
Sugar	11g
Protein	1g

READY WHEN YOU ARE

Keep a stash of frozen bananas and you can make nice cream whenever the craving hits. Start by cutting very ripe bananas into thick slices. Place them on a parchment-lined baking sheet and freeze them. Make a basic dessert with just bananas, or experiment with different add-ins. You can eat nice cream immediately after you make it, when it has a soft-serve ice cream consistency. You can also make a firmer, scoopable nice cream by transferring it to a freezer-safe container and freezing for at least 2 hours.

Easy Skillet Cinnamon Apples

SERVES 2

Per Serving

Calories	340
Fat	16g
Sodium	25mg
Carbohydrates	48g
Fiber	5g
Sugar	38g
Protein	8g

AN APPLE A DAY

Apples are packed with nutrients such as fiber, vitamin C, and antioxidants, which can promote heart health and help to lower cholesterol levels. Additionally, apples contain pectin, a type of soluble fiber that can help to regulate blood sugar levels and keep you feeling full longer. Studies have shown that eating just one apple a day can reduce your risk of developing diabetes by 28 percent.

Sautéed apples make a simple and healthy dessert you can make in no time. For extra flavor, top the apples with slivered almonds and a dusting of cinnamon. Add a few drops of stevia for more sweetness.

2 tablespoons grass-fed butter

3 large apples (any type), peeled, cored, and sliced

1 teaspoon ground cinnamon

1 tablespoon grated lemon zest

3 tablespoons lemon juice

1 teaspoon maple syrup

½ cup whole-milk plain Greek yogurt

1 Melt butter in a large skillet over medium heat. Add apple slices and sauté for 3–4 minutes until softened. Stir in cinnamon, lemon zest, lemon juice, and maple syrup. Remove from heat.

2 Divide apple mixture between two small dessert plates. Top with yogurt and serve.

Gorgeous Vanilla Apple Crumble

You can add extra fruit like raspberries, blackberries, and peaches to this ridiculously tasty apple crumble, which is full of nutrients, fiber, and healthy fats.

4 large Granny Smith apples, cored and thinly sliced

1 cup blueberries

1 tablespoon grated orange zest

3 tablespoons orange juice

1 tablespoon grated lemon zest

3 tablespoons lemon juice

3 tablespoons maple syrup, divided

1 tablespoon cinnamon, divided

1 teaspoon vanilla extract

1 teaspoon grated fresh ginger

1½ cups rolled oats

½ cup desiccated coconut

1 cup chopped walnuts

¼ cup dried cranberries

3 tablespoons organic virgin coconut oil

½ teaspoon sea salt

SERVES 8	
Per Serving	
Calories	390
Fat	23g
Sodium	150mg
Carbohydrates	42g
Fiber	7g
Sugar	21g
Protein	6g

DARK BERRIES

Studies have shown that eating berries can help lower blood pressure and cholesterol levels, as well as assist in maintaining healthy aging and blood sugar levels. Darker berries, such as blackberries, blueberries, cranberries, elderberries, and boysenberries, can have as much as 50 percent more antioxidants compared to their lighter-colored cousins. Mix up your berry intake for nutrient variety, and include darker berries whenever possible.

1 Preheat oven to 325°F. Line a 13" × 9" baking dish with parchment paper.

2 In a large bowl, stir together apples, blueberries, orange zest and juice, lemon zest and juice, 1 tablespoon maple syrup, ½ tablespoon cinnamon, vanilla, and ginger.

3 Spread the apple mixture in the prepared baking dish.

4 Place oats, coconut, walnuts, cranberries, coconut oil, remaining 2 tablespoons maple syrup, salt, and remaining ½ tablespoon cinnamon in a food processor and process for 10–20 seconds. If the mixture isn't sticking together, add 1 more tablespoon coconut oil.

5 Spoon topping in clumps over apples in the baking dish. Press gently with your fingers or the back of a spoon to spread topping evenly across apples.

6 Bake for 25–30 minutes until lightly browned and bubbling.

7 Serve warm or at room temperature.

Peach Melba Parfaits

SERVES 4

Per Serving

Calories	250
Fat	11g
Sodium	25mg
Carbohydrates	33g
Fiber	7g
Sugar	23g
Protein	10g

TWO BRAZIL NUTS A DAY

Just two Brazil nuts a day can help maintain or increase your selenium intake as effectively as a supplement. Getting enough selenium in your diet can help reduce your risk of Hashimoto's disease, Graves' disease, and thyroid cancer. Selenium is also import ant for heart health, as it helps to reduce cholesterol levels and prevent blood clots. In addition, selenium has been shown to boost the immune system and slow the aging process.

As long as peaches are organic, there's no need to peel them. Peach skin is generally healthy and safe to eat for most people and is higher in fiber and antioxidants than peach flesh alone.

4 large ripe organic peaches, pitted and sliced

1 tablespoon grated lemon zest

3 tablespoons lemon juice

1 tablespoon maple syrup

1 cup whole-milk plain Greek yogurt

1 pint raspberries

8 Brazil nuts, chopped

4 sprigs fresh mint

1 In a medium bowl, combine peaches, lemon zest, lemon juice, and maple syrup.

2 In four parfait or wine glasses, spoon some of the peach mixture. Top with a spoonful of yogurt, then some raspberries. Repeat layers, ending with raspberries. Cover and refrigerate for 4 hours.

3 Garnish each parfait with a sprinkle of nuts and a mint sprig before serving.

Lemon Curd Tart

This gorgeous lemon tart is excellent with and without toppings. Try covering the entire surface with blueberries. Blend 1/3 cup blueberries with 1 tablespoon maple syrup to make a glaze to brush over the berries.

1 cup shelled raw pumpkin seeds

½ cup shelled raw sunflower seeds

¼ cup sesame seeds

¼ cup ground flaxseeds

6 large Medjool dates, pitted

½ cup organic virgin coconut oil, divided

2 large lemons

2 cups unsweetened almond milk

¼ cup maple syrup

1 teaspoon vanilla extract

¼ teaspoon ground turmeric

6 tablespoons agar-agar flakes

⅛ teaspoon sea salt

¼ cup kudzu starch

3 tablespoons cold water

SERVES 12

Per Serving

Calories	240
Fat	18g
Sodium	55mg
Carbohydrates	15g
Fiber	3g
Sugar	8g
Protein	5g

1. Grease a 9" round tart pan or springform pan.
2. Place pumpkin seeds, sunflower seeds, sesame seeds, flaxseeds, dates, and ¼ cup oil in a food processor. Process for 1 minute or until the ingredients begin to stick together. Transfer to the prepared pan. Firmly press mixture into the bottom and 1" up the sides. Cover loosely and place in the refrigerator.
3. Zest lemons, then use a sharp knife to remove lemon rinds. Discard rinds. Place zest and fruit in a high-speed blender. Add almond milk, maple syrup, vanilla, turmeric, and remaining ¼ cup oil. Blend on high speed for 30–60 seconds until smooth.
4. Pour the lemon mixture into a medium saucepan. Sprinkle agar-agar and salt over the mixture and bring to a boil over high heat without stirring. Reduce heat to low and cook, stirring frequently, until agar-agar is dissolved, 2–3 minutes.
5. Meanwhile, in a small bowl, whisk together kudzu starch and water. Add to lemon mixture and stir for 30 seconds or until sauce thickens.
6. Remove from heat and set aside to cool for at least 10 minutes. Pour lemon curd into tart shell. Refrigerate for 2–3 hours until set. Serve cold.

GROUND FLAXSEEDS

Whole flaxseeds have a tough outer hull that keeps them from breaking down in your digestive tract. Grinding the brown and golden flaxseeds creates a heart-healthy powerhouse. Flaxseeds are very high in fiber and provide good amounts of protein. They're also one of the best plant-based sources of heart-healthy omega-3 fats. Numerous studies have shown that ground flaxseeds can help to lower cholesterol and blood pressure. Simply add a tablespoon or two of ground flaxseeds to your favorite smoothie, cereal, yogurt, or salad.

Matcha Panna Cotta with Chocolate Sauce

SERVES 4

Per Serving

Calories	450
Fat	37g
Sodium	25mg
Carbohydrates	27g
Fiber	0g
Sugar	16g
Protein	8g

HEALTHIER PANNA COTTA

Panna cotta is an Italian dessert usually made with sugar, cream, and gelatin, and it can be easily made with coconut milk instead of dairy milk. Coconut milk is a good source of healthy fats, which can help to support heart health as well as lower cholesterol and blood pressure levels. It's also a great dairy-free dessert base for the estimated 30–50 million Americans that have some form of lactose intolerance.

This is a beautiful finish to a dinner party or special meal. Chocolate and green tea are both full of heart-healthy antioxidants.

½ cup water, divided

2¼ teaspoons (0.25 ounces) unflavored powdered gelatin

2 cups full-fat coconut milk, divided

1 vanilla pod, split and seeds removed

1 tablespoon matcha powder

3 tablespoons maple syrup, divided

1 tablespoon raw cacao powder

4 ounces 70% dark chocolate, chopped

1 Place ¼ cup water in a shallow bowl and sprinkle gelatin over the surface in single layer. Let stand for at least 5 minutes to soften, then use a fork to mix together. Set aside.

2 Place 1 cup coconut milk in a small saucepan over medium-low heat with vanilla pod and seeds. Gently simmer for 10 minutes or until reduced by a third. Remove from heat.

3 Add gelatin mixture to coconut milk mixture and whisk to combine. Set aside to cool for 5 minutes, refrigerate for 10 minutes or until mixture coats the back of a spoon. Remove and discard vanilla pod.

4 Place matcha and 1 tablespoon maple syrup in a small bowl. Whisk vigorously until smooth. Add 1 tablespoon maple syrup and the remaining 1 cup coconut milk and whisk until smooth again. Pour matcha mixture into the gelatin mixture and stir to combine.

5 Divide mixture among four small metal molds or ramekins and refrigerate for at least 1 hour.

6 Whisk cacao powder with remaining 1 tablespoon maple syrup in a small bowl. Slowly whisk in remaining ¼ cup water. Pour into a small saucepan and bring to a boil over medium-high heat. Remove from heat and stir in dark chocolate. Continue stirring until chocolate is melted and incorporated into the sauce.

7 To serve, dip molds into warm water to loosen, then turn over onto small plates. Top with chocolate sauce and serve immediately.

Chocolate Pudding Heaven

SERVES 4

Per Serving

Calories	210
Fat	16g
Sodium	5mg
Carbohydrates	17g
Fiber	7g
Sugar	6g
Protein	2g

AWESOME AVOCADOS

Avocados are a great source of potassium and heart-healthy fats. Numerous studies have shown that avocados can help to lower cholesterol, triglyceride levels, and blood pressure, as well as improve blood vessel function. Additionally, avocado consumption has been linked to a lower risk of stroke and other cardiovascular problems.

If you want a quick hit of chocolate, all you need is 5 minutes for this lovely, rich chocolate pudding. It's great topped with crushed nuts, such as pistachios, almonds, or walnuts, as well as fresh raspberries.

2 large avocados, peeled, pitted, and chopped

1½ tablespoons grated orange zest

¼ cup fresh squeezed orange juice

1 tablespoon raw honey

3 tablespoons raw cacao powder

1 Place avocados, orange zest, orange juice, honey, and cacao powder in a high-speed blender or food processor. Blend until light and fluffy, 1–2 minutes.

2 Pour into four small ramekins. Serve immediately, or cover and refrigerate for up to 3 days.

Black Bean Chocolate Cupcakes

Top these luscious cupcakes with Coconut Whipped Cream (see recipe in this chapter), diced mango, and shavings of toasted coconut for a beautiful treat.

1½ cups raspberries

1 (15-ounce) can black beans, drained and rinsed

4 large free-range eggs

3 tablespoons raw cacao powder

2 tablespoons grass-fed butter, softened

3 tablespoons maple syrup

2 teaspoons vanilla extract

1 teaspoon stevia leaf powder

½ teaspoon baking powder

⅛ teaspoon salt

5 tablespoons chopped unsalted pistachios

1 Preheat oven to 350°F. Line a twelve-cup muffin tin with paper liners.
2 Place a few raspberries in each muffin cup.
3 Place beans, eggs, cacao, butter, maple syrup, vanilla, stevia, baking powder, and salt in a food processor and process until smooth.
4 Fill each muffin cup ⅔ full with batter. Sprinkle pistachios over cupcakes and bake for 20–25 minutes until a skewer inserted in the center comes out clean.
5 Cool in tin for 5 minutes, then transfer cupcakes to a wire rack to cool completely. Serve or store cupcakes in a covered container in the refrigerator for up to 1 week.

MAKES 12 CUPCAKES

Per Serving (1 cupcake)

Calories	120
Fat	5g
Sodium	90mg
Carbohydrates	13g
Fiber	1g
Sugar	5g
Protein	5g

BEANS IN SWEETS

Beans are not just for savory dishes! Puréed beans are excellent in cake and brownie batters. This allows you to cut out flour completely from most recipes. It seems like a strange concept, baking without flour. However, once you find a replacement for the binding agent, you soon learn how replaceable and expendable flour really is.

Blueberry Almond Muffins

These muffins are jam-packed with nutrients and flavor. They'll leave you feeling full and energized for hours.

MAKES 12 MUFFINS

Per Serving (1 muffin)

Calories	250
Fat	10g
Sodium	115mg
Carbohydrates	35g
Fiber	6g
Sugar	10g
Protein	7g

OATS LOWER CHOLESTEROL

The soluble fiber in oats can help reduce the amount of cholesterol in the body. Oats contain about 12 grams of fiber per cup, and studies have shown that a high-fiber diet can reduce the risk of coronary heart disease. In addition, oats are a good source of magnesium, which is important for maintaining normal blood pressure. Oat flour is a great alternative to all-purpose flour because it contains more nutrients, fiber, and protein.

3 cups rolled oats

1 cup whole raw almonds

1 tablespoon ground cinnamon

1 tablespoon baking powder

1 teaspoon baking soda

1 medium lemon

4 large ripe bananas, peeled and chopped

4 pitted Medjool dates, pitted

2 large free-range eggs

2 tablespoons organic virgin coconut oil

½ tablespoon apple cider vinegar

1 teaspoon vanilla extract

1½ cups blueberries

1 Preheat oven to 350°F. Line a twelve-cup muffin tin with paper liners.

2 Place oats, almonds, cinnamon, baking powder, and baking soda in a high-speed blender. Blend until ingredients reach a flour consistency. Transfer to a large bowl.

3 Zest lemon, then use a sharp knife to remove lemon rind. Discard rind. Add zest and fruit to the blender. Add bananas, dates, eggs, coconut oil, vinegar, and vanilla. Blend until smooth.

4 Pour banana mixture over oat mixture and stir until just combined. Fold in blueberries.

5 Spoon batter into muffin cups. Fill cups to the top. (They won't rise much.)

6 Bake for 23–27 minutes until golden brown.

7 Cool in tin for 5 minutes, then transfer cupcakes to a wire rack to cool completely. Serve, or store in an airtight container for up to 3 days.

Chocolate-Dipped Cardamom Macaroons

These macaroons are great after a meal with a cup of tea or coffee. For a speedier treat, you can omit the chocolate on these tasty mini macaroons.

2 cups unsweetened shredded coconut

1 teaspoon ground cardamom

¼ cup maple syrup

1 teaspoon vanilla extract

3 large free-range egg whites

⅛ teaspoon sea salt

1 (4-ounce) bar 85% dark chocolate, chopped

1 Preheat oven to 350°F. Line a large baking sheet with parchment paper.
2 Combine coconut and cardamom in a medium bowl. Add maple syrup and vanilla. Stir until well combined.
3 In another medium bowl, whisk egg whites and salt until stiff peaks form. Gently fold the coconut mixture into the egg whites. Place bowl in the freezer for 10 minutes or refrigerate for 20 minutes.
4 Scoop batter with a spoon and form 24 small mounds on the prepared baking sheet. Bake for 12–15 minutes until golden brown.
5 Remove from oven and transfer cookies to a wire rack. Let cool completely.
6 Set a large metal bowl over a saucepan of simmering water. Add chocolate to the bowl and stir until just melted. Remove from heat.
7 Line a large serving platter with parchment paper. Dip a macaroon into melted chocolate, covering half the cookie, and place on the prepared platter. Repeat with the remaining macaroons and chocolate. Refrigerate for at least 2 hours.
8 Serve immediately, or store in an airtight container in the refrigerator for up to 7 days.

MAKES 24 COOKIES

Per Serving (1 cookie)

Calories	80
Fat	6g
Sodium	25mg
Carbohydrates	6g
Fiber	1g
Sugar	4g
Protein	1g

EAT SMALL TREATS

It's important to have small treats when you are eating healthfully. Constant self-denial can lead to dietary defiance, which leads to derailing all your good intentions. Chocolate that has 75% or more cocoa solids is a great foundation for a treat, as it's beneficial to have dark chocolate every day. Try having a square of 75% dark chocolate and letting it slowly melt in your mouth when you get your next sugar craving.

Sweet Potato Brownies

These thin brownies have a crisp exterior and gooey interior. They taste great warm, but they get fudgier as they cool.

3 cups diced sweet potatoes (2 medium)

½ cup raw cacao powder

¼ cup organic virgin coconut oil

¼ cup maple syrup

1 tablespoon ground cinnamon

1 teaspoon vanilla extract

¼ teaspoon sea salt

2 large free-range eggs

½ cup chopped walnuts

3 ounces 70% dark chocolate, chopped

1 Preheat oven to 350°F. Line an 8" × 8" baking dish with parchment paper.

2 Place sweet potatoes in a steamer basket in a large saucepan and steam over simmering water for 10–15 minutes until soft. Transfer to a food processor.

3 Add cacao powder, oil, maple syrup, cinnamon, vanilla, salt and eggs and process for 30 seconds or until smooth.

4 Add walnuts and chocolate to the food processor. Pulse for about 3 seconds to gently mix. Batter should be chunky.

5 Pour batter into the prepared pan. Bake for 35 minutes or until the exterior is quite dark and a toothpick inserted into the center comes out clean.

6 Cool for at least 30 minutes before cutting into rectangles.

SERVES 12

Per Serving

Calories	190
Fat	13g
Sodium	80mg
Carbohydrates	18g
Fiber	2g
Sugar	7g
Protein	3g

AMAZING DARK CHOCOLATE

Eating dark chocolate (with 75% or more cocoa solids) on a regular basis can activate stem cells, improve your mood, and increase the health of your gut and brain. It lowers blood pressure, improves blood flow, and lowers your risk of coronary artery disease.

Coconut Whipped Cream

SERVES 4

Per Serving

Calories	110
Fat	4.5g
Sodium	10mg
Carbohydrates	16g
Fiber	0g
Sugar	15g
Protein	0g

COCONUT CREAM

You can buy coconut cream in small cans, or you can simply place a full-fat can of coconut milk in the refrigerator overnight. The cream will separate out from the coconut water. Drain the water to use in a smoothie, and you're left with the coconut cream for your recipe.

Add a spoonful of Coconut Whipped Cream to desserts like chocolate brownies, fruit cobbler, or ice cream for a luxurious creamy topping.

6 tablespoons coconut cream
9 drops liquid stevia
1 teaspoon vanilla extract
½ teaspoon ground cinnamon

1 Place coconut cream in a medium chilled bowl. Beat with an electric mixer or metal whisk until soft peaks form. Add stevia, vanilla, and cinnamon and beat until combined.
2 Serve immediately.

Antioxidant Gummies

These gut-healthy gummies are fruity and lightly sweet. For a little more sweetness, add a few more drops of liquid stevia. Pour the mixture into silicone candy molds for a more authentic looking gummy treat.

1 large lemon

2 cups chopped strawberries

½ cup cold water

2 tablespoons raw honey

15 drops stevia liquid sweetener

½ cup gelatin powder

½ cup boiling water

1 Line a 9" × 9" glass baking dish with parchment paper.

2 Grate zest from lemon and then peel the fruit. Discard peel and roughly chop lemon. Transfer lemon zest and fruit to a high-speed blender.

3 Add strawberries, cold water, honey, and stevia and blend for 1–2 minutes until puréed. Sprinkle gelatin powder over the mixture and set aside for 5 minutes to allow gelatin to bloom.

4 Add boiling water to the gelatin mixture and blend for 10 seconds or until gelatin is fully dissolved.

5 Pour mixture into the prepared baking dish. Refrigerate overnight, then cut into 1" squares. Serve immediately, or store in a covered container for up to 5 days.

SERVES 12

Per Serving

Calories	60
Fat	0g
Sodium	25mg
Carbohydrates	5g
Fiber	1g
Sugar	4g
Protein	11g

BENEFICIAL GELATIN

Gelatin can improve heart health, digestive health, skin health, and mental health. It's a good source of protein and can improve heart health by helping to lower homocysteine, which is a significant risk factor for heart disease. Gelatin is a good source of the amino acid glycine, which helps to balance out methionine levels in the blood (which can otherwise increase homocysteine). Gelatin has also been shown to improve joint health, as it helps to lubricate the joints and reduce inflammation.

CHAPTER 12

Sauces, Spreads, and Condiments

Five-Minute Raspberry Chia Jam

SERVES 4

Per Serving

Calories	90
Fat	4g
Sodium	35mg
Carbohydrates	14g
Fiber	8g
Sugar	6g
Protein	3g

CHIA JAM

Enjoy fruit without the sugar overload by mixing it with chia seeds. When chia dissolves in liquid, it thickens and binds everything together, "setting" the jam. Chia jam has a thick texture, plus added protein and omega-3s, and you don't have to cook the fruit, which preserves more nutrients. Try this method with apricots, kiwis, strawberries, cherries, and peaches.

Jam doesn't get much easier than this! This delicious jam is great on pancakes or toasted protein bread for breakfast. For a lovely snack, spread pumpernickel with cream cheese and top it with a dollop of jam.

1½ **cups raspberries**

1 **tablespoon raw honey**

½ **teaspoon vanilla extract**

3 **tablespoons chia seeds**

1   Place raspberries, honey, and vanilla in a high-speed blender and blend until smooth. Transfer to a small bowl and stir in chia seeds.

2   Cover and refrigerate for at least 30 minutes. Serve immediately, or store covered in the refrigerator for 4–5 days.

Quick Strawberry Syrup

SERVES 4

Per Serving

Calories	30
Fat	0g
Sodium	0mg
Carbohydrates	7g
Fiber	2g
Sugar	5g
Protein	1g

COMBINE SWEETENERS WITH FIBER

This syrup is designed to release sugar much more steadily into your system. It helps you to avoid the damaging blood glucose spikes that you'll get from store-bought syrup, which is stripped of fiber and nutrients. Wherever possible, try to obtain sweetness in meals from whole fruit, dates, or stevia (liquid and powder), which all cause less of a sugar spike.

This syrup is fantastic to drizzle over pancakes, cakes, muffins, and oatmeal. Quick to make, the syrup lasts about 5 days in the refrigerator, but it's so good that it rarely lasts that long!

2 cups chopped strawberries

4 tablespoons water

1 large Medjool date, pitted

¼ teaspoon ground cinnamon

1 Place all ingredients in a high-speed blender. Blend on high for 30 seconds or until smooth.

2 Serve immediately, or cover and store in the refrigerator for up to 5 days.

Thick Creamy Lemon Sauce

This high-protein, luxurious-tasting cream sauce is so versatile. Use it on salads, fruit, fish, baked vegetables, or grilled meat and fish. Make it often and keep it on hand in the refrigerator. Use the thickest Greek yogurt you can find for this sauce.

2 cups whole-milk plain Greek yogurt

1 tablespoon grated lemon zest

1 teaspoon sea salt

1 Combine all ingredients in a medium bowl. Stir vigorously for 10 seconds.

2 Serve immediately, or cover and store in the refrigerator for up to 1 week.

MAKES 2 CUPS

Per Serving (¼ cup)

Calories	70
Fat	3.5g
Sodium	310mg
Carbohydrates	3g
Fiber	0g
Sugar	3g
Protein	6g

SHEEP'S MILK AND LACTOSE

An estimated 68 percent of the world's adult population is lactose intolerant. If you're not sure, but struggle with acne, digestive problems, or autoimmune conditions, try cutting out cow's milk. It contains one protein in particular, A1 beta-casein, which has been linked to inflammation. Organic grass-fed sheep or goat dairy contain little to no A1 beta-casein.

Pomegranate Raita

Per Serving

Calories	130
Fat	6g
Sodium	330mg
Carbohydrates	11g
Fiber	1g
Sugar	9g
Protein	10g

RAITA REDUCES HEAT

Raita is a traditional Indian yogurt dish that has been used for centuries to add nutrients and cool down spicy foods. The sauce is usually made from yogurt, cucumber, and spices. The yogurt in raita sauce is a good source of probiotics, which are beneficial for gut health.

Season this sauce with a little more salt and lots of ground black pepper. Garnish it with chopped cilantro and a few pomegranate seeds.

⅓ cup finely grated cucumber, squeezed to remove liquid

¾ cup pomegranate seeds

1½ cups whole-milk plain Greek yogurt

½ teaspoon ground cumin

½ teaspoon salt

1 Place cucumber in a medium bowl. Add pomegranate seeds, yogurt, cumin, and salt. Stir gently to combine.

2 Serve immediately, or cover and store in the refrigerator for up to 1 week.

Amazing Salad Dressing

This dressing will make you invent reasons to eat vegetables. It adds a luscious mouthfeel to greens while providing necessary healthy fats to help you absorb nutrients. Spoon it liberally over everything.

1 cup extra-virgin olive oil

½ cup nutritional yeast flakes

½ cup tahini

1 medium red apple, peeled, cored, and chopped

⅓ cup tamari

⅓ cup apple cider vinegar

⅓ cup water

2 cloves garlic, peeled

Place all ingredients in a high-speed blender and blend on high for 20–30 seconds until smooth. Store in an airtight jar in the refrigerator for up to 2 weeks.

MAKES 3½ CUPS

Per Serving (2 tablespoons)

Calories	120
Fat	11g
Sodium	210mg
Carbohydrates	3g
Fiber	1g
Sugar	1g
Protein	2g

WHY MAKE DRESSING?

Most salad dressings in the store contain canola or other seed oils that are bad for your health, as well as added sugar and unnecessary ingredients. Homemade salad dressing takes about two minutes to make, tastes so much better, and makes eating tons of vegetables easy and enjoyable.

Quick-Pickled Cucumbers and Onions

These easy pickles are perfect for snacking or adding zing to sandwiches, burgers, and salads. For different flavors, try adding garlic and/or crushed red pepper flakes.

½ medium cucumber, very thinly sliced

1 medium red onion, peeled and very thinly sliced

1 cup apple cider vinegar

1 tablespoon sea salt

2 teaspoons dried dill

2 teaspoons fennel seeds, crumbled between your fingers

8 drops liquid stevia

2 cups hot water

1 Place cucumber slices in a pint-sized canning jar. Place onion slices in another pint jar.

2 In a large measuring cup, mix together vinegar, salt, dill, fennel seeds, stevia, and water. Pour half of the liquid over cucumbers and half over onions. If vegetables are not fully covered, top up jar with additional apple cider vinegar.

3 Set aside for 1 hour. Serve immediately, or store covered in the refrigerator for up to 3 weeks.

SERVES 8

Per Serving

Calories	25
Fat	0g
Sodium	870mg
Carbohydrates	6g
Fiber	1g
Sugar	1g
Protein	0g

APPLE CIDER PICKLING

Pickling cucumbers in apple cider vinegar is a great way to enjoy the health benefits of both cucumbers and vinegar. Cucumbers are a good source of vitamins C and K, as well as fiber. A 2015 study by Athens University Medical School noted that vinegar consumption in general is known for many health benefits, including helping to regulate blood sugar levels and promote gut health. The health benefits of pickled cucumbers also include improved joint health and reduced inflammation.

Hemp Hollandaise

MAKES 1 CUP

Per Serving (¼ cup)

Calories	210
Fat	19g
Sodium	540mg
Carbohydrates	5g
Fiber	2g
Sugar	2g
Protein	6g

USING HOLLANDAISE

Creamy dressings transform most vegetable combinations into a delectable feast. Take a few healthy salad ingredients, like greens, poached eggs, avocados, tomatoes, shredded carrots or beets, small canned fishes (sardines, mackerel, or anchovies), and nuts, and drizzle them all with Hemp Hollandaise.

Spoon this creamy, lemony hollandaise sauce over eggs, fish, or steamed vegetables. It's particularly good with Sweet Potato Latkes Benedict (see recipe in Chapter 3).

¼ cup extra-virgin olive oil

¼ cup shelled hemp seeds

¼ cup nutritional yeast flakes

2 tablespoons tamari

2 tablespoons lemon juice

2 cloves garlic, peeled

1 teaspoon raw honey or maple syrup

1 teaspoon Dijon mustard

¼ teaspoon ground turmeric

1 Place all ingredients in a small food processor or blender and blend on high for 30 seconds or until smooth and creamy. If the mixture is too thick to pour, blend in 1–2 tablespoons water.

2 Serve immediately, or store in an airtight jar in the refrigerator for up to 2 weeks.

Green Herb Pesto

Drizzle this magical green sauce onto soups, salads, and main dishes. It adds a nutrient burst to your meal, and it will earn you endless compliments! Try it with other herb combinations, like basil and cilantro.

1 cup chopped fresh parsley

½ cup chopped fresh mint

¼ cup crumbled feta cheese (preferably sheep's milk feta)

2 tablespoons chopped raw unsalted cashews

1½ teaspoons grated lemon zest

1½ tablespoons lemon juice

1 clove garlic, peeled

1 tablespoon extra-virgin olive oil

¼ teaspoon crushed red pepper flakes

1 Place all ingredients in a small food processor. Process for 30 seconds, stopping once or twice to run a spatula around the edges to push all the ingredients down toward the blade.

2 If the sauce is too thick, add 1 tablespoon water and pulse until the mixture is almost smooth. Serve immediately, or cover and store in the refrigerator for up to 1 week.

MAKES 1½ CUPS

Per Serving (¼ cup)

Calories	60
Fat	5g
Sodium	65mg
Carbohydrates	3g
Fiber	1g
Sugar	1g
Protein	2g

SHAKE UP PESTO!

Pesto is amazing, not only in flavor, but in antioxidant capacity. It's a health bomb formed out of a blended mixture of crushed herb leaves, nuts, garlic, cheese, and olive oil. While basil and pine nuts are the original pesto combination, you can change up the herbs and the nuts to take in more nutrient variety.

Arugula Pesto

MAKES 1 CUP

**Per Serving
(2 tablespoons)**

Calories	170
Fat	17g
Sodium	200mg
Carbohydrates	2g
Fiber	1g
Sugar	0g
Protein	2g

For an easy, fiber-filled appetizer, spread rustic, seedy crackers with hummus and top with a small spoonful of Arugula Pesto. Or use it as a zesty pizza or pasta sauce.

2 cups packed arugula leaves, stems removed

½ cup chopped walnuts

½ cup grated Parmesan cheese

6 cloves garlic, peeled

½ teaspoon salt

½ cup extra-virgin olive oil

1 Place arugula, walnuts, cheese, garlic, and salt in a food processor and process for 30–60 seconds until mixture forms a paste, stopping once or twice to run a spatula around the edges to push all the ingredients down toward the blade.

2 With the motor running, gradually add oil in a thin, steady stream until combined. Serve immediately, or cover and store in the refrigerator for up to 4 days.

Cilantro Pesto

MAKES 1½ CUPS

Per Serving (¼ cup)

Calories	150
Fat	14g
Sodium	200mg
Carbohydrates	2g
Fiber	1g
Sugar	0g
Protein	3g

Serve over konjac flour, shirataki, buckwheat, or kelp noodles, or as an accompaniment to grilled fish or chicken or salad.

1 cup roughly chopped fresh cilantro

½ cup shelled raw pumpkin seeds

¼ cup extra-virgin olive oil

2 tablespoons lime juice

½ small jalapeño pepper, seeded and chopped

1 clove garlic, peeled and minced

½ teaspoon sea salt

1 Place all ingredients in a food processor and process for 30–60 seconds until mixture forms a paste, stopping once or twice to run a spatula around the edges to push all the ingredients down toward the blade.

2 Serve immediately, or cover and store in the refrigerator for up to 4 days.

White Bean and Basil Spread

Spread this thick spread on whole-wheat or rye crostini for a starter, or serve as a side with fish or chicken. It can also be used as a dip with vegetables and crackers.

2 tablespoons extra-virgin olive oil

2 large leeks, trimmed and thinly sliced

1 clove garlic, peeled and minced

1 (15-ounce) can cannellini beans, drained and rinsed

½ teaspoon sea salt

½ teaspoon ground black pepper

¼ teaspoon crushed red pepper flakes

1 cup thinly sliced basil

1 Heat oil in a large saucepan over medium heat. Add leeks and garlic and sauté until softened, 3–4 minutes. Add beans and water to just cover.

2 Increase heat to high and bring to a boil. Reduce heat to medium-low, cover, and simmer for 5 minutes. Uncover pan and stir in salt, black pepper, and red pepper flakes. Simmer uncovered for 2–3 minutes until all liquid has evaporated.

3 Remove from heat and set aside to cool for at least 20 minutes.

4 Stir in basil and mash mixture with a fork to make a chunky paste. Serve immediately, or cover and store in the refrigerator for up to 5 days.

SERVES 6

Per Serving

Calories	150
Fat	6g
Sodium	310mg
Carbohydrates	19g
Fiber	1g
Sugar	2g
Protein	6g

LEEKS

Leeks are part of the allium family, which also includes onions and garlic. They're an excellent source of vitamins K and folate, and they also contain heart-healthy plant compounds that have been shown to reduce inflammation, cholesterol, blood pressure, the formation of blood clots, and your overall risk of heart disease. Leeks can be used as a replacement for onions in most recipes.

Fresh Salsa

SERVES 8

Per Serving

Calories	20
Fat	0.5g
Sodium	150mg
Carbohydrates	5g
Fiber	1g
Sugar	1g
Protein	1g

PEPPER HEAT

The heat in a pepper is concentrated in its seeds and inner membranes. If you prefer a milder taste, just remove and discard the seeds and membranes before mincing. Habaneros and Scotch bonnet peppers are the hottest peppers, while pepperoncini and poblano peppers are milder.

You could make this awesome salsa by hand, cutting everything as finely as you can, but it's super quick to run for 10 seconds in a food processor.

1 medium jalapeño pepper, seeded and minced

1 clove garlic, peeled and minced

½ cup diced red onion

2 cups halved grape tomatoes

2 tablespoons lime juice

1 teaspoon extra-virgin olive oil

½ teaspoon sea salt

¼ cup chopped fresh cilantro

1 Place all ingredients in a food processor. Pulse for 10 seconds until combined but still chunky.

2 Serve immediately, or cover and store in the refrigerator for up to 1 week.

Blueberry and Black Bean Salsa

SERVES 4

Per Serving

Calories	340
Fat	15g
Sodium	840mg
Carbohydrates	38g
Fiber	1g
Sugar	7g
Protein	15g

SURPRISING SALSA

Salsa is not only a delicious condiment, but it also offers some impressive health benefits. It's rich in antioxidants, vitamin C, and fiber. Fiber can help manage blood sugars, reduce cholesterol levels, aid with satiety, and promote good bowel health.

Here's an excellent accompaniment to grilled fish, chicken, and other meats. Try it with Burrito Bowls (see recipe in Chapter 7).

½ cup minced red onion

1 small jalapeño pepper, seeded and minced

2 teaspoons grated lime zest

2 tablespoons lime juice

2 tablespoons balsamic vinegar

1 teaspoon sea salt

2 (15-ounce) cans black beans, drained and rinsed

2 cups blueberries

1 cup chopped roasted red peppers

1 cup chopped fresh cilantro

4 tablespoons extra-virgin olive oil

1 Place onion, jalapeño, lime zest, lime juice, vinegar, and salt in a small bowl. Stir to combine, then set aside for 5 minutes.

2 In a large bowl, combine beans, blueberries, roasted peppers, and cilantro and gently stir.

3 Use a slotted spoon to remove onion and jalapeño from the small bowl and add to the bean mixture. Leave liquid in the small bowl. Add oil to the pickling liquid and whisk until emulsified. Pour over bean mixture and stir to combine.

4 Refrigerate for at least 1 hour (up to overnight) before serving. Store covered in the refrigerator for up to 5 days.

Speedy Blender Pizza Sauce

While this sauce is great on pizza, it's also good on zucchini noodles or spooned over baked chicken. This recipe makes enough sauce for 4 (10") pizzas. If you're not making pizza again soon, freeze the sauce in individual 1/2-cup containers.

1 (15-ounce) can crushed tomatoes

1 (6-ounce) can tomato paste

1/4 small yellow onion, peeled and roughly chopped

2 cloves garlic, peeled

1 tablespoon dried oregano

1 tablespoon dried rosemary

1 teaspoon raw honey

1 teaspoon sea salt

1 Place all ingredients in a food processor and process for 1 minute or until smooth.

2 Serve immediately, or cover and store in the refrigerator for up to 5 days.

MAKES 2 CUPS

Per Serving (2 tablespoons)

Calories	15
Fat	0g
Sodium	210mg
Carbohydrates	4g
Fiber	1g
Sugar	2g
Protein	1g

TOMATO PASTE

Consuming 2 tablespoons of tomato paste daily is an easy heart-health hack. Canned tomato paste, juice, and sauce deliver an impressive amount of lycopene, which is a powerful antioxidant that is ten times more potent than vitamin E. A supplement of lycopene improved and normalized function of the endothelium (the inner lining of blood vessels) in volunteers with cardiovascular disease. Consuming a tomato-containing diet can result in a significant reduction in oxidized LDL cholesterol.

Tartar Sauce

SERVES 8

Per Serving

Calories	35
Fat	2g
Sodium	260mg
Carbohydrates	2g
Fiber	0g
Sugar	1g
Protein	3g

Tartar sauce is great with seafood, but it can also accompany chicken or vegetables. You can even use it as a mayonnaise or salad dressing substitute.

1 cup whole-milk plain Greek yogurt

2 teaspoons Dijon mustard

½ teaspoon sea salt

½ teaspoon ground black pepper

½ teaspoon dried dill

⅛ teaspoon ground cayenne pepper

2 tablespoons minced dill pickle

2 tablespoons minced capers

1 Place all ingredients in a small bowl and stir to combine. Cover and refrigerate for 30 minutes to let flavors develop.

2 Serve immediately or cover and store in the refrigerator for up to 1 week.

Healthy Big Mac Sauce

SERVES 8

Per Serving

Calories	45
Fat	2g
Sodium	400mg
Carbohydrates	4g
Fiber	0g
Sugar	2g
Protein	4g

This sauce is great on sandwiches and with Speedy Burgers (see recipe in Chapter 6).

1 cup whole-milk plain Greek yogurt

¼ cup apple cider vinegar

¼ cup tomato paste

2 teaspoons yellow mustard

½ teaspoon garlic powder

½ teaspoon onion powder

1 medium dill pickle, minced

½ teaspoon sea salt

3 drops liquid stevia

1 Place all ingredients in a small bowl and stir to combine.

2 Serve immediately or cover and store in the refrigerator for up to 2 weeks.

Cheesy Sauce

This delicious vegan sauce is wonderful over steamed cauliflower or pasta. For a nonvegan version, add a sprinkle of Parmesan for extra cheesiness.

1 (15-ounce) can cannellini beans, drained and rinsed

½ cup unsweetened almond milk

½ cup nutritional yeast flakes

1 clove garlic, peeled

1 tablespoon extra-virgin olive oil

½ teaspoon apple cider vinegar

½ teaspoon sea salt

¼ teaspoon ground turmeric

1 Place all ingredients in a high-speed blender and blend on high for 30 seconds or until smooth and creamy.

2 Transfer to a medium saucepan over medium-low heat. Cook, stirring occasionally, for 2–3 minutes until heated through. Serve immediately.

SERVES 6

Per Serving

Calories	100
Fat	3g
Sodium	270mg
Carbohydrates	14g
Fiber	1g
Sugar	1g
Protein	7g

EAT WITH ABANDON

Having healthy fats in a sauce helps to make steamed vegetables feel decadent. Sauces are a vehicle to ensure you love eating your vegetables. Use healthy sauces with abandon. They are designed to be used in generous ¼ cup or more portions, which feels and tastes wonderful. Nutritional yeast is used for cheese flavor, protein, and nutrients in this sauce.

Bread Crumb Substitute

MAKES 3½ CUPS

Per Serving (¼ cup)

Calories	70
Fat	2g
Sodium	460mg
Carbohydrates	10g
Fiber	1g
Sugar	4g
Protein	3g

PARMESAN CHEESE

Parmesan is a good source of nutrients like calcium, phosphorus, and nitrogen. It also contains high levels of folate, vitamin K, and B vitamins. These nutrients are important for bone health, blood clotting, and cell growth. Parmesan cheese also contains conjugated linoleic acid, which has been linked to lower cholesterol levels and improved heart health.

Use this breading to coat fish, chicken, and vegetables before frying. To use, whisk an egg in a shallow bowl and place Bread Crumb Substitute in another shallow bowl. Dip the item in egg first, then crumbs, before frying.

2 cups (5 ounces) dehydrated onion

2 teaspoons sea salt

1 teaspoon dried rosemary

1 teaspoon dried thyme

1 teaspoon dried coriander

½ teaspoon ground sage

½ teaspoon dried oregano

½ teaspoon paprika

½ teaspoon ground black pepper

¼ teaspoon crushed red pepper flakes

1¼ cups Parmesan cheese

1. Place onion in a food processor and process for 1 minute. Add salt, rosemary, thyme, coriander, sage, oregano, paprika, black pepper, and red pepper flakes. Process for 30 seconds. Add Parmesan and pulse briefly to blend.
2. Serve immediately or refrigerate in an airtight container for up to 2 weeks.

Start Here: 2-Week Eating Plan

		Week 1		
	Breakfast	**Snack**	**Lunch**	**Dinner**
Monday	Protein Scramble (Chapter 3)	Sunshine Smoothie (Chapter 2)	Asian Lunch Bowl (Chapter 5)	Best Basic Salad (Chapter 9) and Tahini Sweet Potatoes with Chicken and Broccoli (Chapter 5)
Tuesday	Chocolate Mint Protein Smoothie (Chapter 2)	Carrot Cake Energy Balls (Chapter 4)	Tahini Sweet Potatoes with Chicken and Broccoli (Chapter 5)	Best Basic Salad (Chapter 9) and Tzatziki Salmon with Quinoa (Chapter 6)
Wednesday	Savory Quinoa Muffins (Chapter 4)	Strawberry Grapefruit Beauty Boost Smoothie (Chapter 2)	Strawberry Sweet Potato Bowl (Chapter 5)	Magical Kale and Cannellini (Chapter 6) and Baked Teriyaki Tofu (Chapter 5)
Thursday	Easy Chia Breakfast Pudding (Chapter 3)	Essential Green Smoothie (Chapter 2)	Grapefruit and Avocado Salad (Chapter 5)	Carrot, Goji, and Mint Salad (Chapter 9) and Salmon with Creamy Kale (Chapter 6)
Friday	Raspberry Coconut Smoothie (Chapter 2)	Matcha Protein Balls (Chapter 4)	Red Lentil Lunch Curry (Chapter 5)	Speedy Burgers (Chapter 6) and Sweet Potato Fries with Harissa Dip (Chapter 8)
Saturday	Broccoli and Feta Egg Bake (Chapter 3)	Red Chili Hummus (Chapter 8) with carrot sticks or baby carrots	Tomato and Fennel Soup (Chapter 10) and Easy Protein Bread (Chapter 5)	Blueberry Beet Salad with Walnuts (Chapter 9), Green Olive–Roasted Salmon (Chapter 7), and Chocolate Pudding Heaven (Chapter 11)
Sunday	Almond Breakfast Cake (Chapter 3)	Spiced Edamame and Nut Mix (Chapter 4)	Garlic Shrimp with Zucchini Pasta (Chapter 6)	Best Kale Salad (Chapter 9), Za'atar Roast Chicken, (Chapter 7) Parmesan Truffle Mash (Chapter 8), and Blueberry Banana Nice Cream (Chapter 11)

Week 2

	Breakfast	Snack	Lunch	Dinner
Monday	Whirlpool Crustless Quiche (Chapter 5)	Tropical Spirulina Smoothie (Chapter 2)	Energizing Pesto Zoodles (Chapter 5)	Best Basic Salad (Chapter 9) and Meatballs and Roasted Cauliflower (Chapter 5)
Tuesday	Blueberry Buckwheat Bowl (Chapter 3)	Chocolate Peanut Protein Cookies (Chapter 4)	Meatballs and Roasted Cauliflower (Chapter 5)	Best Basic Salad (Chapter 9) and Baked Fish with Tomatoes and Capers (Chapter 6)
Wednesday	Pumpernickel Toast with Cream Cheese (Chapter 3)	Five-Minute Protein Balls (Chapter 4)	Roasted Orange Veggies and Baked Teriyaki Tofu (Chapter 5)	Za'atar Chicken Thighs with Spinach Mash (Chapter 6)
Thursday	Strawberry Walnut Oatmeal (Chapter 3)	Sunshine Smoothie (Chapter 2)	Sardines on Avocado Toast (Chapter 5)	Lemon Asparagus Tomato Bake (Chapter 6)
Friday	Blueberry Kale Crunch (Chapter 2)	Rosemary Olive Bread (Chapter 4)	Open-Faced Tomato Basil Sandwiches (Chapter 5)	Lemony Tabouleh with Salmon (Chapter 6) and Coconut Quinoa (Chapter 8)
Saturday	Egg-Stuffed Mushrooms with Feta (Chapter 3)	Roasted Chickpeas (Chapter 4)	Broccoli and Walnut Soup (Chapter 10)	Pumpkin Seed–Crusted Trout with Lime Salad (Chapter 7) and Matcha Panna Cotta with Chocolate Sauce (Chapter 11)
Sunday	Sweet Potato Latkes Benedict (Chapter 3)	Awesome Artichoke Dip (Chapter 8) and Buckwheat Olive Crackers (Chapter 4)	Umami Bounty Bowl (Chapter 10)	Toasted Walnut Starter Salad (Chapter 9), Beef Bolognese on Zucchini Noodles (Chapter 7), and Sweet Potato Brownies (Chapter 11)

STANDARD US/METRIC MEASUREMENT CONVERSIONS

VOLUME CONVERSIONS

US Volume Measure	Metric Equivalent
⅛ teaspoon	0.5 milliliter
¼ teaspoon	1 milliliter
½ teaspoon	2 milliliters
1 teaspoon	5 milliliters
½ tablespoon	7 milliliters
1 tablespoon (3 teaspoons)	15 milliliters
2 tablespoons (1 fluid ounce)	30 milliliters
¼ cup (4 tablespoons)	60 milliliters
⅓ cup	90 milliliters
½ cup (4 fluid ounces)	125 milliliters
⅔ cup	160 milliliters
¾ cup (6 fluid ounces)	180 milliliters
1 cup (16 tablespoons)	250 milliliters
1 pint (2 cups)	500 milliliters
1 quart (4 cups)	1 liter (about)

WEIGHT CONVERSIONS

US Weight Measure	Metric Equivalent
½ ounce	15 grams
1 ounce	30 grams
2 ounces	60 grams
3 ounces	85 grams
¼ pound (4 ounces)	115 grams
½ pound (8 ounces)	225 grams
¾ pound (12 ounces)	340 grams
1 pound (16 ounces)	454 grams

OVEN TEMPERATURE CONVERSIONS

Degrees Fahrenheit	Degrees Celsius
200 degrees F	95 degrees C
250 degrees F	120 degrees C
275 degrees F	135 degrees C
300 degrees F	150 degrees C
325 degrees F	160 degrees C
350 degrees F	180 degrees C
375 degrees F	190 degrees C
400 degrees F	205 degrees C
425 degrees F	220 degrees C
450 degrees F	230 degrees C

BAKING PAN SIZES

American	Metric
8 × 1½ inch round baking pan	20 × 4 cm cake tin
9 × 1½ inch round baking pan	23 × 3.5 cm cake tin
11 × 7 × 1½ inch baking pan	28 × 18 × 4 cm baking tin
13 × 9 × 2 inch baking pan	30 × 20 × 5 cm baking tin
2 quart rectangular baking dish	30 × 20 × 3 cm baking tin
15 × 10 × 2 inch baking pan	30 × 25 × 2 cm baking tin (Swiss roll tin)
9 inch pie plate	22 × 4 or 23 × 4 cm pie plate
7 or 8 inch springform pan	18 or 20 cm springform or loose bottom cake tin
9 × 5 × 3 inch loaf pan	23 × 13 × 7 cm or 2 lb narrow loaf or pate tin
1½ quart casserole	1.5 liter casserole
2 quart casserole	2 liter casserole

Index